The Art of Governance

The Art of Governance

*Analyzing Management
and Administration*

Patricia W. Ingraham

Laurence E. Lynn, Jr.

Editors

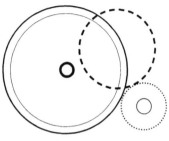

Georgetown University Press • Washington, D.C.

Georgetown University Press, Washington, D.C.
© 2004 by Georgetown University Press. All rights reserved.
Printed in the United States of America

10 9 8 7 6 5 4 3 2 1   2004

This book is printed on acid-free, recycled paper meeting the requirements of the American National Standard for Permanence in Paper for Printed Library Materials.

Library of Congress Cataloging-in-Publication Data

The art of governance : analyzing management and administration / Patricia W. Ingraham and Laurence E. Lynn, Jr., editors.
    p.   cm.
    Includes bibliographical references and index.
    ISBN 1-58901-034-5 (pbk. : alk. paper)
    1. Public administration—Research. 2. Human services—Management—Research. 3. Public administration—Evaluation. 4. Human services—Management—Evaluation.
I. Ingraham, Patricia W. II. Lynn, Laurence E., 1937–
    JF1338.A2A.78 2004
    351—dc22
                                                    2004005617

Contents

Figures and Tables

Contributors

Amy K. Donahue is an assistant professor of pubic administration at the University of Connecticut. Professor Donahue is also senior advisor to the administrator at the National Aeronautics and Space Administration. Her research focuses on the influence of management on the productivity of emergency services organizations and on the nature of citizen demand for public safety services.

Jo Ann G. Ewalt is associate professor and chair of the Department of Government at Eastern Kentucky University, Richmond, where she teaches courses on research methods and public policy analysis in the graduate programs in public administration and political science. She is also an associate of the Institute of Government at Eastern Kentucky. Her research interests include intergovernmental policy management, welfare policy, and program evaluation.

Meg Patrick Haist is a doctoral candidate in the Martin School of Public Policy and Administration at the University of Kentucky. Her dissertation research is funded under the auspices of the assistant secretary for planning and evaluation, Department of Health and Human Services, through a fellowship awarded by the University of Kentucky Center for Poverty Research. Ms. Haist's research interests include race and gender issues in social welfare policy, implementation and performance measurement, federalism, political behavior, and organizational innovation.

Carolyn J. Heinrich is an associate professor at the LaFollette School of Public Affairs and associate director at the Institute for Research on Poverty, at the University of Wisconsin–Madison. Heinrich's primary areas of research expertise are in social welfare policy, public management, and econometric methods for social program evaluation. Her work on performance management in public organizations includes a number of journal articles and two books, *Improving Governance: A New Logic for Empirical Research* (with Laurence E. Lynn, Jr., and Carolyn J. Hill) and *Governance and Performance: New Perspectives* (with Laurence E. Lynn, Jr.).

Carolyn J. Hill is an assistant professor of public policy at the Georgetown University Public Policy Institute. She received her Ph.D. from the Harris Graduate School of Public Policy Studies at the University of Chicago. Professor Hill's research focuses on the design and management of publicly supported programs, particularly those that serve poor families. She is coauthor—with Laurence E. Lynn, Jr., and Carolyn J. Heinrich—of *Improving Governance: A New Logic for Empirical Research*. She has coauthored studies with Howard Bloom and James Riccio, of MDRC, on implementation and performance in welfare-to-work programs and with Bloom and Charles Michalopoulos, also of MDRC, on the use of propensity score methods.

Patricia W. Ingraham is Distinguished Professor of Public Administration at the Maxwell School of Citizenship and Public Affairs, Syracuse University. Her most recent book is *Government Performance: Why Management Matters* (with Philip Joyce and Amy Donahue). She is the author or editor of ten other books. She has published extensively on issues related to civil service systems, administrative reform, and performance in public organizations. Her current research focuses on leadership and organizational effectiveness.

Willow S. Jacobson is an assistant professor at the School of Government at the University of North Carolina at Chapel Hill. She specializes in human resource management, organizational theory, and public management. Her research has appeared in *Public Administration Review* and *Public Personnel Management*.

Edward T. Jennings, Jr., is a professor in the Martin School of Public Policy and Administration at the University of Kentucky. His research interests include the policy process, social policy, and performance management. He is a former president of the American Society for Public Administration.

Laurence E. Lynn, Jr., is the George Bush Chair and Professor of Public Affairs at the George Bush School of Government and Public Service at Texas A&M University. His recent publications include *Improving Governance: A New Logic for Empirical Research* (coauthored with Carolyn J. Heinrich and Carolyn J. Hill) and *Governance and Performance: New Perspectives* (coedited with Carolyn J. Heinrich). In addition, he is the author or coauthor of numerous articles and book chapters on public management and governance. He is a past president of the Association for Public Policy Analysis and Management and a winner of the *Journal of Policy Analysis and Management*'s Vernon Prize.

Kenneth J. Meier is the Charles Puryear Professor of Liberal Arts in the Department of Political Science at Texas A&M and a professor of public management at Cardiff University (Wales). He has multiple research agendas on governance, public management, and public policy. With Laurence J. O'Toole, he is engaged in a multiyear project to estimate when management matters and under what conditions it matters for public organizations. He is directing a national study of minority education covering 1,800 school districts in the United States with a focus on questions of educational equity. He is also working on book-length projects on the relationship between bureaucracy and democracy and how gender issues are represented in street-level bureaucracies.

Donald P. Moynihan is an assistant professor at the George Bush School of Government and Public Service at Texas A&M University. He studies public management reforms, especially in the areas of performance management, homeland security, and citizen participation. He has published in a number of edited volumes and journals, including *PAR, J-PART, Administration & Society*, and the *American Review of Public Administration*. In 2002, he was recognized for writing the best journal article from the Public and Nonprofit Division of the Academy of Management. He received his Ph.D. in public administration from the Maxwell School at Syracuse University.

Laurence J. O'Toole, Jr., is the Margaret Hughes and Robert T. Golembiewski Professor of Public Administration in the Department of Public Administration and Policy, School of Public and International Affairs, at the University of Georgia. He is also head of that department. He is widely published, especially on the subjects of policy implementation in networked settings, environmental policy and management, and the impact of public management on program performance.

Hal G. Rainey is Alumni Foundation Distinguished Professor in the Department of Public Administration and Policy in the School of Public and International Affairs at the University of Georgia. A third edition of his book *Understanding and Managing Public Organizations* was published in 2003.

Mark D. Robbins is an associate professor of public administration at the University of Connecticut. His current research projects focus on municipal bond issuance and citizen preferences for taxation and spending.

Ellen V. Rubin is a senior analyst on the strategic issues team at the U.S. General Accounting Office (GAO), where she specializes in strategic human capital management. This work includes developing conceptual models for human capital management, identifying government-wide trends, and applying those lessons to agency-specific management reviews. Prior to joining GAO, she served as a research assistant on the Government Performance Project at Syracuse University.

Jay Eungha Ryu is an assistant professor of public administration in the Department of Political Science at Ohio University, where he teaches public budgeting and finance and public management. He has been especially interested in how to improve productivity of the public sector while facilitating the creation of public values and ethics. His recent research areas include the evaluation of public revenues and expenditures such as education policy and finance, job training programs, and investment in public infrastructures, budgetary politics, organizational performance and its determinants, and state privatization studies.

Sally Coleman Selden is an associate professor of management at Lynchburg College. Dr. Selden's articles have appeared in *American Journal of Political Science, Administration and Society, American Review of Public Administration, Review of Public Personnel Administration, Journal of Public Administration Education, Public Administration Review,* and *Journal of Public Administration Research and Theory.*

Jessica Sowa is an assistant professor in the Department of Political Science at the University of South Carolina at Columbia. She received her Ph.D. in public administration from the Maxwell School of Citizenship and Public Affairs at Syracuse University in 2003. Her research interests include public and nonprofit management and the implementation of policies for children and families. Her current research agenda focuses on the use of alternative service delivery mechanisms to deliver public services, and she is currently examining the use of interagency collaborations to deliver full-day, year-round early care and education services.

Preface

The performance of public and nonprofit organizations is an increasing focus of concern to citizens, elected officials, and managers of the organizations in the hot seat. How, when, and under what conditions performance occurs—and what difference it all makes—are questions that have captured analysts' attention. The questions have been explored in the literatures of political science, public management, and economics. It is not surprising that consensus about how best to approach the questions' pursuit and analysis has been difficult to achieve. A common theme in the analytic controversy is that the subjects are so complex as to defy conclusive analysis.

At the same time, the need for "approaches to research design and interpretation that will promote a body of knowledge whose value equals or exceeds the sum of its numerous parts" (Heinrich, Hill, and Lynn, this volume) is clearly recognized. Discovering the paths to these approaches—and the potential for new common paths—is a necessary component of contemporary management research agendas. Coherent exploration of consequences for performance of how public programs are organized and managed is very important. Lynn, Heinrich, and Hill began to frame and explore cumulative research agendas in *Improving Governance: A New Logic for Empirical Research*. A group of scholars—meeting at the University of Arizona, Syracuse University, and, most recently, Texas A&M University—have combined their research efforts to explore elements of a shared agenda. Although the identification of specific links to performance and, ultimately, to improved governance remains somewhat elusive, the synergies of the group's interests, disciplinary and policy perspectives, and research designs are compelling, and the cumulative learning emerging from the group's efforts is clearly significant. Questions explored are compelling and timely. They include:

- Does a logic of governance (based on the reduced form model) and the location of public management within such a logic move us forward or distract us? In what ways is it helpful or unhelpful to research design, evaluation, and synthesis? For example, is it too hierarchical? Is it useful as an ex ante framework for research design? As an ex post interpretive or meta-analytic scheme? As both?
- Is research bearing on governance producing findings that indicate governance and, in particular, public management matter? Does research suggest more than that—that is, are there useful substantive findings concerning what matters? Are we learning anything—or enough—to

justify efforts to influence the discourse over governmental effectiveness?
- What are the consequences of organization and management of public programs for governmental performance? Does management matter, and, if so, how? Are some forms of organization better than others for accomplishing public purposes? If so, for whom, when, and where?
- Is it possible and useful to learn across substantive and disciplinary boundaries? To what extent does research concerning the governance of welfare reform, mental health services, economic and regulatory policy, and other substantive domains conducted by economists, sociologists, and organizational theorists have implications for the general problem of governance? What are the implications for theory and for research agendas of the cumulative findings from governance research?
- What is, or should be, the role of a priori, explanatory theory in governance and public management research?
- An objective of empirical governance research is to open "black boxes" at the various levels of governance to identify variables that have demonstrable effects at hierarchically subordinate or superior levels. How well are we meeting this objective?

This book presents the most current thinking and work from a group of leading scholars. Although the book is an edited collection, it brings unusual synthesis and coherence in analytic perspectives and cumulative learning. The authors have worked closely together for more than six years, refining questions, testing methodologies and models, and exploring scholarly capacity to answer questions of great significance to public policy makers. The book breaks new ground in exploring efforts to link alternative institutional and administrative structures to program performance in different policy areas. It also explores the extent to which important, but difficult to capture, influences such as political direction and leadership can be incorporated into the empirical examination of performance and governance. Fundamentally, the book synthesizes the current state of the art in governance and performance issues and poses critical questions for the future agenda.

Financial support for research appearing in earlier publications associated with this project and for the conferences at which continuing work was presented was provided by the Pew Charitable Trusts, the University of Arizona's Eller College of Business and Public Administration, the Maxwell School of Citizenship and Public Affairs at Syracuse University, and the George Bush School of Government and Public Service at Texas A&M University. Additional support for the present volume was provided by the Bush School, with special thanks to Professors Laurence E. Lynn, Jr., and Kenneth J. Meier. The editors and authors would like to express appreciation to Gail Grella of Georgetown University Press for her encouragement and support of this work. The editors would also like to thank Jennifer Cook and Maria Fernanda Ariceta for their assistance in getting this manuscript into production.

Part I

Choosing a Conceptual Lens

One

Governance as an Organizing Theme for Empirical Research

Carolyn J. Heinrich • Carolyn J. Hill • Laurence E. Lynn, Jr.

Beginning in the early 1990s, it became popular to argue that the field of public administration must be repositioned on new intellectual and practical foundations to avoid collapsing into a rubble of irrelevance (Wamsley et al. 1990; Barzelay 1992; Osborne and Gaebler 1993; Frederickson 1997). Many of the field's leading scholars began to embrace the idea of "governance" as an organizing concept (Garvey 1997; Peters and Pierre 1998; Kettl 2000, 2002; Salamon 2002). The momentum behind this idea has surged such that Frederickson and Smith could suggest that governance had become "a virtual synonym for public management and public administration" (2003, 225).

The intellectual movement toward governance as an organizing concept is associated with the widespread belief that the focus of administrative practice has been shifting from the bureaucratic state and direct government to the "hollow state" (Milward and Provan 1993; Milward 1994) and "third-party government" (Salamon 1981). In this view, public management is now about arms-length, indirect relationships with dispersed and diverse entities rather than about the supervision of civil servants who are organized by agency and governed by employment contracts.

To Peters and Pierre (1998), for example, the idea of governance encompasses the predominance of network relationships, deregulation, hybridization of public and private resources, and use of multiple instruments in policy implementation. In *The Transformation of Governance*, Kettl employs the idea of governance to confront the realities of administrative roles that require "capacities that lie far beyond the standard responses, structures, and processes that have gradually accumulated within American government" (2002, 123). Kettl argues that devolution, globalization, and hyperpluralism are examples of the tectonic forces that are forcing revolutionary change on administrative practice and concludes that governments must have new theories to explain and guide practice. Salamon (2002) proposes a paradigm that he calls the "new governance," which shifts the unit of analysis from programs and agencies to tools of action; and the focus of administration from hierarchy to network, from public versus private to public plus private, from command and

3

control to negotiation and persuasion, from management skills to enablement skills.

The perception that separation of ownership (by citizens) and control (by unelected officials) of public policy administration is growing has spurred intellectual and practical efforts to address the accountability problems associated with new approaches to the publicly sponsored provision of goods and services. "Governance" is a general concept that captures attempts to address these problems. The concept of public governance (including the study of public management in a governance context), however, remains conceptually less well developed than the older subject of corporate governance. Public governance is arguably harder to study because of the sheer complexity of both normative and positive analyses of why and how to govern in a democracy. Further, useful heuristics in the study of corporate governance (e.g., principal-agent theory) seem to leave out too much of what many scholars and practitioners regard as central to governance in a democratic polity: the growing importance of collaboration among largely or partially autonomous organizational units.

Nevertheless, the problems of hierarchy and agency that are endemic to republican forms of government cannot be relegated to histories of the field. If anything, such problems are exacerbated by the growing importance of practices that seem to threaten the very notion of accountability to constitutional institutions: to legislatures, the courts, and the Madisonian interplay of interests. The question addressed in this chapter is how both old and new realities might be incorporated into an analytic framework adequate to guide and interpret empirical research on governance that is useful to practice.

In what follows, we first survey both older and newer concepts of governance and the issues they raise. Next, we discuss the use of governance as a multilevel analytic framework for evaluating empirical research. We argue that, to be useful, the concept of governance must recognize both hierarchical and associational forms of administrative practice. We then summarize a number of recent multilevel empirical studies that investigate the tensions between vertical and horizontal dimensions of public governance. We conclude with comments on the prospects for governance research.

Defining Public Governance

Governance—whether public or private—has been defined simply as "the general exercise of authority" (Michalski, Miller, and Stevens 2001, 9), where authority refers to systems of accountability and control. It includes global and local arrangements, formal structures and informal norms and practices, and spontaneous and intentional systems of control (Williamson 1996). The Twenty-Fifth International Congress of Administrative Sciences, held in July 2001 in Athens, had as its theme "Governance and Public Administration in

the 21st Century: New Trends and New Techniques." At the Athens conference, governance referred to the public interest and public service, the rule of
law and the *état de droit,* citizens and civil society. Despite the breadth of these
concerns, a growing number of scholars around the world, including the contributors to this volume, are attempting to give greater precision to the subject.

Private, or corporate, governance has long been an active area of research,
where it has been defined broadly as "the design of institutions that induce or
force management [that is, agents] to internalize the welfare of stakeholders
[that is, principals]" (Tirole 2001, 4).[1] Thus, governance in the private sector generally applies to the steering function, for example, as performed by
corporate (for-profit and nonprofit) boards, by structures that assign property
rights, and by international overhead organizations. The subject was brought
to a level of analytic refinement in the principal-agent literature and the analysis of contracts (for an overview, see Arrow 1985) as well as in Williamson's
(1996) *The Mechanisms of Governance,* in which he employed transaction
cost analysis to predict why certain forms of governance emerge in a market
economy.

An analogous approach might be useful in studying public sector governance: such an approach might encompass institutions that induce public managers—agents—to internalize the public's interests—principals—or to realize
net positive value from public expenditures. Most public administration and
management scholars, however, recognize a need to embrace a concept of public governance that is broader than one characterized by formal contracts, by
assignments of property rights, or by discrete economic calculations. According to Frederickson and Smith, for example, "Governance refers to the lateral
and interinstitutional relations in administration in the context of the decline
of sovereignty, the decreasing importance of jurisdictional borders, and a general institutional fragmentation" (2003, 222).[2] Most scholarship on public
governance emphasizes coordination and collaboration—manifest in the emergence of associational networks—as fundamental to democratic governance.

Underscoring this shift, Frederickson and Smith argue that "the administrative state is now less bureaucratic, less hierarchical, and less reliant on central authority to mandate action. Accountability for conducting the public's
business is increasingly about performance rather than discharging a specific
policy goal within the confines of the law" (2003, 208). They further state
that governance theories that incorporate ideas about the role of conjunctions
or associations among organizational entities are especially promising in over-
coming the centrifugal forces that are fragmenting administrative practice.

What, then, of the constitutional scheme in which public governance is embedded? What of legislatures and courts, politics and the rule of law, and accountability to citizens through electoral processes? Frederickson and Smith
acknowledge that "hierarchy is necessary for conjunction to exist" (224) because the American political scheme remains hierarchical and jurisdictional. As
noted below, other scholars also recognize this tension between hierarchical

and associational aspects. Much recent work on governance, however, is comparatively silent on this tension and on how it might be formally addressed.

Governance as an Analytic Framework

Despite the apparent fragmentation of the administrative state, devolution and loose or partial association are constrained by political and judicial demands for accountability to centralized authorities. Acknowledging that indisputable reality, we earlier defined public sector governance as "regimes of laws, rules, judicial decisions, and administrative practices that constrain, prescribe, and enable the provision of publicly supported goods and services" through formal and informal relationships with agents in the public and private sectors (Lynn, Heinrich, and Hill 2001, 7). This definition of governance links constitutional institutions with the realities of policymaking and public management. Underlying this concept is recognition that governance involves means for achieving direction, control, and coordination of individuals or organizational units on behalf of their common interests (Vickers 1983; Lynn, Heinrich, and Hill 2001).

Political Economy as a Logic of Governance

From this fundamental starting point of the rule of law, we have proposed an analytic framework—a "logic of governance"—that can provide some conceptual order to the systematic empirical study of governance (Lynn, Heinrich, and Hill 2000a, 2000b, 2001). This logic links several aspects of collective action and may be expressed in the following set of hierarchical interactions:

- Between (a) citizen preferences and interests expressed politically and (b) public choice expressed in enacted legislation or executive policies;
- Between (b) public choice and (c) formal structures and processes of public agencies;
- Between (c) the structures of formal authority and (d) discretionary organization, management, and administration;
- Between (d) discretionary organization, management, and administration and (e) core technologies, primary work, and service transactions overseen by public agencies;
- Between (e) primary work and (f) consequences, outputs, or results;
- Between (f) consequences, outputs, or results and (g) stakeholder assessments of agency or program performance; and
- Between (g) stakeholder assessments and (a) public interests and preferences.

Employing the entirety of this logic in more than a descriptive way in a single empirical study is likely to be intellectually and practically infeasible. Some research communities tend to focus either on narrower bands of causal relationships (for example, public choice research focuses on public opinion, interests, and legislative behavior; organizational studies on structures and processes; management studies on managerial behavior and its consequences; human services fields on treatments and outcomes); or to focus on two or three (not necessarily adjacent) levels within a particular policy domain (for example, public health research focuses on how laws affect individual behavior; or non-profit research on how ownership affects efficiency and service distribution). Yet interdependencies across levels undoubtedly exist in all fields.

To facilitate comprehension of the possibilities in empirical governance research, a reduced-form expression can serve as a framing device:

$$O = f(E, C, T, S, M),$$

where
    O = outputs/outcomes (individual or organizational);
    E = environmental factors (political, economic, and so on);
    C = client or consumer characteristics;
    T = treatments (primary work, core processes, or technology);
    S = structures (administrative or organizational); and
    M = managerial roles, strategies, or actions.

Governmental outputs or outcomes, in other words, may depend in the general case on several classes of variables. The intellectual challenge for an individual researcher is to specify a causal model postulating how different kinds and levels of variables are directly and indirectly related in the particular aspects of governance under investigation. The resulting model will become the basis for empirical analysis that tests hypothesized relationships while controlling for other influential factors.

Neither this logic of governance nor its reduced form expression constitutes a "theory" of governance, but rather an organizing device for conceptualizing and interpreting empirical research. In particular, they are useful for at least two reasons. First, this logic of governance assists in integrating the findings of dispersed but conceptually related literatures. Does governance matter to governmental performance? Are there substantive, useful findings concerning what specific factors matter? What are the implications of these findings for theory building, research agendas, and practice? (See Hill and Lynn, forthcoming, for an analysis.)

Second, the logic enables investigators—and readers of their analyses—to locate individual research projects in a framework that identifies factors with potential influence on the results. It encourages discussion of limitations of findings that are attributable to the models, methods, and data used, as well as discussion of competing explanations that may be consistent with empirical observations. To the extent that researchers can locate their more specifically focused models or research agendas within a broader logic of governance such as this, and thereby be more explicit about the biases that may arise when factors at other levels cannot be modeled or when the nature of their effects is uncertain, we think the logic serves an important purpose. This purpose can be recognized in framing and interpreting research, even though it may not be fully incorporated in formal models and data analyses. Thus, this framework serves as a reminder of the endogeneity of complex governance processes, and in particular of the various hierarchical (and political) aspects that are fundamental to a constitutional scheme.

The logic of governance just described is, however, only one of many that might be employed to frame public governance research. As we have suggested elsewhere (Lynn, Heinrich, and Hill 2001, 88–92), other logics, employing different theories, might instead be used:

- Salamon's "new governance" framework, which uses as its unit of analysis the tools of government action (e.g., regulation, grants, fees, contracting, vouchers) and their operational political characteristics (1981, 2002);
- Systems frameworks, which view governance regimes as production or transformation processes that link inputs to outputs via organizations, managers, and technologies (e.g., Barnow 1979; Scott 1998; O'Toole and Meier 2000);
- Socialized choice frameworks, which emphasize information flows and actions mediated by social relations among actors (e.g., Laumann and Knoke 1987).

This last type of governance logic—especially one that focuses on "networks" or conjunctions of organizations—is a principal alternative to a logic based in a more hierarchically ordered political economy. Because practitioners and scholars of public governance increasingly signal a shift toward relational networks in the "hollow state," "third-party government," or "the new governance," we focus on this logic for understanding governance and framing research.

Networks as a Logic of Governance

"Networks" are, in fact, a particular form of the more generic concept of *collaboration:* the voluntary participation in interorganizational (horizontal) relationships that involve agreements or understandings concerning the allocation of responsibilities and rewards among the collaborators. Logics of governance that revolve around collaborative or networked arrangements emphasize the centrality of continuing social and political relationships and communications among stakeholders and other actors. These networked actors may be both internal and external to executive agencies and bureaucracies or hybrids that cross agency boundaries.

As noted at the beginning of this chapter, a number of scholars have emphasized the growing importance of such collaborative relationships in the production and delivery of public goods and services and the associated shift in emphasis for the study of public management and governance. Examples include:

- O'Toole's (1986) review of the implementation literature, in which he focuses on "multi-actor" implementation and corresponding issues for practitioners and researchers, and, later (1997), the need to "treat networks seriously" by incorporating network concepts to a greater degree in public administration research and practice;
- Kooiman's concept of "socio-political governance," in which "private actors do not act separately but in conjunction, together, in combination . . . in 'co' arrangements . . . [and] patterns that emerge from governing activities of social, political and administrative actors" (1993, 2);
- Milward's (1994) and Milward and Provan's (1993) description of the "hollow state" where goods and services are increasingly delivered through webs of nongovernmental providers while core functions remain the responsibility of governmental bureaucracies;
- Bardach's (1998) explication of "craftsmanship theory" as an attempt to "create value through collaboration" of provider networks;
- Kettl's (2002) depiction of a "transformation of governance" spurred by the idea that hierarchy and authority no longer are adequate characterizations of theory or practice in public management and administration; and
- Frederickson and Smith's (2003) argument that hierarchical relationships are waning as collaborative forms and alternative delivery systems emerge, thus requiring a shift in how public administration is studied—a shift toward studying governance.

These and other scholars emphasize the challenges and opportunities that networked forms of governance present; however, a concern is that the motivating core of the systematic study of governance—democratic accountability—can be lost or demoted in paradigms that focus solely or primarily on innovations, tools, networks, or any one feature of a system of governance (even hierarchy). That public policies and programs in the United States and elsewhere are being administered to an increasing extent through networks and collaborative relationships does not imply that hierarchical governance is no longer of practical or theoretical importance.

Some discussions of the network-focused paradigms do acknowledge that constitutional, hierarchical structures exist. For example, in addition to Frederickson and Smith's point about the necessity of hierarchy even within the shift they describe, Kettl notes that transformations in governance have "made government both *horizontal*—in search of service coordination and integration with nongovernmental partners in service provision—and *vertical*—through both traditional, hierarchical bureaucracies and multilayered federalism. It is not so much that the horizontal relationships have supplanted the vertical ones, but rather that the horizontal links have been added to the vertical ones" (Kettl 2002, 128).

In general, however, scholars that emphasize the ascendant role that networked relations play in governance tend to downplay, diagnose as a problem, or fail to acknowledge the realities of hierarchical governance in a federal, constitution-based system.

Hierarchy and Networks: A Continuum

"Hierarchy" and "network" may usefully be considered as the two ends of a continuum. "Hierarchy" consists of classic command-and-control relationships within organizational units or programs; across national, state, and local governments in a federal system; and between elected officials and the products of their political control. "Network" consists of spontaneous collaboration without formal governance. In between these two extremes are most of the interesting problems of governance in practice, where networks are hierarchical "tools of government" (for example, delegated cooperation).

A familiar argument among those describing the transformation of governance is that the lines of authority and control have become blurred for public managers (or private managers of the public's business), who no longer perform their work within the traditional structures of bureaucracy. As Meier and Krause (2003) and Kettl (2002) note, however, the separation of powers in the United States has long made the lines of bureaucratic authority unclear. "Authority leakages," as described some time ago by Tullock (1965), are common. Thus, the limitations of administrative governance have long been recognized and the subject of considerable study, although some of these problems are, as some suggest, becoming more acute as administrative structures evolve or dissolve.

Hierarchical relations and a logic of governance rooted in the rule of law remain realities in public governance and are in many ways its defining features. These features are most often present to assure democratic accountability or, less loftily, to permit the control by politicians of the exercise of administrative power. As Moe (1989, 267) has commented, "The bureaucracy arises out of politics, and its design reflects the interests, strategies, and com-

promises of those who exercise political power." Thus, multiple and sometimes conflicting goals in legislation can lead to vague mandates or divided
factions within bureaucracies and among competing authorities.

It is thus useful—and necessary—to temper the charge toward network
governance with a logic of governance that does not privilege either hierarchy
or network, but allows for theoretical and empirical exploration of the existence of, and implications of, both. To ignore the role of hierarchical structures and management in network performance would be a primary error;
command and control remain central to governance within a constitutional
framework, albeit with a much expanded (in many ways more problematic)
set of tools or instruments of policy and administration (Salamon 2002).

Recent treatments of the rise of network forms often acknowledge the difficulties these forms present for accountability in a democratic system. Milward and Provan (1993) raised these kinds of issues when they first described
the hollow state: "To the extent that governments are unwilling to invest in
adequate management, accountability for the expenditure of public funds by
private organizations will be compromised. And even if sufficient funds for
oversight are provided, entirely new governance structures will need to be developed" (234). More recently, Kettl acknowledges that, "for public administration, the challenge is reconciling the management and accountability challenges of these networks with the bedrock ideas that hierarchical authority
has long provided. How can government ensure accountability in extended
service networks where administrative responsibility is widely shared and
where no one is truly in charge? How can government, structured and staffed
for an era when vertical relationships dominated, build the capacity to manage horizontal partnerships effectively?" (Kettl 2002, 129–30).

Kettl goes further by saying that "the first governance problem is *adaptation:* fitting traditional vertical systems to the new challenge of globalization
and devolution and integrating new horizontal systems into traditional vertical ones" (2002, 147).[3] Despite the acknowledgement of accountability and
governance challenges associated with networked forms of public governance,
the conundrum remains of exactly how to accomplish the kind of adaptation
that Kettl and others suggest.

In light of these practical difficulties with governance and accountability in
changing times, the "new" governance forms are a mirage without also tackling head-on the realities of hierarchy and law that accompany them. Many
researchers of governance in this era debate a related question: are the theories of governance or public administration lagging behind, or are they also
evolving as government itself "reinvents" or "transforms"? We suggest, and
the examples that follow confirm, that elements of traditional theories of public administration will continue to usefully shape the study of governance and
guide administrative practice, just as new conceptualizations of governance
expand our approaches both to research and public management.

The Logic of Governance in Recent Research

Many recent studies of governance apply more than one type of theory, melding old and new, to frame issues, problems, research hypotheses, and analyses.

There are few areas of policy that have seen greater changes in organization, structure, program administration, and other aspects of governance than public health care systems. Banting and Corbett describe the struggle of governments everywhere to "balance the needs and expectations of citizens, the demands of health care professionals and the pressures of public budgets" as health policy administration becomes more complex and tradeoffs among stakeholders become more painful. At the same time, they stress the importance of meeting these challenges through political institutions that foster the participation and cooperation of "at least two levels of government" (e.g., federal and state), with implications for a "wider range of multi-level systems" (2002, 2).

In their study of health policy in Australia, Belgium, Canada, Germany, and the United States, Banting and Corbett specifically suggest that the role of different levels of government in defining basic policies that shape health services is a key variable determining policy impacts. Some related governance questions in health care that they identify include "Who sets the range of services to be covered and the terms of access to them? Who regulates the training, standards and reimbursement of service providers? Who sets the regulatory framework and funding mechanisms for health institutions such as hospitals and clinics? And who decides how the system as a whole will be financed?" (6).

In their recent work, Milward and Provan (2002) address some of these health care governance questions. They study the evolution of two mental health managed care systems in Arizona, one "governed" by a nonprofit agency and the other by a for-profit firm, in a "mental health authority" model. The mental health authorities in Arizona are regional behavioral health authorities (RBHAs) that render behavioral health services from general health care funded by the states and federal government under the Medicaid program. All but one RBHA are nonprofit organizations (the other being a for-profit firm). Thus, the primary providers of services are nongovernmental partners in fairly complex, nontraditional administrative arrangements.

Milward and Provan locate these provider systems within a broader logic of governance and, in doing so, gain further traction on their problem and make it more transparent for practitioners and researchers in other areas. They specifically discuss the "political economy of public health," noting that the for-profit and nonprofit "regimes" exist within the institutional structure of the state government's mental health care program. In figure 2 in their essay, they map out hierarchical linkages among the federal government (via block grants and Medicaid), the state government, the Arizona Health Care Cost Containment System, and multiple levels of the contracted, nongovernmental regimes. Medicaid and the state's "subvention funds" are the primary sources of funding for mental health care services, and, thus, the legislature controls appropriations for the mental health care system. The politics of Medicaid, therefore, are elemental in the governance of these programs. Milward and Provan note that Arizona was the last state to adopt Medicaid and the first state to make Medicaid a managed care program.[4]

Milward and Provan draw on theories of collaboration—employing a logic of cooperation, partnerships, alliances, and services integration—but also principal-agent theory in their analysis of relationships and arrangements among the system actors. Thus, both network and hierarchy are central concepts in explaining the relationships they examine. For example, the level of funding for services (determined by federal Medicaid funds and state government matching allocations) influences the risks for contractors involved in service provision and access to program services among eligible clients, which is controlled by the RBHAs. They also describe a hierarchical system of service provision within the for-profit RBHA that facilitates the integration of key functions performed by various affiliate organizations. Thus, at multiple levels of analysis, hierarchical and network governance theories together enrich the analysis of the complex set of political, administrative, and contractual relationships and arrangements that govern the delivery of mental health care in Arizona.

Brown and Potoski (2003) similarly draw from different (and sometimes competing) theories to study how county and municipal governments choose among service delivery modes that are increasingly less likely to involve direct service provision. They begin by using transactions costs theory to investigate government choices among five different service modes: direct service provision, joint contracting, complete contracts with other governments, complete contracts with for-profit firms, and complete contracts with nonprofit organizations.

Employing Williamson's (1981) orthodox economic theory of transactions costs, they categorize government services according to their amenability to contracting, based on asset specificity and metering (or the ability to monitor performance). Their central argument is that rationally bounded governments choose among the different modes of service provision with the goal of moderating variable production and transactions costs. On the basis of this theoretical framework, they derive a series of hypotheses about the types of service arrangements governments will choose, depending primarily on the characteristics of the service provided. Are these service delivery mechanisms endogenous to a logic of choice based on transactions costs, as Williamson's theory proposes?

Rather than proceeding directly to their municipal and county government survey data to test their hypotheses, however, Brown and Potoski first turn to theoretical frameworks of institutional governance to consider institutional and market explanations for how governments organize to deliver services.

From institutional theory, they draw upon institutional rules and norms, and history and path dependence, to consider the role of organizational structure, management capacity, and politics in determining service delivery modes and contract arrangements. For example, they hypothesize that governments with low human resource and fiscal capacity are more likely to engage in complete contracts. At the same time, they recognize that political and fiscal pressures from the states—e.g., in the form of property tax limitations—will influence the service delivery modes chosen by municipal governments. In their empirical analysis, Brown and Potoski merge data characterizing historical-political development patterns of the cities and state policies with the municipal-county survey data to test these alternative hypotheses.

Brown and Potoski find that transactions costs alone do not explain these decisions, and that organizational capacity and state policies that affect fiscal resources are also important determinants of service delivery arrangements. They accordingly conclude that modeling these decisions as simple economic choices between contracting and service provision is unwise and that governments that invest in management capacity may be better positioned to reap the benefits of effective contracting.

Sowa, Selden, and Sandfort (forthcoming) are concerned with the expanding role that nonprofit (and other private) organizations are playing in the delivery of publicly funded services. In particular, they note that questions about nonprofits' effectiveness in addressing complex social problems have become increasingly important to funders, clients, and the public. Turning to the literature on organizational effectiveness, they review alternative theories that provide guidance on how to conceptualize organizational effectiveness, define criteria by which performance should be judged, and identify frameworks and tools to assess effectiveness.

Although they comment that there are nearly as many models as there are studies of organizational effectiveness, Sowa, Selden, and Sandfort (forthcoming) distinguish among several types of approaches. First, they explain that some scholars focus on internal organizational factors in defining criteria of effectiveness—e.g., organizational goals or procedures for accomplishing goals. These are commonly known in the literature as closed system models, where there are typically a small number of variables for managers to control, relationships among the variables can be reliably predicted, and organizational objectives or outcomes are verifiable. They note that this approach may be more relevant in practice to nonprofit managers who are increasingly required to track goal achievements to secure or maintain funding.

The open system modeling approach is a second alternative that encompasses a broader array of variables that relate the structure and characteristics of organizations to their contexts or environments. Included are what Sowa, Selden, and Sandfort (forthcoming) describe as system resource models, where inputs into an organization are more important than their outputs, and an "effective" organization is one that survives. Another is the ecological model that defines organizational effectiveness in terms of stakeholder or constituency satisfaction.

Rather than viewing these diverse measures (and the theories and values that underlie them) as necessarily in conflict, Sowa, Selden, and Sandfort (forthcoming) suggest an alternative (theory-based) multidimensional, hierarchical framework for the analysis of nonprofit organizational effectiveness that combines some aspects of each approach. They describe this framework as hierarchical in the sense that it depicts organizational effectiveness as comprised of both management and program dimensions. In their model, management more broadly refers to both organizational characteristics and the actions of managers within them, including structure and process. Program dimensions include the specific services or intervention of the organization. In effect, their model focuses on what Lynn, Heinrich, and Hill (2001) describe as organizational and technical governance or the managerial and primary work levels. They also link these levels of analysis to management outcomes and program outcomes and incorporate open-systems measures of effectiveness.

Sowa, Selden, and Sandfort (forthcoming) apply their model in a study, Investigating Partnerships in Early Childhood Education (IPIECE), that explores early childhood organizations that are blending multiple sources of public dollars to provide full-day, full-year care for children and their families. They report that as their study progressed, however, they discovered more hierarchical levels than anticipated among organizations operating the programs. For example, clients were grouped into classrooms in different sites, and multiple sites were sometimes operated by a single organization. Thus, they expanded their conceptual framework to include additional levels and units of analysis.

To reflect these complex realities of organizational structure and services delivery in IPIECE, Sowa, Selden, and Sandfort (forthcoming) apply multilevel structural equation modeling: a technique that goes beyond many standard methods for analyzing organizational effectiveness by not only allowing for multiple levels of analysis, but also facilitating the modeling of reciprocal causation. More specifically, they explain that multilevel structural equation models "combine the full strength of structural equation modeling with multilevel or hierarchical modeling because they allow for estimation of multilevel path analysis, wherein within-group level parameters are modeled as a function of between-group variables following their own path models" (Sowa, Selden, and Sandfort forthcoming). The problem of measurement error in the variables, which arises when many of the variables are directly or indirectly related to outcomes that may also be simultaneously related to each other, is likewise addressed. In the end, their proposed empirical model for the IPIECE analysis includes five different levels of analysis and multiple measures of management and program outcomes. Sowa and Selden (forthcoming) more fully develop the measures and empirical tests of effectiveness for these organizations.

More generally, their work suggests that both theories and methods can keep up with the growing complexities of governance in practice.

There are a number of other examples of recent studies that demonstrate scholars' skills and creativity in adapting theories, models, and methods of governance research to the changing realities of public managers and their administrative responsibilities and agency functions. Some of this work appears in this volume and in the winter 2004 issue of the *Journal of Policy Analysis and Management*. Others, such as Roderick, Jacob, and Bryk (2000), presented their research in the preceding volume edited by Heinrich and Lynn (2000), and their work has advanced since then (Jacob 2002; Jacob and Lefgren 2002; Roderick, Jacob, and Bryk 2002). What is perhaps most impressive about the work of Roderick et al. is that they examine the performance of the Chicago Public School system as a whole, despite the complex set of policies (i.e., administrative reforms, promotional gate policies, summer study programs, high-stakes testing, and so forth) that are being implemented in the system by various policy actors. They draw from multiple bodies of theory and spearhead advances in research methodologies to accommodate these complexities, deriving important findings with direct relevance to the daily work of public managers and program administrators.

Progress in governance research is undoubtedly uneven across policy areas, and, of course, public administrators and scholars themselves have different metrics by which they judge progress in the field. And the issues and concerns raised by those alarmed by the transformation of governance in practice—democratic accountability, shifting public and private risks and responsibilities, competition and quality, citizen satisfaction, and so forth—are serious and call for new or more creative approaches to research. We suggest, nonetheless, that the fields of public administration and management are on a solid foundation and are advancing to produce the types of knowledge that will be useful to policymakers and public managers as they struggle to meet more complex public responsibilities and demands with fewer resources.

Prospects for Governance Research

As we noted in our earlier work (Lynn, Heinrich, and Hill 2001), specific research studies necessarily adapt theories, models, and methods to issues that arise in particular organizational and political contexts and to the limitations of available data sets. While such adaptations make accumulation of findings across context more difficult, the emergence of patterns of approaches and findings despite variations in research contexts is especially encouraging to those seeking a broader, empirically based view of governance. Thus we regard the fact that so many studies, including those included in the present volume and a great many others as well, are using multilevel frameworks or models to explore the complexities of administrative practice as a positive development for the field. The general thrust of the findings, to the effect that public managers are necessarily preoccupied with reconciling the centrifugal forces of service complexity and administrative fragmentation with the centripetal forces of political and judicial accountability, should, moreover, be reassuring to those who view the American administrative state as responsive to evolving circumstances within its constitutional framework. The alternatives—lurching from one new "paradigm" to the next or succumbing to the forces of inertia, both of which are characteristic of other advanced democracies—are hardly what we aspire to when attempting to both respect individual rights and promote collective justice.

Notes

1. Corporate governance has also been defined more narrowly as "ways in which suppliers of finance to corporations assure themselves of getting a return on their investment" (Shleifer and Vishny 1997, 737).

2. As another example, Canada's Institute of Governance (2002) states, "Governance is the process whereby societies or organizations make important decisions, determine whom they involve, and how they render account."

3. Likewise, Salamon (2002) acknowledges the accountability problems that accompany "third-party-government" and the use of tools: "Indeed, to operate most effectively, third-party tools require that program managers have wide latitude to bargain with their third-party partners, in direct opposition to the prohibitions on ex parte contacts stipulated in administrative law. . . . How to square these new approaches with the more traditional procedural safeguards of administrative law, however, is still far from settled, leaving administrators and courts alike significantly adrift" (605).

4. A Harvard case study describes the development of the Arizona Health Care Cost Containment System and the politics and institutional issues that shaped its design and administration. See Varley (1988).

References

Arrow, Kenneth. 1985. "The Economics of Agency." In John W. Pratt and Richard J. Zeckhauser, eds., *Principals and Agents: The Structure of Business*. Cambridge, Mass.: Harvard Business School Press, 37–51.

Banting, Keith G., and Stan Corbett. 2002. "Multi-Level Governance and Health Care: Health Policy in Five Federations." Paper presented at the American Political Science Association annual meeting, Boston, August 29–September 1.

Bardach, Eugene. 1998. *Getting Agencies to Work Together: The Practice and Theory of Managerial Craftsmanship*. Washington, D.C.: Brookings Institution Press.

Barnow, Burt S. 1979. "Theoretical Issues in the Estimation of Production Functions in Manpower Programs." In F. Bloch, ed., *Evaluating Manpower Training Programs*. Research in Labor Economics, Supplement 1. Greenwich, Conn.: JAI Press, 295–338.

Barzelay, Michael. 1992. *Breaking Through Bureaucracy: A New Vision for Managing in Government*. Berkeley: University of California Press.

Brown, Trevor L., and Matthew Potoski. 2003. "Transactions Costs and Institutional Explanations for Government Service Production Decisions." *Journal of Public Administration Research and Theory* 13:441–68.

Frederickson, H. George. 1997. *The Spirit of Public Administration*. San Francisco: Jossey-Bass.

Frederickson, H. George, and Kevin B. Smith. 2003. *The Public Administration Theory Primer*. Boulder, Colo.: Westview Press.

Garvey, Gerald. 1997. *Public Administration: The Profession and the Practice*. New York: St. Martin's Press.

Heinrich, Carolyn J., and Laurence E. Lynn, Jr., eds. 2000. *Governance and Performance: New Perspectives*. Washington, D.C.: Georgetown University Press.

Hill, Carolyn J., and Lynn, Laurence E., Jr. 2005. "Is Hierarchical Governance in Decline? Evidence from Empirical Research." *Journal of Public Administration Research and Theory*.

Institute of Governance. 2002 [www.iog.ca/]. Nonprofit Canadian organization that aims to promote effective governance with research and analysis, advisory services, professional development, and more.

Jacob, Brian A. 2002. "Accountability, Incentives and Behavior: The Impact of High-Stakes Testing in the Chicago Public Schools." NBER Working Paper 8968.

Jacob, Brian A., and Lars Lefgren. 2002. "Remedial Education and Student Achievement: A Regression-Discontinuity Analysis." NBER Working Paper 8918.

Kettl, Donald F. 2000. *The Global Public Management Revolution: A Report on the Transformation of Governance*. Washington, D.C.: Brookings Institution Press.

———. 2002. *The Transformation of Governance: Public Administration for the Twenty-First Century*. Baltimore: Johns Hopkins University Press.

Kooiman, Jan. 1993. "Social-Political Governance: Introduction." In J. Kooiman, ed., *Modern Governance: New Government-Society Interactions*. London: Sage, 1–6.

Laumann, Edward O., and David Knoke. 1987. *The Organizational State: Social Choice in National Policy Domains*. Madison: University of Wisconsin Press.

Lynn, Laurence E., Jr., Carolyn J. Heinrich, and Carolyn J. Hill. 2000a. "Studying Governance and Public Management: Challenges and Prospects." *Journal of Public Administration Research and Theory* 10 (2):233–62.

———. 2000b. "Studying Governance and Public Management: Why? How?" In C. Heinrich and L. Lynn, eds. *Governance and Performance: New Perspectives*. Washington, D.C.: Georgetown University Press, 1–33.

———. 2001. *Improving Governance: A New Logic for Empirical Research*. Washington, D.C.: Georgetown University Press.

Meier, Kenneth J., and George A. Krause. 2003. "The Scientific Study of Bureaucracy: An Overview." In George A. Krause and Kenneth J. Meier, eds., *Politics, Policy and Organization: Frontiers in the Scientific Study of Bureaucracy*, 1–19.

Michalski, Wolfgang, Riel Miller, and Barrie Stevens. 2001. "Governance in the 21st Century: Power in the Global Knowledge Economy and Society." In *Governance in the 21st Century: Power in the Global Knowledge Society*. Paris: Organization for Economic Cooperation and Development, 7–26.

Milward, H. Brinton. 1994. "Nonprofit Contracting and the Hollow State." *Public Administration Review* 54:73–77.

Milward, H. Brinton, and Keith G. Provan. 1993. "The Hollow State: Private Provision of Public Services." In H. Ingraham and S. R. Smith, eds., *Public Policy for Democracy*. Washington, D.C.: Brookings Institution Press, 222–37.

———. 2002. "Private Principals, Nonprofit Agents." Paper presented at the American Political Science Association annual meeting, Boston, August 29–September 1.

Moe, Terry M. 1989. "The Politics of Bureaucratic Structure." In John E. Chubb and Paul E. Peterson, eds., *Can the Government Govern?* Washington, D.C.: Brookings Institution Press, 267–92.

O'Toole, Laurence J., Jr. 1986. "Policy Recommendations for Multi-Actor Implementation: An Assessment of the Field." *Journal of Public Policy* 6 (2):181–210.

———. 1997. "Treating Networks Seriously: Practical and Research-Based Agendas in Public Administration." *Public Administration Review* 51:45–52.

O'Toole, Laurence J., Jr., and Kenneth J. Meier. 2000. "Networks, Hierarchies, and Public Management: Modeling the Nonlinearities." In Carolyn J. Heinrich and Laurence E. Lynn, Jr., eds., *Governance and Performance: New Perspectives*. Washington, D.C.: Georgetown University Press, 263–91.

Osborne, David, and Gaebler, Ted. 1993. *Reinventing Government: How the Entrepreneurial Spirit Is Transforming the Public Sector*. New York: Penguin.

Peters, B. Guy, and John Pierre. 1998. "Governance without Government? Rethinking Public Administration." *Journal of Public Administration Research and Theory* 8:223–44.

Roderick, Melissa, Brian A. Jacob, and Anthony Bryk. 2000. "Evaluating Chicago's Efforts to End Social Promotion." In Carolyn J. Heinrich and Laurence E. Lynn, Jr., eds., *Governance and Performance: New Perspectives*. Washington, D.C.: Georgetown University Press, 34–67.

———. 2002. "Summer in the City: Achievement Gains in Chicago's Summer Bridge Program." In G. D. Borman and M. Boulay, eds., *Summer Learning: Research, Policies and Programs*. Mahwah, N.J.: Erlbaum, 73–102.

Salamon, Lester M. 1981. "Rethinking Public Management: Third-Party Government and the Changing Forms of Public Action." *Public Policy* 29:255–75.

Salamon, Lester M., ed. 2002. *The Tools of Government: A Guide to the New Governance*. Oxford: Oxford University Press.

Scott, W. Richard. 1998. *Organizations: Rational, Natural, Open Systems*, 4th ed. Upper Saddle River, N.J.: Prentice Hall.

Shleifer, Andrei, and Robert W. Vishny. 1997. "A Survey of Corporate Governance." *Journal of Finance* 52:737–83.

Sowa, J. E., and S. C. Selden. Forthcoming. "Testing a Multi-Dimensional Model of Organizational Performance: Prospects and Problems." *Journal of Public Administration Research and Theory*.

Sowa, J. E., S. C. Selden, and J. R. Sandfort. Forthcoming. "No Longer 'Unmeasurable'?: A Multidimensional Integrated Model of Nonprofit Organizational Effectiveness." *Nonprofit and Voluntary Quarterly*.

Tirole, Jean. 2001. "Corporate Governance." *Econometrica* 69:1–35.

Tullock, Gordon. 1965. *The Politics of Bureaucracy*. New York: McGraw-Hill.

Varley, Pamela. 1988. "Matters of Life and Death: Defunding Organ Transplants in the State of Arizona." *Kennedy School of Government Case Program*, C15-88-821.0.

Vickers, Geoffrey. 1983. *The Art of Judgment: A Study of Policy Making*. London: Harper & Row.

Wamsley, Gary L., and James F. Wolf. 1990. "Introduction: Can a High-Modern Project Find Happiness in a Postmodern Era." In Gary L. Wamsley et al., *Refounding Public Administration: Modern Paradoxes, Postmodern Challenges*. Newbury Park, Calif.: Sage, 1–37.

Wamsley, Gary L., Robert N. Bacher, Charles T. Goodsell, Philip S. Kronenberg, John A. Rohr, Camilla M. Stivers, Orion F. White, and James F. Wolf. 1990. *Refounding Public Administration: Modern Paradoxes, Postmodern Challenges*. Newbury Park, Calif.: Sage.

Williamson, Oliver. 1981. "The Economics of Organization." *American Journal of Sociology* 87:548–77.

———. 1996. *The Mechanisms of Governance*. New York: Oxford University Press.

Two

Framing High Performance and Innovativeness in Government

A Review and Assessment of Research

Hal G. Rainey • Jay Eungha Ryu

In the past two decades, numerous books and articles have focused on high performance, excellence, and innovativeness of government agencies and programs. Their authors have tried to identify the characteristics of the agencies that bring about such desirable results. These books and articles have appeared in sufficient numbers and with sufficient similarity in theme and objectives to amount to something of a genre. This chapter summarizes and assesses many of these contributions. In addition to bringing them together and examining them, we seek to understand how well these studies validate their conclusions about excellence, high performance, and innovation. We examine their methods and the strength of the support for their conclusions. The studies focus on individual organizations as the unit of analysis. Although about half of them emphasize the challenge of managing relations with the political authorities and influences in the environments of the organizations, as well as with other stakeholders, the studies for the most part do not adhere to a multilevel, multiorganizational "governance" perspective that is a central theme in this book and in the work of the contributors to it. All the studies we review here, however, seek to analyze the effectiveness of one important part of such a framework—the individual organizations and the leaders and professionals within them. All the studies seek to understand how we might conceive and elaborate excellent performance and innovativeness at this level, the organizational level, of a governance framework. We identify points of consensus among the studies to contribute to such an elaboration. In turn, the limits of some of the studies, such as the limited attention to external political institutions and processes by some of the authors, suggest the value of expanding future research on this topic to include more of the contextual factors that a governance framework would include.

Validation and Verification: The "Take My Word for It" Challenge

The summaries and review will show that the contributions to this stream of literature vary widely among themselves, in methods, samples and sampling, and especially in their conceptual frameworks. Many of them draw on case studies and case observations and some on even more informal or inexplicit methods involving highly subjective conclusions. Some of them represent or resemble "best practices" research, which has been so widely practiced and extolled as to achieve buzzword status. In this type of inquiry, consulting firms or academic researchers identify the best practices in organizations on the basis of what they observe or hear from organizations about things the organizations do well that purportedly lead to high performance. This method has some strengths and attractions, but also some obvious weaknesses, such as problems in firmly validating the conclusions. The studies typically lack comparison groups, representative samples, and replicable methods and results. In effect, the reports of such results ask us to "take my word for it" in accepting their conclusions. In a sense, all social research raises this challenge in varying degrees, and excellent, influential case studies and ethnomethodological research in the social sciences have often raised this issue of how much we have to rely on the researcher's judgments and perceptions. Even empirical research reporting a great deal of data and explicit methodological and analytical procedures often cannot relate all details of the data collection, analysis, and interpretation, and their relation to each other.

Whether or not we label it best practices research, the form of conclusion drawing in many of these high performance studies has had immense influence on the popular and academic literature on management in recent decades. Peters and Waterman's (1982) highly successful *In Search of Excellence*, probably the single most important wellspring of much of this activity, told us that the authors had identified excellent corporations using a set of criteria that they listed (without explaining the exact methods of employing these criteria). They then enunciated a set of aphoristic observations about the characteristics and practices that made the firms excellent (including "stick to the knitting," "stay close to the customer," and "employ simultaneous loose-tight properties"). They illustrated these points with examples of how some of the firms displayed such behaviors, thus begging the questions of how much variation there was among the firms and how one validated the connection between these behaviors and the successes of the firms. Indeed, some of the excellent firms foundered, or at least floundered, in years following the publication of the book.

The success of *In Search of Excellence* appears to be the primary reason for the explosion of management books offering either explicitly "best practice" information for managers, or kindred lists of aphoristic advisory statements, usually based on case observations (e.g., Collins and Porras, 1994). It certainly influenced Osborne and Gaebler's *Reinventing Government* (1992) and many more recent articles and books on excellence and high performance in government such as those summarized below. As mentioned, these contributions vary, with some of them relying on observations about best practices and others drawing on survey research and other evidence. Most of those that carry excellence, high performance, or innovation in their titles tend to rely to significant degrees on the judgment of the author, without clear, direct empirical evidence to support this judgment.

An easy resolution would be to condemn much of this body of research as insufficiently rigorous, poorly validated, and excessively disparate to support well-substantiated conclusions. If, however, we demand high levels of scientific rigor—large representative samples, clear conceptualization of concepts and variables and their hypothesized relations, very explicit empirical measures and analyses—we will be crying in the wilderness for a long time. Such conditions will remain difficult and expensive to attain for many reasons, such as the difficulty in establishing clear, widely accepted, and measurable performance indicators for many government organizations.

At the same time, we need to consider the challenges in designing and carrying out research that clearly resolves such questions. We need to avoid easy critiques and to sincerely seek to assess how much these contributions offer. Even if we aspire to find a rich source of funding to design the supreme study we might all want, we can look at these contributions for points of consensus and insight that we can use to develop models and theories and to guide future research. Even the less methodologically explicit studies can be regarded as sources of evidence and insight, akin to case studies and other forms of "qualitative" research. Limitations of these studies can also provide reminders of matters definitely to be accounted for in future studies.

The Methods and Conclusions of the Studies

As a first step in summarizing this literature, we invite attention to the set of propositions about effective public organizations listed in appendix A. The propositions are based on a review of studies like the ones examined in this chapter, but also of many other sources of propositions about effective public organizations. For example, the review drew on Meier's (2000; see also Rourke 1984) observations about factors that increase an agency's power, such as leadership and expertise, and the agency's relations with external authorities and groups, such as legislative bodies and interest groups. Meier did not directly propose that these factors lead to high performance, but appendix A posits that agencies with higher levels of them are more likely to perform effectively. Below, we will return to these matters about relations with external political authorities and attach much significance to the scant attention they receive in the studies we summarize and review here.

Appendix A thus provides a set of assertions about many different factors that should be related to a government organization's effectiveness and that should be taken into account in studying organizational performance. In this sense, appendix A provides a framework that we can use in assessing the studies reviewed below, and in making various points about them. In turn, the contributions reviewed below sometimes indicate matters missing from appendix A and often show ways of elaborating factors in appendix A. The propositions in the appendix have many limitations, such as the need for more clarification of many of them, but they can serve as a framework and checklist in this way.

Next, we need to begin examining the methods and conclusions of the studies summarized in appendix B (in alphabetical order of the first author's last name). Appendix B includes both the research on high performance and innovation, even though we later discuss evidence that those two outcomes can have very different implications for organizations. We keep the two types of studies together in the appendix and the review below because they overlap in various ways. The studies of high performance sometimes conclude that those organizations are innovative, and the studies of the innovative organizations tend to assume or conclude that those organizations perform very well (see, for example, the entries in appendix B for Behn, Denhardt, and Holzer and Callahan). The two types of studies often find similar organizational characteristics. Later, however, we discuss research on innovation and performance in the private sector that indicates differences between the organizational implications of performance versus innovativeness.

Reading appendix B, one encounters many similarities among conclusions of different studies, but obviously the studies vary a great deal in methods, conceptualization, and conclusions. The sprawling character of the studies creates challenges in drawing conclusions about what we learn from them about high performance and innovation. Figure 2.1 illustrates one major challenge. The figure will be easier to understand after reading appendix B and the review to follow, but it can be introduced now to emphasize a point that the summaries and review will illustrate. The studies vary in the size and representativeness of their samples and in the degree to which they provide quantitative evidence that supports assessment of their internal validity and the strength of association among variables. By the dimension of validity and strength of association, we mean that some authors—such as Borins (1998) and Wolf (1993)—report quantitative measures of variables and analysis of relations among variables that provides evidence about internal validity (by statistical controls for variables that rule out alternative explanations, for example) and about the strength of the relationships among the variables.[1] Holzer and Callahan (1998), by contrast, report a study of a large sample of successful innovators but provide no quantitative evidence of relationships among variables involved in their main conclusions about successful innovators, although they do provide evidence from a survey, about some of the conclusions in their study. Although they examine only a small sample of organizations or a single organization, we classify Linden (1990, 1994) and Behn (1991) as high on this dimension because they report outcome measures or evaluations at different times that provide evidence of effective organizational performance. All of the studies classified in the lower left quadrant concentrate on one or a small sample of organizations and report case analyses in which the authors provide no clear quantitative evidence of the internal validity of their conclusions or the strengths of the associations between organizational performance and innovation and the factors the authors conclude to be important determinants of these two outcomes. The authors often offer evidence in the form of examples or quotations, but otherwise report their conclusions in a manner that places the studies high on the "take my word for it" dimension.

As noted in figure 2.1, classification in any quadrant of appendix B does not indicate an assessment of the quality or value of the study. Case studies of one unit of analysis or a small sample of them have provided some of the most important insights in the social sciences. Yet, by themselves—in advance of further confirmation—they have obvious limitations in generalizability and validation. Large-sample, more quantified studies can offer more explicit evidence supporting generalizability and validity, but they can lack fidelity to individual circumstances and richness of insight. The classification illustrates the challenge mentioned earlier, that the studies are disparate and they raise the classic issue in the social sciences of trading off between rich case and qualitative analysis against more quantified analysis, and small samples versus larger ones. This makes it difficult to evaluate the set of studies to determine ultimate conclusions, but we will try to do so anyway. Even if ultimate conclusions prove difficult, reviewing the range of findings and the alternatives and the trade-offs can support the design of future studies. We also emphasize that the classification scheme may trample certain nuances. For example, the dimensions would be better conceived as continua rather than dichotomies.

We also invite attention to table 2.1 now, even though we discuss it below, in relation to drawing conclusions. It illustrates an attempt at locating points of consensus by noting the points at which the conclusions of the studies coincide with factors listed in the propositions in appendix A (as indicated by the Xs in table 2.1). The review to follow will refer to aspects of this figure, in leading up to the effort to draw conclusions.

Case Studies of Small Samples of Organizations

The Gold (1982) study, one of the earliest in this stream of research, drew on a sample of five government organizations (three federal agencies and two city governments) and five private organizations. According to Gold, he chose the organizations because each had a good product, each was a good place to work, and each had been sound and healthy for a long time. He then con-

Provision of Quantitative Data on Validity or Statistical Association

		Low	High
	High	Holzer and Callahan (1998) Wilson (1989) Rainey and Steinbauer (1999)	Borins (1998) Wolf (1993) Greve (1999) Greve and Taylor (2000) Staw and Epstein (2000)
	Low	Moore (1995) DiIulio (1994) Popovich (1998) Peters and Waterman (1982) Gold (1982) Denhardt (1993)	Light (1998) Linden (1990, 1994) Behn (1991) Thompson (2000)

Representativeness of Samples labels the left axis.

Figure 2.1
Representativeness and Provision of Quantitative Data in the Studies of Organizational Performance and Innovation

Note: Classification of a study on this table does not indicate evaluation of the individual study's quality or value. A study low on representativeness, for example, can produce creative insights. The classifications in this table illustrate methodological and analytical tradeoffs that researchers face.

cluded that each of the organizations attributed their success to the emphases and conditions summarized in appendix B. The study offers no clear description of how evidence on the organizations was gathered, but implicitly involves contacts and interviews with members of the organization and reviews of their documents. It is clear that the reader has to rely heavily on the author's judgment about the adequacy of the evidence, about both the organizations' success and the factors leading to it and the degree of uniformity among the organizations in displaying success and its causes. Thus, the study offers stimulating ideas and suggestions about achieving success but, as research, has value only as one person's loosely justified observations about successful organizations that can contribute to developing propositions to be further confirmed. As an example of contributing to such consensus, Gold emphasizes the importance of clarifying organizational mission and goals, of valuing and empowering the people in the organization, as do many of the other studies in this group. By contrast, comparing this study to the list of propositions and factors in appendix A raises the interesting point that Gold's conclusions make no reference to the aspects of external political environment

Table 2.1

Comparison of Findings from the Innovation Studies with Propositions from Appendix A

Propositions from Appendix A	Behn (1991)	Borins (1998)	Denhardt (1993)	DiIulio (1994)	Gold (1982)	Hale (1996)	Holzer & Callahan (1998)	Light (1998)	Linden (1990)	Linden (1994)	Moore (1995)	Popovich (1998)	STEP (1985)	Wilson (1989)	Wolf (1993)
Effective relations with oversight authorities	X										X				
Effective relations with other stakeholders		X												X	
Responsive autonomy in relation to oversight							X	X	X		X	X	X		
Mission valence	X		X		X	X		X				X		X	X
Strong organizational culture			X	X		X	X								X
Effective leadership	X	X	X			X		X	X			X		X	
Effective task design	X	X		X	X	X		X	X			X		X	X
Effective utilization of technology		X					X				X		X		
Effective development of human resources	X				X	X	X	X							
High levels of professionalism among members		X	X			X						X	X	X	
High levels of motivation among members			X	X	X			X	X		X	X		X	X

of the organizations, such as external political support and oversight, to which other authors such as Meier (2000) devote much attention.

In a similar methodological vein, the STEP (Striving Towards Excellence in Performance) program in Minnesota relied on "hypotheses" about high-performance organizations that appendix B summarizes, developed in ways that are not systematically explicated (Hale 1996).

Hale's (1996) related discussion of high-performance public organizations also drew on the STEP hypotheses, additional literature such as discussions of organizational learning (Senge 1999), and points of consensus with other reports, such as that of Denhardt (1993). She proposed the characteristics summarized in appendix B.

In *The Pursuit of Significance*, Denhardt (1993) provides more explicitness about the method and source of his conclusions, which are also summarized in appendix B. He describes his observations of a movement away from a traditional and rational approach in public administration, toward a newer alternative that involves common themes of a commitment to values, serving the public, empowerment and shared leadership, pragmatic incrementalism, and a dedication to public service. Appendix B provides further examples of his conclusions about effective practices in public organizations. Denhardt describes his method as involving interviews with public managers and leaders of public administration professional associations in Australia, Canada, Great Britain, and the United States. In interviews, he asks about the public managers who were making an important difference and making significant improvements. The themes and conclusions he identifies, he says, emerged with regularity in the interviews. He then illustrates the meaning of the themes and the practices related to them by describing examples of managers he observed or interviewed, including documents they issued and used, such as mission and value statements. This approach provides more clarity about the way the author drew conclusions and what they mean, and the result is a stimulating depiction of excellent, innovative public management. Methodologically, of course, we are again reliant on the opinions and observations of public managers and professionals about what is effective and how. The study provides no independent measure of effectiveness or of the link between the practices and effectiveness. Simply put, this leaves open the possibility that the respondents merely report on what appears to them to be innovative and effective, and they may be influenced by the appearances of the practices rather than their actual impacts. In other words, they may be wrong. In addition, we are heavily reliant on the author's assimilation of the information obtained, and there is no systematic reporting on that process, such as frequency counts and percentages of respondents offering a particular type of observation.

Popovich (1998) and his colleagues in the Alliance for Redesigning Government, under the auspices of the National Academy of Public Administration, offer conclusions about a set of public organizations identified as high-performance organizations. They base the conclusions on case examples, a literature review of articles, papers, books, and presentations, professional experience, and "field testing" in the form of obtaining reactions to their conclusions from "frontline innovators" that they met with through professional associations. The group reports that they identified forty cases of high-performance government organizations, including sixteen local, fifteen state, and nine federal organizations. They provide no clear explanation of how these organizations were selected for the sample. They provide illustrations of practices employed by the organizations in their sample that display the characteristics of high-performance organizations. These organizations, they say, "are clear on their mission; define outcomes and focus on results; empower employees; motivate and inspire people to succeed; display flexibility and adjust nimbly to new conditions; are competitive in terms of performance; restructure work processes to meet customer needs; and maintain communications with stakeholders" (Popovich 1998, 16). Here again, the study provides stimulating suggestions and conclusions, but based on an assemblage of examples and essentially a best practices approach. Again, the literature and state of knowledge will be advanced by more evidence supporting the conclusions that these characteristics actually cause the differences between more and less effective government agencies, and that they actually cause higher performance on measures of outcomes and impacts.

Two books by Linden (*Seamless Government* [1994] and *From Vision to Reality* [1990]) provide yet another approach to identifying effective and innovative practices in public management by targeting a set of case examples and providing extensive description of them, including evidence of their success such as reports of quantitative success indicators. Linden (1990) derives the seven characteristics of innovative managers summarized in appendix B by examining the cases of four federal, two state, and one local government manager. He offers no explanation of how he selected these cases, but he does explain the criteria used in identifying innovations, such as a focus on people and program innovations, perceived success of the innovation by staff members affected, and innovations that had been in effect for at least three years. Linden then describes the cases of innovations and the evidence of their success, and rates each case on the extent to which it illustrates the use of each of the seven approaches. We must rely on the program representatives to report the evidence of success accurately. We must rely on Linden's judgment to identify the characteristics of the effective, innovative programs and to assess how importantly they figured in the cases. The design amounts to an informal version of an ex post facto design, with the attendant threats to validity. Linden's (1994) examination of seven government organizations applying practices related to reengineering concepts, described in appendix B, provides similar methodological advantages and disadvantages relative to the other alternatives summarized in this set.

Moore (1995), in his analysis of how leaders in public agencies "create public value," emphasized the points summarized in appendix B. As indicated there, he devotes more attention to the need to manage and respond to the political environment than do some of the other authors cited in appendix B.

Also in the set of relevant studies are single case studies, such as those of DiIulio (1994; see appendix B) and Behn (1991; see appendix B). They provide intensive case information in support of insights and conclusions such as those summarized in appendix B. They do raise the issues that single case studies involve methodologically, however, including generalizability of results to other cases and settings and verification of the authors' interpretation of the case information.

Studies with Larger Samples

Systematic Analysis of Multiple Award-Winning Organizations

Borins (1998) combined the approach of analyzing award winners with content analysis of multiple cases. Borins selected a sample from the 350 semifinalists for the Ford Foundation–Kennedy School of Government's State and Local Government Innovation Awards from 1990 to 1994. The award program receives 1,500 applicants annually and the top 5 percent in the ratings become the semifinalists (seventy-five each year). Semifinalists are chosen based on four criteria: novelty of innovation, significance in addressing an important problem, value the innovation brings to citizens/clients, and transferability (feasibility of replication elsewhere).

From the 350 semifinalists, the author selected 217 cases, by use of a stratified sampling method. The five categories used for the stratified sample included innovations in information technology, organizational change or restructuring, energy or environmental policy, community building, and social programs. The stratified sampling procedure assured a reasonable size of the sample for each category of innovation. The author argued that, because the award program is nationally prominent, various organizations have strong incentives to participate in it. Therefore, the samples used in this study may be quite representative of the population of organizations who are prepared to contend that they have a significant innovation.

Semifinalists who compete for the award must respond to twenty-one open-ended questions. The author coded answers to the questions into statistical categories to conduct a broad quantitative analysis of the innovations with statistical distributions, correlations, and regression analysis. The findings and analyses are complex but included such findings as these (see also appendix B):

- Politicians who initiate innovations often are responding to publicly visible crises. Agency heads initiate innovations when they take over an agency. Middle and frontline public servants initiate innovations as responses to internal problems and technological opportunities.

- When innovations need the coordination of several organizations, line agency coordination and interdepartmental committees are important. When innovations need partnerships, line agency coordination and interdepartmental committees are also important.
- Three methods of outcome evaluation show significant relations to success in winning the award: formal surveys, experimental design, and no formal evaluation (a negative relation). Growing demand from clients and cost reductions are also significant determinants of winning the award.
- Innovative programs are initiated at many organizational levels and almost half the time by career civil servants in middle management.

As in other studies analyzing award winners, the procedure prompts questions about the validity of the award selection process, the representativeness of the sample, and possible problems in assessing determinants of innovation in the absence of comparisons with failed innovations or ineffective programs. Nevertheless, the analysis of multiple cases with a systematic procedure for choosing them as innovative, the systematic methodology for analyzing the cases, and the reporting of statistical analyses among the variables provides superior methodological reassurance to many of the alternatives summarized here.

Appendix B also summarizes conclusions about "best practices and model programs" from Holzer and Callahan's *Government at Work* (1998). They examined 140 award winners, from 1989 to 1995, of the Exemplary State and Local Awards Program (EXSL), conducted by the National Center for Public Productivity. Awardees are selected from a pool of nominees based on rigorous criteria: program outputs, impact on quality of life of population served, cost-effectiveness, client support/satisfaction, innovative nature, obstacles or encumbrances that had to be overcome, nature of the problem addressed, degree of difficulty, and transferability. As does Borins's analysis, this analysis involves a systematic and explicit method of identifying the high-performance organizations, by examining programs that have been selected for an award. In addition, the authors report on a process of surveying the award winners that provides some insights beyond their main analysis.

Of course, as Holzer and Callahan discuss, analyzing award winners raises methodological questions. The sample is obviously not representative of government agencies and programs in general and does not permit comparisons of more and less effective organizations. This in turn diminishes the evidence that the practices identified have a well-validated causal relation to performance. Nevertheless, the approach provides more reassurance than some of the other studies that the effective organizations have been identified on the basis of a systematic procedure involving a review of evidence of their effectiveness.

Holzer and Callahan conclude that the effective practices of the award winners consistently reflect five approaches to management. They apply quality management principles, use performance measurement in decision making, invest in human resource development and organizational learning, adopt new technologies, and develop partnerships. The authors neither describe how they identified these categories of practice nor provide data on how they analyzed the different agencies to come to these conclusions. They provide additional detail about these practices and supporting practices, by providing descriptions of award winners that exemplified the practices. More systematic evidence of how the award winners were content analyzed to support these conclusions would enhance their validity.

Holzer and Callahan also report on an ongoing process of surveying the award winners, and the survey results provide interesting findings. For example, in rank orderings of the resource factors important to innovation, the respondents gave the highest rankings to support from top agency executives and to "committed personnel." With regard to motivations important to innovation, they gave the highest ranking to "do[ing] the right thing." Although these results raise various methodological issues, they provide evidence of the perceived importance to respondents from award-winning agencies of factors emphasized in other research on successful organizational change—the importance of top leaders and employee support and commitment—and in other research, including other studies in this set, of the importance of an altruistic and/or public spirited service ethic in effective and innovative government activity.

Case and Survey Analysis of Successful Innovators

Light (1998), in *Sustaining Innovation,* reports an analysis of organizations in Minnesota selected as organizations that sustained innovations and innovativeness, leading to the conclusions summarized in appendix B. From 1991 to 1995, the Surviving Innovation Project sought to determine "how nonprofit and government organizations can increase the odds that innovation will occur and endure." The study analyzed twenty-six detailed case examples of Minnesota nonprofit and government organizations, with data from more than 200 face-to-face interviews and nearly a year's worth of site visits. More than 100 nominees were selected on the basis of the judgment from focus groups composed of funders, practitioners, evaluators, and community leaders. To get the final sample, Light used four criteria: history of innovations, commitment to innovativeness as a product of organizational design, yielding a compelling story on how nonprofit and government organizations can innovate, and the receptiveness of the participants to site visits for in-depth interviews.

Light conducted 220 face-to-face interviews with board members, frontline staff, funders, and clients. He then used an "interrogation instrument" to draw information from the interviews for answers to eighty-four questions about the organization's environment, internal structure, leadership, and management systems. He cross-tabulated these four factors with five control variables: subsector (nonprofit or government), type of innovativeness (how or what), budget size, total full-time staff number, and age of organizations. The results are tabulated with percentages reported for each cell of appendix B. Light also reports, however, that the conclusions were also based on his personal observations and observations based on information from individual interviews.

Content Analysis of Multiple Case Studies

Wolf (1993) reported an elaborate content analysis of forty-four case studies of federal agencies and his construction of measures of agencies' characteristics and their relations to agency effectiveness, leading to the conclusions summarized in appendix B. This method provides a more systematic analysis of multiple cases, with measures of interrater reliability for the raters performing the content analysis. It thus provides more methodological accountability than does the less systematically and explicitly analyzed case reports. It obviously draws on a broader sampling of organizations than many of the other studies summarized in the present review.

Toward Conclusions: Chaos or Consensus?

The diversity of the studies makes it difficult to draw general conclusions about consensus and about the most strongly supported findings among the contributions. One might conclude that the research is too divergent to support clear general conclusions. Table 2.1, however, illustrates some points of convergence. We emphasize that this classification is crude, indicating apparent points of very explicit and clear correspondence between an author's main conclusions and the propositions from appendix A that we use as a general framework. The assignments do some injustice to a number of subtleties (and authors). For example, virtually all of the authors refer to empowerment, shared values, or effective incentive systems. Thus, they imply that the high-performance and innovative organizations have effective cultures and employees with high levels of motivation. Only where the author placed an explicit emphasis on highly motivated employees as a driving factor in high performance or innovation, however, does "X" mark that spot. For example, DiIulio explicitly emphasizes the strong motivation of the "principled agents" in the bureau he examines as a central factor in the performance of the agency. Several other authors point to the effectiveness with which leaders in well-performing agencies managed relations with external stakeholders, and this could of course include political oversight authorities. Others mention that political officials' support for innovations is a very important factor in their success (e.g., Borins 1998; Holzer and Callahan 1998). Nevertheless, these authors do not place a heavy emphasis on analyzing the ways in which agency leaders managed relations with political oversight authorities such as legislators and chief executives. The emphasis on such matters is much stronger in other contributions reviewed here and sources not included here (e.g., Meier 2000). Thus, the Xs in the appendix reflect judgments about those authors who placed a heavy, explicit emphasis on matters pertaining to the factors in the propositions from appendix A. They reflect our best judgments and may do injustice to some contributions.

In spite of the imprecision just noted, even this rather crude categorization of the studies indicates generalizations about their conclusions that tend to echo through the entries in appendix B. As illustrated by the number of Xs in the rows, these studies have tended to emphasize the following topics, mentioned here roughly in order of the frequency of emphasis in the studies:

- Effective leadership, exemplified in many ways in the entries in appendix B.
- Effective task design, in which we included such matters as the authors' conclusions about the importance of redesigning and clarifying work tasks, organizational structures, and work and production processes; utilization of performance measurement goals and systems and such arrangements as internal competition.
- Effective relations with stakeholders by, for example, developing and maintaining external support, partnerships, and relations with customers and suppliers.
- Organizational "mission valence" as reflected, for example, in the members' valuation of the mission and the mission's motivating influence and in references to clear goals, shared values, and ethical standards as part of the mix of values and in customer orientation or public service as a part of the mission.
- Effective development of human resources, including developing the human resource management systems and incentive systems themselves; investing in employee training, development, and learning; empowering employees and providing autonomy and flexibility; valuing employees through fair, respectful, participative, communicative relations with them.
- Strong, effective organizational cultures.

In their treatment of these topics, the studies also expose limitations of the propositions from appendix A. Those propositions fail to cover certain topics explicitly enough, and their overgeneralized character fails to reflect many of the nuances in the entries in appendix B, about how leadership, task design, mission, and other important factors actually manifest themselves in effective and innovative organizations. For example, organizational structural design and redesign should be included as a major factor, independent of task design. The entries in appendix B also present many conclusions about employee empowerment, autonomy, learning, teamwork, and other practices that show the propositions in appendix B need more elaboration and further research to provide clarification and verification of the importance of such practices.

As indicated in table 2.1, receiving less attention in the studies were relations with oversight officials, maintaining autonomy in relation to them, utilization of technology, and professionalism. The lower frequency of attention to professionalism may simply result from semantics—some researchers simply use other terms for commitment and service orientation. It may result from awareness of the social scientific literature on professionalism that would treat it as a characteristic of certain advanced occupational specializations and therefore only applicable to certain agencies that are highly professionalized in this sense (i.e., with many attorneys or scientists). The lower frequency of attention to utilization of technology suggests that many of these studies have a human relations orientation, with heavy emphasis on leadership, culture, mission, and employee empowerment, as opposed to utilization of new technologies. This may reflect legitimate findings by the researchers that technology does not figure as importantly in high performance and innovation as do leadership, mission, and the way employees are treated and motivated, or it may reflect a methodological and conceptual bias in that direction—some researchers may not look for technological applications and improvements as carefully as they should.

More important is the low level of attention to effective relations with oversight authorities and to autonomy with respect to such oversight. This general lack of attention to these matters raises fundamental issues about this body of research and about the nature of performance and innovation in government as well. One of these issues concerns the apparent inward and downward orientation of many of the studies. Although frequently mentioning effective relations with external stakeholders, most of the studies concentrate on how the organizational leaders lead and manage the organization and on the conditions inside the organization that purportedly influence performance and innovation. Perhaps the lack of attention to how leaders deal with external authorities results from the researchers' primary objective of explaining how a well-performing organization is managed—that is, it results from the perspective and orientation of the researcher.

A related issue raises a more fundamental question. The entries in appendix B echo with references to autonomy, empowerment, freedom, flexibility, clarification of goals and mission and employee task goals, motivation, challenge, and change. These conditions imply that these organizations and their leaders have a high level of authority and capacity to bring these conditions about. For decades, however, the literature and lore on governmental bureaucracy and the scholars, experts, and critics focused on it, including governmental managers themselves, have repeatedly asserted or complained that government agencies and their leaders face severe disincentives and constraints on their ability to bring about that list of desirable conditions recited just above (e.g., Niskanen 1971; Warwick 1975; Barton 1980; National Academy of Public Administration 1986).[2] Where and how, then, do these high-performing and innovative agencies and their leaders attain the capacity and authority to make themselves exceptions to decades of observations about performance problems in government?

Are these agencies simply lucky? Some agencies have more public support for their functions and missions than others, and some have clearer missions and stronger expertise than others. Other agencies face sharply conflicting public and political demands on them, vague and uncertain mandates and missions, unpopular clientele (prisoners, indigent clients that can be stereo-typed as lazy), and other difficulties (Wilson 1989; Hargrove and Glidewell 1990; Meier 2000). The innovative and well-performing agencies in these studies may be those that exist in the most favorable conditions. This possibility is heightened by the practice in some of these studies of selecting organizations because of their records, reputations, or awards for high performance or innovation. The set of studies contains virtually no explicit comparisons of high-performing and innovative organizations to organizations that are not. The "lucky" interpretation also coincides with positions taken by some organization theorists who study all types of organizations, not just government agencies, and question whether leadership and management really matter or whether evolving technological, social, economic, and other conditions determine the performance of organizations of all types.[3]

On the other hand, could the organizations and their leaders simply be skillful? Behn (1991) describes success in an employment-training program in a department of public welfare, and DiIulio (1994) describes high motivation and commitment in a corrections agency. These are hardly public agencies born with silver spoons in their mouths (Hargrove and Glidewell 1990). Borins (1998) and Light (1998) analyze successful innovations in a variety of different types of organizations. These results suggest that the skills, abilities, practices, and motivation of leaders and members of the organization can overcome environmental constraints to achieve high performance—it is not just the luck of the draw. Yet, in a sense it would still be the luck of the draw, because the studies reviewed here and other research do not provide conclusive answers about where such leaders and members come from and why. Must we wait passively for heroic leaders and government employees to come along and save organizations? How do we identify, attract, and provide them with conditions that support their skills? Moreover, the lack of attention in many of these high-performance and innovation studies to the leaders' and members' behaviors toward oversight authorities leaves us with little explanation of how they attain the authority and capacity to provide flexibility, empowerment, and the other desirable conditions that many of these studies conclude to be the determinants of high performance and innovation.

This situation poses an important issue for future research and for reanalysis of previous research where possible. More comparisons among different types of agencies and programs with different levels of public support, clarity of mandate and mission, and levels of expertise, and more comparisons of high-performance organizations to less successful ones can support analysis of whether fortunate circumstances drive performance and innovation. The same types of comparisons, with more attention to behaviors of leaders and leadership cadres toward external authorities, can support analysis of how organizations attain those conditions that in turn allow them to establish the desirable internal practices and conditions, described in the entries in appendix B, that are allegedly scarce in government agencies.

Innovation and Performance as Different Outcomes?

Another issue for theory and research concerns the question of whether innovative organizations and high-performance organizations should be analyzed separately rather than treated as synonymous or related, as this review does. As mentioned earlier, many of the studies reviewed here combine attributes of high performance with those of change and innovation. Recent studies of leadership and innovation in private sector organizations, however, have found that innovation and organizational performance do not necessarily go together. For example, Staw and Epstein (2000), based on an empirical analysis of data on 100 largest American corporations in 1995, conclude that "core" organizational changes, such as the adoption of popular management techniques, have positive impacts on the corporation's reputation but very weak impacts on organizational performance. From an empirical study of U.S. radio markets from 1984 to 1992, Greve (1999; see also Greve and Taylor 2000) concludes that organizational performance declines after core organizational changes and that larger and high-performing organizations incur greater losses from core changes. These studies on organizational performance in the private sector, in which the researchers can have access to clearer and more readily quantifiable performance indicators than are available for most public and nonprofit organizations, indicate that organizational innovations or changes do not necessarily lead to higher organizational performance. These studies suggest that researchers on innovation and performance in the public sector need to more carefully examine and validate the relation between the two outcomes over time.

Thompson's (2000) analysis of the implementation of the recommendations of the National Performance Review (NPR) at the federal and regional levels comes to a conclusion generally similar to those of the private sector studies cited above. He concludes that the NPR initiatives did not contribute significantly to the improvement of government performance. Thus, the NPR recommendations appear to play a role similar to that of the popular management techniques or fads that Staw and Epstein (2000) found to be ineffectual in relation to organizational performance. This further suggests the need to study the relationship between innovation and long-term performance, but also raises an additional issue for research on the effects of innovation. The studies of successful innovation reviewed in this chapter, such as Linden (1990), usually focus on innovations responding to a need or a performance gap perceived by actors in or around a particular organization. This suggests the possibility of a contrast between successful innovations that respond to "felt needs" by actors in an organization and unsuccessful attempts at innovation by way of broad, general recommendations from a central source to a wide array of government organizations with diverse needs and conditions. This suggests the value of future research that is sensitive to this distinction and of research that actually contrasts different types of innovation initiatives along these lines.

The Potential for High Performance and Innovation in Government

The latter suggestion about distinctions between successful "felt need" innovations and less successful general reform initiatives in turn suggests that many of the more negative observations that government organizations perform poorly and resist innovation overgeneralize and oversimplify. This review has emphasized many conceptual and methodological complications in drawing firm conclusions from the set of studies it covers. In spite of such complications, we need to recognize the most important general conclusion that these diverse studies support, and that justifies the attention to them here. Government organizations can and do perform well and innovate successfully. The challenge now is to build on the contributions reviewed here and to continue the analysis of when, where, how, and why they do.

Appendix A
Propositions about Effective Public Agencies (Revised and Adapted from Rainey and Steinbauer 1999)

Public agencies are more likely to perform effectively when there are higher levels of the following conditions.

Effective Relations with Oversight Authorities (Legislative, Executive, Judicial). Authorities Are:
- Attentive
- Demanding
- Supportive
- Delegative

Effective Relations with Other Stakeholders:
- Favorable public opinion and general public support
- Multiple, influential, mobilizable constituent and client groups

- Effective relations with partners and suppliers
  - Effective management of contracting and contractors
  - Effective utilization of technology and other resources
  - Effective relations with networks

Responsive Autonomy in Relation to Political Oversight and Influence

Mission Valence (The Attractiveness of the Mission):
- Difficult but feasible
- Reasonably clear and understandable
- Worthy/worthwhile/legitimate
- Interesting/exciting
- Important/influential
- Distinctive

Strong Organizational Culture, Linked to Mission

Effective Leadership:
- Stability of leadership
- Multiplicity of leadership—a cadre of leaders, teams of leaders at multiple levels
- Leadership commitment to mission
- Effective goal-setting in relation to task and mission accomplishment
- Effective coping with political and administrative constraints

Effective Task Design:
- Intrinsically motivating tasks (interest, growth, responsibility, service and mission accomplishment)
- Extrinsic rewards for tasks (pay, benefits, promotions, working conditions)

Effective Utilization of Technology

Effective Development of Human Resources:
- Effective recruitment, selection, placement, training, and development
- Values and preferences among recruits and members that support task and mission motivation

High Levels of Professionalism among Members:
- High levels of special knowledge and skills related to task and mission accomplishment
- Commitment to task and mission accomplishment
- High levels of public service professionalism

High Levels of Motivation among Members:
- High levels of public service motivation among members
- High levels of mission motivation among members
- High levels of task motivation among members

Appendix B
Studies of High Performance and Innovative Government Organizations

Behn (1991):
Behn's case study of the successful implementation of an Employment and Training Program (ET CHOICES) by the Massachusetts Department of Public Welfare from 1983 to 1988 concluded that the following factors are crucial for successful organizational performance:
- Support from external stakeholders and advocacy community
- Redesign of organizational structure, rewards systems, and human resource management pursuant to new program needs
- Increased resources
- Loose properties that allow autonomy, entrepreneurship, and innovation in accomplishing mission as well as tight properties for mission
- Clarification of the long-term vision or mission of programs
- Most of all, energy and initiative from leadership, or "departmental adrenaline," positively orchestrates these factors for successful public performance

Borins (1998):
Borins reports a statistical analysis of data on a large sample of winners of the Ford Foundation–Kennedy School of Government's State and Local Government innovation awards from 1990 to 1994. His analysis shows that these winners shared common innovative characteristics. Public sector innovation tends to be characterized by:
- Systematic thinking
- Delivery of multiple services
- Partnerships among organizations
- Application of new technology
- Process improvement
- Organizational redesign
- Empowerment
- Incentives instead of regulation
- Prevention instead of remediation
- The use of private sector
- Voluntarism
- Internal competition

Three important paths to public innovation include:
- Politicians responding to crises
- Newly appointed agency heads restructuring organizations
- Middle-level and front-line workers responding to internal problems and taking advantage of opportunities

Denhardt (1993):
On the basis of interviews with public managers and leaders of public administration professional associations in Australia, Canada, Great Britain, and the United States and observations of their practices, Denhardt concluded that the following practices characterize high-performance public organizations:

- Dedication to public service and understanding public intent
- Serving the public, which represents democratic values
- Leader demonstrates commitment to mission
- Manager builds sense of community in organization
- Manager clearly articulates values
- Managers insist on high ethical standards
- Empowered and shared leadership
- Employees accept responsibility and performance accountability
- Pragmatic incrementalism (change is natural, appropriate)
- Approach to change is creative and humane
- Commitment to values

DiIulio (1994):

On the basis of observations of the behaviors of employees in the Federal Bureau of Prisons, DiIulio concludes that rational choice intepretations, including principal-agent perspectives, do not account for social, moral, and symbolic incentives for that behavior in that bureau. He further concludes that performance of public organizations is enhanced by:

- Organizational members adhering to a right mode of action stricter than formal policy directives
- Symbols valued by employees throughout the organization
- A long history of careerist leaders with strong public service mentalities

These nonpecuniary and other intangible incentives are important for explaining the performance of public servants in government.

Gold (1982):

Interviews and observations of five public and five private organizations, which Gold identified as high performers, indicated that they have the following characteristics:

- Emphasize clear mission and objectives
- Employees take pride in the organization and its product
- Focus on treating employees fairly and respectfully through honest and open communication
- Emphasize delegation of responsibility and authority as widely as possible
- Management aims at challenging and encouraging people
- Management emphasizes innovative ways of managing
- Places great value on the people in the organization
- Job task and goals are clear

Hale (1996):

On the basis of a review of previous research, such as Denhardt (1993), and literature, such as Senge (1999), Hale advances the following propositions about the characteristics of high-performance public organizations:

- Focused mission that is clarified and communicated to organization members
- Enabling leadership that emphasizes learning, communication, flexibility, sharing, and vision development
- Emphasize learning and carefully support learning, risk taking, training, communication, and work measurement

- Nurturing community culture that is supportive and emphasizes teamwork, participation, flexible authority, and effective reward and recognition

Holzer and Callahan (1998):
Factors that characterize the winners of the Exemplary States and Local Award Program (EXSL) from 1989 to 1995 are developed into an integrated model for organizational behavior that includes:
- Focus on the customer
- Build partnerships with public and private organizations and citizens
- Manage for quality using long-term strategies planning with support from top leadership
- Develop human resources and empower employees through team building, systematic training, recognition, and balancing employee and organizational needs
- Adapt technologies to achieve open access to data, automation for productivity, cost-effective applications, and cross-cutting techniques that deliver on public demands
- Measure for performance by establishing goals and measuring results, justifying and allocating as necessary resource requirements, and developing organizational improvement strategies

Fiscal pressure, discretionary resources, and a public service ethic drive innovation in the public sector. The study also gives three agendas to reinvigorate public bureaucracy:
- Have a positive impact on government's personnel resources
- Utilize low-cost or no-cost innovations
- Move beyond the base of existing innovations

Light (1998):
Case studies of nonprofit and public organizations in Minnesota between years 1991 and 1995 (the Surviving Innovation Project) identify the following factors that trigger and sustain innovation:
- Release of creativity in the organization such as lowering or removal of internal and external barriers and debunking myths
- Understanding their environment and how to manage, exploit, and even manipulate it
- Organizational designs and leadership
- Internal management systems linking these factors to the innovation system: mission, pay/personnel, learning, idea generation, budget, and accountability/governance
- Innovative organizations display adherence to core values of trust, honesty, rigor, and faith

Linden (1990):
Linden reports intensive case studies of four federal, two state, and one local innovators, including interviews with innovating managers, to investigate how a single manager can make an organization more effective. Innovative managers share in common seven characteristics:

- Strategic action
- "Holding on and letting go"
- Creating a felt need for change
- Starting with concrete change
- Employing structural changes
- Dealing with risk
- Utilizing political skills

Successful innovation involves both rational and intuitive thinking and is a function of many small starts and pilot efforts. The successful innovation initiatives tended to:
- Employ multifunction teams
- Provide time, freedom, flexibility, and access to resources
- Offer autonomy, control, protection against turf warfare and flak
- Support committed champions

Linden (1994):
Studying one regional medical center, two federal agencies, two city governments, one state agency, and the Government Performance and Results Act of 1993, the author found that, as U.S. society shifts from the mass production era to the consumer society, process-, or outcome-based, organizations outperform traditional organizations compartmentalized according to functions.
Process-based organizations:
- Organize around outcomes, not functions
- Substitute parallel for sequential processes
- Bring downstream information upstream
- Capture information once at the source
- Provide a single point of contact for customers and suppliers whenever possible
- Focus on activities that add values to end-users
- Try first to reengineer and then automate

Moore (1995):
Moore analyzed two federal, two state, and two local agency cases to suggest a new way of delivering public services. The strategic triangle—creation of public value, political management, and reengineering organizations—is crucial for successful public performance. The provision of public goods should be evaluated in terms of the political marketplace of citizens and the collective decisions of representative democratic institutions rather than the economic marketplace of individual consumers. Public managers need to have the capacity to manage environments in a way that is adaptive to the external authorizing (and coproducing) environment. When public values for organizations are identified, public managers need to reorganize structures, exert additional efforts, and maintain activities compatible with the new public values.

Popovich (1998):
Analysis of sixteen local, fifteen state, and nine federal government organizations based on four study approaches, case studies, literature review, professional experience, and field testing found the following factors for high performance:
- Mission clarity and understanding
- Maintain open and productive communication among stakeholders

- Empowered employees
- Organizations allocate resources for continuous learning
- Employees accept accountability to achieve results with rewards and consequences
- Motivate and inspire people to succeed
- Defined outcomes and focus on results (performance measures)
- Institute new work processes as necessary
- Flexible and adjust nimbly to new conditions
- Competitive in terms of performance

STEP (see Hale 1996):
Minnesota's STEP program sought to encourage the following practices in state agencies, based on "hypotheses" about high-performance organizations:
- Closer contact with customers to better understand their needs
- Increased discretionary authority for managers and employees for greater control over accountability
- Increased employee participation taps their knowledge, skills, and commitment
- Partnerships to allow the sharing of knowledge expertise and other resources
- State-of-the-art productivity improvement techniques
- Improved work measurements to provide a base for planning and implementing service improvements and worker evaluation

Wilson (1989):
Drawing on many case studies, the author investigated the extent to which management systems or administrative arrangements are well suited to the tasks that agencies actually perform. He observed that well-performing government organizations tend to have the following characteristics:
- Mission is clear and reflects a widely shared and warmly endorsed organizational culture
- External political support
- Executives command loyalty, define and instill a clear sense of mission, attract talented workers, and make exacting demands of subordinates
- Leaders make peer expectations serve the organization
- Maximize discretionary authority for operators
- Executive takes responsibility for organizational maintenance
- Bottom-up implementation perspective
- Clearly defined goals
- Widespread agreement on how critical tasks are performed
- Agency autonomy to develop operational goals from which tasks are designed
- Ability to control or keep contextual goals in proper perspective

Wolf (1993):
Meta-analysis of randomly selected forty-four cases of 4,000 executive studies on federal agencies concludes that the following variables are associated with bureaucratic effectiveness:
- Leadership
- Political autonomy
- Strong sense of mission and adaptability significantly affect agency performance

- Increased motivation caused by competition is more important for effectiveness than the environmental control that monopolistic situations can bring

Various theoretical perspectives and interpretations can all play a part in explaining agency performance, including leadership theory, professionalism, economic responsiveness, population ecology, and the political theory of the firm.

Notes

1. Obviously, internal validity and strength of association can be separated into two distinct criteria, but we combine them because the classification is imprecise at best and we simply want to emphasize a general difference among the studies in explicit quantification of variables and explicit analysis of relations among them.

2. Significantly, in relation to this point, Light (1998) concludes from his study that small nonprofit organizations are the organizations most likely to sustain innovation, thus implying that the governmental organizations in his sample face particular difficulties in doing so.

3. See Aldrich (1999) for discussion of theoretical perspectives that take such positions or variants of them.

References

Aldrich, H. E. 1999. *Organizations Evolving*. Thousand Oaks, Calif.: Sage.

Barton, A. H. 1980. "A Diagnosis of Bureaucratic Maladies." In C. H. Weiss and A. H. Barton, eds., *Making Bureaucracies Work*. Thousand Oaks, Calif.: Sage, 27–36.

Behn, R. D. 1991. *Leadership Counts*. Cambridge, Mass.: Harvard University Press.

Borins, Sanford. 1998. *Innovating with Integrity: How Local Heroes Are Transforming American Government*. Washington, D.C.: Georgetown University Press.

Collins, J. C., and J. I. Porras. 1994. *Built to Last: Successful Habits of Visionary Companies*. New York: HarperBusiness.

Denhardt, R. B. 1993. *The Pursuit of Significance*. Belmont, Calif.: Wadsworth.

DiIulio, J. J. 1994. "Principled Agents: The Cultural Bases of Behavior in a Federal Government Bureaucracy." *Journal of Public Administration Research and Theory* 4:277–320.

Gold, K. A. 1982. "Managing for Success: A Comparison of the Public and Private Sectors." *Public Administration Review* 42:568–75.

Greve, H. R. 1999. "The Effect of Core Change on Performance: Inertia and Regression toward the Mean." *Administrative Science Quarterly* 44:590–614.

Greve, H. R., and A. Taylor. 2000. "Innovations as Catalysts for Organizational Change: Shifts in Organizational Cognition and Search." *Administrative Science Quarterly* 45:54–80.

Hale, S. J. 1996. "Achieving High Performance in Public Organizations." In J. L. Perry, ed., *Handbook of Public Administration*, 2d ed. San Francisco: Jossey-Bass, 136–50.

Hargrove, E. C., and J. C. Glidewell, eds. 1990. *Impossible Jobs in Public Management*. Lawrence: University Press of Kansas.

Holzer, M., and K. Callahan. 1998. *Government at Work: Best Practices and Model Programs*. Thousand Oaks, Calif.: Sage.

Light, Paul C. 1998. *Sustaining Innovation: Creating Nonprofit and Government Organizations That Innovate Naturally*. San Francisco: Jossey-Bass.

Linden, Russell M. 1994. *Seamless Government: A Practical Guide to Re-engineering in the Public Sector.* San Francisco: Jossey-Bass.

———. 1990. *From Vision to Reality: Strategies of Successful Innovators in Government.* Charlottesville, Va.: LEL Enterprises.

Meier, K. J. 2000. *Politics and the Bureaucracy.* New York: Harcourt College Publishers.

Moore, M. H. 1995. *Creating Public Value: Strategic Management in Government.* Cambridge, Mass.: Harvard University Press.

National Academy of Public Administration. 1986. *Revitalizing Federal Management.* Washington, D.C.: National Academy of Public Administration.

Niskanen, W. A. 1971. *Bureaucracy and Representative Government.* Chicago: Aldine.

Osborne, D., and T. Gaebler. 1992. *Reinventing Government.* Reading, Mass.: Addison-Wesley.

Peters, T. J., and R. H. Waterman. 1982. *In Search of Excellence: Lessons from America's Best-Run Companies.* New York: Harper & Row.

Popovich, Mark G., ed. 1998. *Creating High Performance Government Organizations.* San Francisco: Jossey-Bass.

Rainey, H. G., and P. Steinbauer. 1999. "Galloping Elephants: Developing Elements of a Theory of Effective Government Organizations." *Journal of Public Administration Research and Theory* 9:1–32.

Rourke, F. E. 1984. *Bureaucracy, Politics, and Public Policy.* New York: Little, Brown.

Senge, P. M. 1999. *The Fifth Discipline.* New York: Doubleday.

Staw, B. M., and L. D. Epstein. 2000. "What Bandwagons Bring: Effects of Popular Management Techniques on Corporate Performance, Reputation, and CEO Pay." *Administrative Science Quarterly* 45:523–56.

Thompson, J. R. 2000. "Reinvention as Reform: Assessing the National Performance Review." *Public Administration Review* 60 (November/December):508–21.

Warwick, D. P. 1975. *A Theory of Public Bureaucracy.* Cambridge, Mass.: Harvard University Press.

Wilson, J. Q. 1989. *Bureaucracy.* New York: Basic Books.

Wolf, P. J. 1993. "A Case Survey of Bureaucratic Effectiveness in U.S. Cabinet Agencies: Preliminary Results." *Journal of Public Administration Research and Theory* 3 (April):161–81.

Part II

Social Program Service Delivery:
Identifying the Linkages in Diverse Settings

Three

Alternative Governance Structures for Welfare Provider Networks

Jo Ann G. Ewalt

Were Max Weber and Woodrow Wilson suddenly to appear on the landscape of modern public administration, normative theories in hand, some might argue that they would be unable to recognize the field. The comprehensive, functionally uniform, hierarchical organizations governed by strong leaders who are democratically responsible and staffed by neutrally competent civil servants who deliver services to citizens (Ostrom 1973)—to the extent they ever existed—are long gone. They have been replaced by an "organizational society" in which many important services are provided through multiorganizational programs. These programs are essentially "interconnected clusters of firms, governments, and associations which come together within the framework of these programs" (Hjern and Porter 1981, 212–13).

These implementation structures operate within a notion of *governance* about which a surprising level of consensus has been reached. There is a pervasive, shared, global perception of governance as a topic far broader than "government."Governance is seen as a "new process of governing, or a changed condition of ordered rule; or the new method by which society is governed" (Stoker 1998, 17). Similarly, in the scholarship that has followed the "reinventing government" themes of public effectiveness, much has been written of "new public management" (NPM) practices—such as privatization, contracting out, and public-private partnerships—through which governance theory is put into action (Kettl 1995, 1997; Frederickson 1996; Kamensky 1996; Mathiasen 1996; Peters and Pierre 1998).

In this complex, devolved mode of service delivery, the unit of analysis for some scholars of policy implementation is the network of nonprofit organizations, private firms, and governments. As Milward and Provan note, in policy arenas such as health, mental health, and welfare, "joint production and having several degrees of separation between the source and the user of government funds . . . combine to ensure that hierarchies and markets will not work and that networks are the only alternative for collective action" (2000, 243).

This chapter establishes a framework for evaluating the effectiveness of two distinct governance structures that implement welfare-to-work programs and applies this framework to two Kentucky works program implementation models. One program, operating throughout counties in most of the state, uses a centralized authority (the county office of the Kentucky Cabinet for Families and Children) to create and administer a network of support agencies whose mission is to provide a variety of services to move welfare clients from public assistance to work. The model with which this "traditional service network" is being compared is the Local Investment Commission operating in Fayette and surrounding counties. Known as LexLinc, it is a citizen-directed community collaborative. It is self-governed, with public, private, nonprofit, and community leadership and autonomous budgetary authority. LexLinc is modeled after an innovative human services collaborative called the Local Investment Commission (LINC) implemented in Kansas City and Jackson County, Missouri, in 1992. The "Kansas City model," as it has become known, is a citizen-based governance structure responsible for delivery of human services in Jackson County.

The primary research question addressed in this study is whether one governance model is more effective than the other is at moving clients into work. This chapter makes two contributions to the field of public management. First, the research seeks to extend the "logic of governance" described by Lynn, Heinrich, and Hill (1999) and Heinrich and Lynn (2000). This logic, or "reduced-form" governance model, defines individual and/or organizational outcomes (O) as a function of environmental factors (E), client characteristics (C), treatments (T), organizational and/or institutional structures (S), and managerial roles and actions (M), as well as the interdependencies that exist among and within these factors. This chapter examines the welfare work policy outcomes (O) of two distinct service delivery system models (S), evaluates the structures and managerial roles and actions of these systems (M), and explores the interrelationships of these factors with client characteristics (C) and environmental factors (E).

The second contribution is in the area of empirical modeling. The methodology employed in this study, hierarchical linear regression modeling (HLM), acknowledges and takes advantage of the hierarchical nature of the data in estimating work outcomes. One of the problems associated with empirical models of governance that has become clearer in the past few years is the inadequacy of ordinary least squares (OLS) regression when data are hierarchically structured (Bryk and Raudenbush 1992; Singer 1998; Heinrich and Lynn 2001). In many social science settings, individual-level observations are nested within groups (i.e., schools, hospitals, or counties). HLM, and generalized hierarchical models for the study of noncontinuous outcome measures, are very useful in these cases. They are particularly well suited to exploring the interactions among governance factors that exist at different levels.

Glazer (1995) summarizes the gap in the literature on the governance of welfare work programs. He notes that we have moved from trying to create incentives to work and then imposing requirements to work to a period where the most important task is to elaborate the governance structures that put work requirements into effect (1995, 23). In essence, the present study is an attempt to address one of the major questions posed in this volume: what are the consequences for governmental performance of how public programs are organized and managed? It examines which governance structures work best in helping clients go to work, stay on the job, and earn relatively higher wages. To place the research question within a theoretical context, governance and NPM literatures are briefly summarized to draw expectations of what post-bureaucratic models of governance should look like. Concepts of welfare-to-work networks are then integrated into this literature to define specific expectations about how local service delivery networks operate and to define key service delivery coordination and integration issues. Then, the two Kentucky Works implementation networks studied here are described and compared. Finally, an empirical design is specified to test whether one network structure is more effective than the other in achieving work outcomes for welfare clients. We begin with a brief description of the current environment in which welfare programs are implemented.

Welfare Policy Implementation

It would be difficult to find a policy arena in which the sheer number of local, regional, and state organizations involved in the implementation of programs and policies was greater, and in which the organizational interdependencies and dynamics were more varied, than is the case in welfare policy. The complexity and variation of welfare program structures are due in large part to the flexibility given to states by the Personal Responsibility and Work Opportunity Reconciliation Act of 1996 (PRWORA).

Although there are many models of welfare implementation, welfare is essentially administered at either the state level (centralized administration) or at the local or county level (decentralized administration). Regardless of the administration status, PRWORA has brought together public, nonprofit, and private agencies that had been largely autonomous in their operations and more narrowly focused in their organizational mission. For example, in theory, private industry councils (PICs) and departments of employment services (DESs) were to have been working closely with welfare agencies implementing the Job Opportunity and Basic Skills (JOBS) program in the late 1980s and the first half of the 1990s. The reality was that for most states, there was very little involvement from employment-related public agencies in implementing welfare programs (Ewalt 1998).

In the current environment, local welfare implementation involves a host of public and nonprofit organizations offering a variety of services to recipients (Meyers, Gornick, and Peck 2001). Regardless of whether the organization is centralized or decentralized, a variety of agencies are contracted with to provide case management, as well as basic services, such as eligibility assessment, needs assessments, job training, employment training, education, transportation, child care, job retention, housing assistance, medical assistance, and rehabilitation. Numerous agencies also provide supportive services such as crisis counseling, alcohol and drug abuse services, child abuse prevention, and parenting services (Edin and Lein 1997; Danziger et al. 1998). In addition, although most welfare recipients are children and their mothers, noncustodial parents (usually fathers) are also an important, if ancillary, program target (Federle 1999). Important goals of welfare programs relate directly to the legislation and to state implementing regulations. All states are subject to statutory requirements about the percent of welfare clients who must be engaged in "countable" work activities, among other rules, and these requirements drive many of the organizational relationships states and localities establish.

One of the pervasive problems associated with implementing welfare programs within a network structure is the difficulty of achieving consensus on goals among all network partners (Meyers, Riccucci, and Lurie 2001). A broad array of federal, state, and local employment, education, and training services is linked to welfare programs. These include the Job Training Partnership Act (JTPA) programs, state employment services, community colleges, other vocational and adult education providers, and vocational rehabilitation providers. The Workforce Investment Act of 1998, aimed at integrating funding streams and workforce programs geared to the economically disadvantaged, requires that these employment service providers coordinate activities, and also requires the inclusion of employment training and education services provided by community service block grants, housing and urban development programs, and the Department of Veterans Affairs. In some states and local jurisdictions, including some areas of Kentucky, welfare-to-work programs operated under the Temporary Assistance for Needy Families (TANF) program are included in these broader workforce development systems that serve all disadvantaged individuals. In others, there is no formal link between welfare and workforce development programs although welfare agencies can and do refer clients to non-TANF programs (Barnow and Trutko 1997). Another layer in the complex fabric of employment services for welfare clients is the welfare-to-work competitive and formula grant program authorized by the Budget Reconciliation Act of 1997. These grants are used by states and localities to help the least employable welfare recipients and noncustodial parents of recipient children move into jobs with potential for upward mobility (Nightingale, Trutko, and Barnow 1999). The grants are administered through the JTPA system of local PICs, but must be coordinated with state and local TANF agencies. The Kentucky jurisdictions under study here have received welfare-to-work grants.

In addition to federal and state employment programs operated both as part of and in conjunction with welfare programs, the network of welfare service providers is made much more complex by the vast number of public, nonprofit, and private organizations operating at the local level that also have contracts to serve welfare clients. In the Louisville/Jefferson County and North Central Kentucky Workforce Investment Area, for example, welfare clients are served by as many as eighteen different nonprofit and private providers offering services that range from crisis intervention to legal aid, alcohol and drug treatment and intervention, childcare, consumer debt counseling, job training, job retention, emergency transportation, and computer training (Jefferson County Department of Human Resources 2000).

Welfare programs are delivered at the local level, but the logic of their current implementation structures comes from much broader forces at work in public administration. In a very real sense, what is happening at the local level in welfare policy today can be viewed as evidence of new governing structures and program management arrangements predicted by the governance and NPM literatures.

Understanding Welfare-to-Work Networks: Applying Governance Theories and NPM Concepts

The (mostly European) literature on governance and the increasingly international scholarship on NPM describe two models of public service that reflect a "reinvented" form of government that is better managed and that takes its objectives not from democratic theory but from market economics (Stoker 1998).[1] Although some use the terms interchangeably (for example, Hood 1991), most of the research makes distinctions between the two. Essentially, governance is a political theory, whereas NPM is an organizational theory (Peters and Pierre 1998).

Stoker attempts to bring order to the wide-ranging and complex debate on governance by focusing on how the rise of governance challenges many of the traditional notions of public administration. He contends that a governance perspective offers an organizing framework for comprehending the changing processes of governing. In particular, he draws five propositions to frame our understanding of the critical questions that governance theory should help us answer:

1. Governance refers to institutions and actors from within and beyond government.
2. Governance identifies the blurring of boundaries and responsibilities for tackling social and economic issues.
3. Governance identifies the power dependence involved in the relationships between institutions involved in collective action.
4. Governance is about autonomous self-governing networks of actors; however, the emergence of self-governing networks raises difficulties over accountability.

5. Governance recognizes the capacity to get things done that does not rest on the power of government to command or use its authority (1998, 18).

The dilemma is that, even when nongovernmental entities are involved in delivering government services, government failures may occur. It is in this proposition that we find a natural progression from the more encompassing theory of governance to the more prescriptive notions of NPM. Stoker notes that, within governance, there is a concerted emphasis on new tools and techniques to steer and guide. The language is taken directly from reinventing themes. The dilemma of governance in this context is that there is a broader concern with the very real potential for leadership failure, differences among key partners in time horizons and goal priorities, and social conflicts, all of which can result in governance failure.

Networks and Welfare Work Systems

In meeting program goals, welfare agencies must establish both informal and formal relationships with numerous organizations (Provan and Milward 1995; O'Toole 1996; Agranoff and McGuire 1998). In many of these multi-organizational networks of linked agencies and other units, the linkages are not particularly well established. Rather, they are in a state of continual re-formulation because of shifts in providers, new program emphasis or problems, or other internal or external shocks to the environment (O'Toole and Meier 2000).

The practice of contracting out government services to networks of non-profit (and some private) organizations has been referred to as the "hollow state." As Milward and Provan (2000) have noted, hierarchical bureaucracies are generally considered more predictable and stable because networks must coordinate, negotiate, monitor, enforce, and hold accountable a variety of organizations with varying funding streams and levels of authority and responsibility. In a link to governance theory, they point out that networks may threaten the legitimacy of governance because of the distance between government and policy action.

In their study of four mental heath networks, Provan and Milward theorized that network structure could be linked in predictable ways to client outcome. They tested their theory by use of measures of network density (the extent to which all network organizations are interconnected—i.e., network "integration") and network centralization (the extent to which cohesion is organized around a particular core network member). Provan and Milward conclude that the most effective networks are integrated and centralized, with strong and direct external control, where change to network organizations' external environment (a measure of stability) is minimal (1995, 25–26).

O'Toole, however, notes that program administrators cannot easily control complex networks. "Intergovernmental ties, and increasingly horizontal inter-agency and public-private links, are not subject to unilateral, authoritative supervision by those charged with program responsibilities" (1996, 241). He concludes that more-open and market-oriented networks may be more effective.

Another critical issue is whether network arrangements are mandated or emerge as part of the evolution of program implementation. Mandated networks may have an enhanced immediacy but emerging networks generally exhibit more flexibility in addressing both client needs and stresses on the network system itself (Alter and Hage 1993; Alexander 1995).

Milward and Provan note that there are at least four perspectives on evaluating network effectiveness:

- Clients and advocacy groups favor flexible network structures at the level of the service provider.
- Agency managers and network administrators favor stability, which presumably leads to agency and network growth and increases in resources.
- Local officials and community leaders look for structures that promote efficiency, cost reductions, and the containment or reduced visibility of social problems.
- Funding sources and regulators favor network structures that permit control and monitoring and thus reduce the likelihood of their being blamed for poor outcomes (2000, 255).

These perspectives raise questions both about the impetus to structure networks in specific ways and about the relative effectiveness of any given structural arrangement. In light of the enormous range of programs providing employment, education, and training to welfare clients, numerous studies have focused on the operation of these networks and models of service coordination. These studies identify patterns in the organization of service delivery networks and suggest factors that will hamper the ability of networks to help clients achieve work goals. In a study of human service programs for welfare clients, the General Accounting Office (GAO) categorized service networks as either *system oriented* or *service oriented,* depending upon their goals (U.S. GAO 1998). System-oriented networks have ambitious coordination goals aimed at developing new delivery systems or altering the structure of existing agencies and creating new services to fill service gaps or unmet community needs. The primary vehicles that system-oriented networks use to accomplish these goals are changes in funding streams (often linking funding to performance outcomes) and changes in the entities charged with leading strategic planning for welfare client employment needs. In many cases, this has meant a move away from the county or state social services agency and has resulted in the creation of a new governing body (Grubb et al. 1999; Pindus et al. 2000).

Service-oriented models, which are the most prevalent of welfare service networks, attempt to link clients to existing services and collaborate with various service providers without altering program funding streams, agency responsibilities, or organizational structure (U.S. GAO 1999). State and/or county welfare offices generally lead coordination efforts, establish goals and objectives, are responsible for client placements in work activities and supportive services, and monitor the welfare caseload to ensure that both individual-level and state-level participation requirements are being met.

The 1998 GAO study found that system-oriented networks were less effective at delivering employment services to welfare clients. System-oriented networks can also be linked to the question of network stability examined in the literature on public networks (Provan and Milward 1995; Meier and O'Toole 2001), in which higher levels of change (instability) has been linked to reduced network performance. The Lexington LexLinc network is an example of a system-oriented network, whereas the Louisville/Jefferson County and North Central Kentucky Workforce Investment Area are examples of service-oriented networks.

Another dimension along which network models can vary is *top-down* or *bottom-up* integration (Martinson 1999). The question here is where the impetus to coordinate welfare services comes from. Although coordination occurs at the local level, the initiative to coordinate can be encouraged or imposed by federal and/or state officials (top down) or may originate with local administrators or community activists (bottom up) without reference to higher jurisdiction mandates. Key issues here generally focus on principal-agent problems (Trutko et al. 1999). Numerous studies have reported that top-down integration can reduce network effectiveness. In particular, bureaucratic turf battles, differences in philosophies or missions, differences in performance measures, incompatible management information systems, and different eligibility criteria among various agencies and providers hamper service coordination and can be expected to affect client work outcomes adversely (Leonard 1999; Martinson 1999; Hasenfeld 2000; Pindus et al. 2000).

By contrast, bottom-up integration with the presence of strong local advocates for network coordination can be a major factor in facilitating coordination and diminishing the impacts of coordination barriers. The problem is that, by definition, federal or state officials have far less control over bottom-up networks, and they cannot expect these networks to demonstrate a consistent pattern of behavior or outcome achievement (Martinson 1999). LexLinc is a bottom-up initiative, whereas Louisville/Jefferson County and the North Central Kentucky Workforce Investment Area are top-down initiatives.

Moving Clients from Welfare to Work in Kentucky: Two Models

The reduction in the welfare caseload in Kentucky since the implementation of welfare reform has kept pace with national figures. The number of individuals and families on welfare in Kentucky fell 50 percent from January 1996 to June 2001, the time period of the present study. As of June 2001, there were 35,398 welfare families in the state, and 79,722 individual clients (U.S. Department of Health and Human Services 2002). If the baseline is drawn in 1993, three years before the implementation of welfare reform, but at the point when welfare caseloads were at their highest, Kentucky's family and individual caseloads have dropped by 55 percent and 62 percent, respectively.[2]

Welfare reform called for states to submit plans to the Department of Health and Human Services' Agency for Families and Children outlining how PRWORA would be implemented. Like most states, Kentucky required each county to prepare a county-level plan, which was to be approved and in place by October 1996. From the beginning, Lexington and Louisville had different ideas about what welfare reform would look like. Louisville-Jefferson County's welfare administration is the dominant model in the state. The Jefferson County office of the Kentucky Cabinet for Families and Children coordinates with public and nonprofit welfare service providers, as well as with local employers in the area, but the management function, policies and program priorities, and funding decisions are made by the local families and children office in consultation with the state. Performance standards are set, but a benchmarked, fee-for-service system is not in place.

In Lexington, representatives of the city-county welfare reform committee, led by then-director of Lexington social services, Barbara Curry, visited Kansas City to learn about that city's LINC, a citizen-run collaborative that had been in place since 1992 and was dramatically changing the way welfare programs were run at the local level (Hobbs 1996; Center for the Study of Social Policy 1998). Curry and her colleagues decided to pattern the Lexington-Fayette County area's welfare program after the Kansas City model. The Kansas City LINC is an example of a local governance partnership, but its organizational structure is founded on the premise that citizens, rather than public administrators, should determine the services local communities need (Center for the Study of Social Policy 1998; Local Investment Commission 2000).[3]

LexLinc was formed in 1998. It is a significantly scaled-back version of the Kansas City LINC. With two staff members and an annual budget of $700,000, most of LexLinc's activities take the form of coordinating services, setting performance standards and evaluating providers, and providing assistance by funneling money to service providers for specific program functions. LexLinc's structure is similar to LINC's, with one important distinction. Social service professionals are members of the operating commission, along with business and community leaders and welfare recipients. The commission sets performance standards and benchmarking levels for service providers and negotiates contracts based on these standards.

LexLinc's two initiatives include welfare-to-work activities and a program aimed at enhancing the emotional and financial support of noncustodial fathers of welfare children. The welfare initiative is administered through a

Table 3.1

Governance, NPM, and Welfare Networks: Two Kentucky Welfare Models

Governance, NPM Concepts	Network Implications	Impact Questions	Lexington and Louisville Area Models
Public and private boundaries are blurred. Private, nonprofit institutions have new role in public service delivery.	Networks—not agencies—as public service delivery mechanisms.	How should public interest be determined?	LexLinc's Commissioners include citizens who set policy goals. Louisville's county welfare office determines strategies based on state directives.
Involvement of multisector institutions and actors means decentralized management.	Privatization, contracting out, opportunities for service duplication, competition and collaboration.	Are agency linkages strongly integrated or loosely coupled? Is network cohesively structured around a core member?	LexLinc's mission includes facilitating strong interagency linkages. Louisville's structure is hierarchical; its goal is interagency information sharing.
Emphasis on market efficiencies. Government authority and sanctions deemphasized; network interactions viewed as market transactions.	Providers become payers. Funding streams based on performance, negotiations; pay for performance and outcome goals emphasized.	How to enforce policy, hold providers accountable for performance? How to avoid unintended consequences (e.g., "creaming")?	LexLinc: performance-based contracts with sliding-scale compensation. Louisville: contracts not renewed if performance subpar.
Self-governing networks.	Changing role for policymakers: network partners also set policy and goals.	Is network mandated—top-down integration? Or is network emerging—bottom-up integration?	LexLinc: collaborative is emerging, bottom-up. Louisville: delivery system is mandated, top-down.
Power dependencies among institutions and actors.	Outcomes may depend upon quality of service of more than one provider. Changes in partners, environment create instability.	Is network systems-oriented: new coordination strategy, delivery structure and/or funding stream? Or service-oriented: no big change in collaborative structure or funding?	LexLinc: systems-oriented. Louisville area: service-oriented.
Communitarianism: new roles for citizens.	Citizens act as their own agents; advocate for services, more flexible implementation structures.	Can the poor be effective self-advocates? Does network structure include citizens and/or target population in governing?	LexLinc: citizens and clients with decision-making authority. Louisville area: clients consulted but lack authority. No citizen involvement.

memo of understanding with the Cabinet for Families and Children, which gives LexLinc the authority and responsibility of developing and overseeing a community strategy utilizing TANF funds. Kentucky's welfare program is called the Kentucky Temporary Assistance Program (KTAP). KTAP participants may also benefit from two Lexington welfare-to-work grants from the U.S. Department of Labor. Funds in use include a $2.8 million competitive grant and a formula grant of approximately $450,000, with subsequent funding available. To enhance collaboration, the local grant administrators have remitted to LexLinc the authority to approve policy, budget, strategy, and implementation of the services funded through these grants.

Initially, LexLinc was viewed with skepticism by local welfare service providers, who worried that the collaborative would compete with them in providing direct services to clients (Smith 1999). Instead, through LexLinc, welfare recipients are first screened and then instructed about the service providers in the community. Recipients are ultimately responsible for deciding which agency to work with and what kinds of activities (for example, job skills or employment training) to pursue. The selected intermediary or participating employer is then responsible for linking their customer to services involving transportation, child care, healthcare, working attire, food stamp allotments, savings accounts, life/parenting skills, and mentoring relationships that are all part of the LexLinc network. The selected agency is also responsible for helping their customers retain their jobs and work toward long-term self-sufficiency.

Testing Research Questions

Table 3.1 synthesizes key policy implementation issues from the governance, NPM, and welfare network literatures and identifies the questions that stem from these postbureaucratic configurations of public management. The broad themes of governance and NPM lead to strategic management conditions that structure the ways in which networks will evolve (Mintzberg 1996), and these conditions lead to questions about the impact of various network configurations on client outcome. These questions will be used to provide a framework for examining the relative effectiveness of the two Kentucky welfare models.

A few points about table 3.1 should be noted. LexLinc's commissioners are responsible for setting strategies to move clients into work as well as for setting the overall goals of welfare reform in the area. Members of the commission believe their decision making is more broadly representative of the public because citizens serve as commissioners. The Louisville-Jefferson county office of the Cabinet for Families and Children is responsible for strategic planning and goal setting. Its program emphasis is based on state directives.

In addition, part of LexLinc's mission is to provide unity among social-service providers. It meets regularly with representatives from all agencies and with representatives of a client committee and representatives of a local employers committee. Its goal in facilitating these meetings, according to the executive director, is to enhance the collaboration among agencies. It is attempting to establish strong interagency linkages.[4] Louisville-Jefferson County also meets regularly with provider agency representatives, but the goal is to share information about caseloads, new programs, and services. County human services officials believe the hierarchical structure, in which the county welfare office serves as the core member of the network, is accepted and approved of by most network partners.[5] Agencies look to the county welfare office for programmatic guidance and collaborative strategies.

This study asks which governance structures work best in helping clients earn relatively higher wages. As described above, the two models of welfare being studied here differ along several dimensions. Table 3.2 summarizes these dimensions and specifies key issues and theoretical expectations of various network configurations. It should come as no surprise to social scientists that the literature suggests theories that conflict at times.

Table 3.2
Dimension of Welfare Service Network Configurations

Welfare Policy Network System Characteristics	Configuration Impacts
Network stability	The more stable the linkages among agencies, the more effective the network. Linkages are more stable in "traditional service networks" such as the Louisville area than they are in local collaboratives like LexLinc.
Network integration	The extent to which all network organizations are interconnected is predicted to positively impact effectiveness. LexLinc works to facilitate collaboration, but agencies are in a competitive environment relative to the Louisville area model.
Network centralization	The extent to which cohesion is organized around a particular core network member (in this case, the county-level welfare office) is predicted to positively impact effectiveness.
Mandated vs. emerging	Emerging networks such as LexLinc are predicted to have more flexibility in meeting client needs than are mandated networks such as that in the Louisville area.
System- vs. service-oriented	System-oriented networks such as LexLinc are associated with much greater instability due to wholesale changes in funding streams and strategic planning responsibilities and strategies. Thus, they are predicted to be less effective than service-oriented systems such as the Louisville area model.
Top-down vs. bottom-up integration	Studies suggest that, when the impetus for coordination is imposed by higher intergovernmental levels, as it is in the traditional model, network effectiveness is reduced.

Data and Study Design

Administrative Data

The Kentucky Automated Management and Eligibility System (KAMES) administrative database is the primary source of client-level demographic data for this analysis. In addition, several other data files gathered from other administrative sources are linked with (and in some cases used to check the reliability of) the KAMES data. These include the Kentucky Works System Tracking for Employability Program (STEP) database, which reports the component in Kentucky Works that the client occupies, and the Department of Employment Services (DES) database containing quarterly earnings from all jobs held by KTAP recipients.

This study contains data on five cohorts of KTAP clients: 48,235 adult cases who were on the former welfare program—Aid to Families with Dependent Children—as of October 1996, when the KTAP program was implemented; 24,441 new adult cases coming on KTAP from November 1996 through October 1997; 12,252 adult cases new to the program from November 1997 through October 1998; 10,620 new adult cases entering the program from November 1998 through October 1999, and 10,250 new adult cases from November 1999 through October 2000. The study looks at annual earnings for KTAP recipients in 1999, 2000, and 2001. It includes only those who are active in the program during the time period and does not include recipients who have been exempted from program work requirements.

Qualitative Field Assessment

The qualitative component of the data consists of extensive field study of welfare program implementation at the county level. Field analysis was conducted at KTAP offices at the Cabinet for Families and Children in Frankfort and in Louisville and Lexington. The objective of this analysis was to understand the nature of, and primary differences in, the implementation of KTAP and the Kentucky Works program in the two models of interest here. With regard to the integrated public-private (Kansas City) model, interviews were conducted with the director and staff of LexLinc, as well as with members of the board of directors, personnel from collaborating public agencies, employers in the region, and with Kentucky Works clients. Second, the role of community leaders and the private sector is considered critical to the operations of the Kansas City model. Interviews were conducted with private and nonprofit sector members of the board and with employers not associated with LexLinc operations to determine the process by which clients were assisted in finding work and the nature of the interaction between employers and LexLinc. In Louisville, field interviews showed that, although the Kentucky Works program clearly has adopted a network structure, governance is the responsibility of the state-level

Cabinet for Families and Children and is implemented through the county office of the KTAP administration.

Dependent and Independent Variables

The outcomes examined here are total annual earnings of recipients who have earnings, not including income maintenance, food stamps, or other supplemental payments, in 1999–2001. Clients who are exempt from the Kentucky Works program because of incidence of domestic violence, a child under one in the household, or a verified inability to find childcare are excluded from the analysis. Average earnings for recipients during this time period were $3,910, $4,273, and $4,191, respectively.

Client (Level 1) Predictors

The individual-level client characteristics used here are fairly standard in welfare-to-work studies. They include age, number of children, youngest child under six, education level, race, prior year earnings, KTAP receipt history, work experience, client's cohort, and indication of substance abuse. Client characteristics of interest in this study include race, education, and prior work experience.

Age is operationalized as teen head of household, 20–29, 30–39, and 40 or over, where 20–29 is the omitted variable. Race is a dummy variable, where 1 equals nonwhite. Education level is a series of indicator variables for less than 10 years, 10 years to less than high school or GED, high school/GED, and post–high school (which is the omitted variable). KTAP recipient history is an indicator variable for active participation in welfare for at least six consecutive months during the prior year. Work experience is an indicator variable for limited work, as identified by less than $500 in earned income in the prior year.

County (Level 2) Predictors

The policy variable of primary interest here is "Program," a series of indicator variables for the Louisville-Jefferson County area's traditional social services model, the Lexington-Fayette County and surrounding county area's integrated public-private (Kansas City) model, north central Kentucky counties, and the other counties in the commonwealth. The north central Kentucky program is similar in administrative structure to the Louisville model and should show similar effects. In addition, both areas received welfare-to-work formula and competitive grants during the study period, as did LexLinc, whereas most other welfare offices in the state did not. As noted earlier, LexLinc was formed in 1998. Thus, I do not expect this program variable to show any effect in the earliest time period. The key question is whether the variable has any effect at all and in what direction.

To capture environmental and economic conditions that vary across sites, county-level socioeconomic variables, as well as the county work participation rate for the year under review, are included in the full model. County-level control variables include the county unemployment rate and median household income for the outcome year and the number of retail and service jobs in the county in 1997. Although some studies use per capita county KTAP transfer payments as an additional control, it is not included here because it is highly correlated with other economic variables.

Methodology

In this study, KTAP clients (level 1—individual-level data) are nested within counties (level 2 group data). The crux of the modeling issue is that when individual-level observations are nested within defined groups, which may themselves be nested within other groups, cross-level interactions may be present but ignored in OLS modeling. One problem is that, when hierarchical structures are present, individual observations may not be independent. It is likely that there will be significant intraclass correlations, and these large between-group variances should be explored to determine the extent to which differences in average outcomes between groups are accountable for by organizational differences or by other characteristics of the individuals being studied. It is also possible that this between-group variance differs, for different types of individuals. Hierarchical regression explicitly models the clusters in the data and provides statistically efficient estimates of regression coefficients and more precise standard errors, confidence intervals, and significance tests. In general, these will be more conservative than OLS estimates (Goldstein et al. 1993; Goldstein 1995).

In the analyses presented here, the level 1 model is specified as follows:

$$Y_{ij} = \beta_{0j} + \beta_{1j}X_{1j} + \ldots + \beta_{nj}X_{nj} + r_{ij} \qquad [1]$$

and includes client characteristics defined above.[6] The variation in the adjusted average outcome for each site, β_{0j} is modeled as follows:[7]

$$\beta_{0j} = \gamma_{00} + \gamma_{01}W_{1j} + \ldots + \gamma_{0n}W_{nj} + \mu_{0j}. \qquad [2]$$

Finally, the effects of clients' race, education, and prior work experience, are modeled as varying randomly across offices:

$$\beta_{mj} = \gamma_{m0} + \gamma_{11}W_{1j} + \gamma_{m2}W_{mj} + \ldots + \gamma_{0k}W_{kj} + \mu_{j}. \qquad [3]$$

This will estimate the average influence of the specific client characteristic m in office j and, in particular, the overall effect of client characteristic m and the effect of site-level characteristics on the average influence of client characteristic m. The other client-level characteristics are assumed to be fixed across sites. HLM computations were performed using the PROC MIXED procedure in SAS (see Singer 1998).

Findings

The variation across sites for recipient annual income for all years analyzed is statistically significant for overall average earnings (controlling for client characteristics) and for race, education, and prior year work experience. This variation may be due to economic factors, welfare office characteristics, and/or other unobservable factors. I estimated an unconditional model that indicated about 5 percent of the total variation in client earnings occurs at the office level for the first two characteristics and about 2 percent for the race variable. This is a variation that remains to be explained after controlling for observable client characteristics.

The preferred models that include all controls for client- and office-level characteristics are presented in table 3.3. Coefficient estimates for fixed-effect client characteristics are shown in the first panel. The second panel shows overall average estimates for the overall model intercept and for client characteristics of race, education, and prior work experience. In 2000, for example, the overall impact on annual earnings of having minimal work experience is a reduction in earnings of $208. Below these intercepts is the coefficient estimate for the impact of the site-level program design variables of interest. The last panel indicates the percent of level 2 variance explained for the variables modeled as varying randomly at level 2 (i.e., race, education, and work history). Although, in all three years, a number of the level 1 and level 2 control variables are substantially and statistically significant, and almost all are in the expected direction, for this review we shall focus only on the policy variables of interest.

Looking first at overall average annual earnings across sites, the results for 1999 show no impact for the welfare implementation variables. In 2000, clients in the LexLinc model saw decreased average earnings of $155 compared with clients in other offices. For 2001 earnings, average earnings in the LexLinc model were $206 lower than in other offices. The Louisville model coefficient is positive in all three years and in 2001 is marginally significant. The north central Kentucky model is also consistently positive, and its average impact in 2001 was an increase of $133.

We turn next to the client characteristics that were allowed to vary randomly across sites (i.e., controlling for other individual characteristics and for site characteristics; we are assuming that the impact of race, education, and

Table 3.3
Hierarchical Linear Model of KTAP Clients' Earnings Outcome (1999 dollars)

Predictors	1999 Coefficient	1999 t Score	2000 Coefficient	2000 t Score	2001 Coefficient	2001 t Score
Level 1 Variables:						
Age teen head of household	−39	−.36	−53	−.63	−122	−.91
Age 30–39 years	160	1.91	190	2.26	210	1.66
Age >39 years	−320	−2.26	−410	−1.77	−403	−1.88
Education <10 years	−526	−3.70	−447	−3.24	−455	−1.68
Education 10 years +, less than high school or GED	−214	−.53	−168	−.55	−177	−.63
Substance abuser	−677	−2.05	−488	−2.26	−488	−2.02
No. of children	−42	−1.07	−63	−.89	−62	−.89
Youngest child <6 years old	−144	−1.77	−191	−1.64	−104	−1.22
Received KTAP at least 6 months in prior year	55	.98	46	.27	48	.55
Earnings in prior year	427	9.24	466	8.35	478	8.57
Level 2 Variables:						
Overall average (constant)	2036	8.36	2022	6.77	2143	6.99
Program: LexLinc model	−63	1.10	−155	−1.77	−206	−1.96
Program: Louisville–Jefferson Co. model	75	1.60	89	1.09	127	1.63
Program: Northern Kentucky model	103	1.55	110	1.23	133	1.88
Work participation rate	312	6.55	214	3.46	188	4.21
Unemployment rate	−26	−1.16	−7	.55	12	.23
Median household income	196	1.08	94	.99	138	1.66
No. of retail jobs in 1997	153	1.99	163	1.66	160	1.50
Nonwhite:	140	.55	133	.77	155	1.02
Program: LexLinc model	84	.88	92	.64	105	.33
Program: Louisville–Jefferson Co. model	266	1.62	267	1.47	249	1.68
High school graduate GED:	488	6.34	522	6.95	513	5.34
Program: LexLinc model	290	.85	232	1.06	252	1.07
Program: Louisville–Jefferson Co. model	322	1.13	208	1.96	244	1.73
Minimal work history:	−227	−3.26	−210	−3.13	−277	−3.32
Program: LexLinc model	98	.86	−66	1.22	−23	−1.66
Program: Louisville–Jefferson Co. model	114	1.29	98	1.66	143	1.89
% Level-2 variance in intercept explained		74		77		81
% Level-2 variance in nonwhite explained		32		32		44
% Level-2 variance in HS/GED explained		58		65		67
% Level-2 variance in work history explained		72		70		76

work history will vary across sites). The impact of race is the weakest of the three variables, as is its explanatory power. In fact, only between 32 and 44 percent of across site variation in the race effects is explained by these models, although the variation across sites is statistically significant. Although the LexLinc variable shows no effect, the Louisville model is marginally significant in 1999 and shows that, in 2001, earnings for nonwhite recipients were $249 greater than for nonwhites in other sites.

As expected, having a high school diploma or GED is clearly related to increased earnings, with the impact ranging between $488 and $522 for the three years. In addition, the effect of the Louisville variable is positive and statistically significant in 2000 and 2001. Between 58 and 67 percent of the variation in education effects across sites is explained in the models.

Minimal work experience is related to reduced earnings, and the overall effect ranges from $210 to $277. The traditional welfare model best serves those clients who are harder to place because of a lack of work history. Although there is no impact for the policy variables in 1999, in 2000, and 2001, the Louisville model increase in earnings is significant and ranges from $98 to $143. Though these magnitudes are fairly weak, in 2001 the impact of the LexLinc policy variable is to reduce annual earnings by $23. Finally, between 70 and 76 percent of the variation in the effect of work history across sites is explained in the models.

Conclusion

The intent of this study was to examine alternative organizational structures in welfare-to-work governance policy. It offers a preliminary comparison of the impact on client earnings of the different network configurations outlined. The study is consistent with others that have found that network stability, integration, and centralization associated with the Louisville-Jefferson traditional welfare model are related to positive program outcomes. The LexLinc model is an emerging network with bottom-up integration, two factors that some predict should improve outcomes; however, its system-oriented framework, associated with changes in funding streams, fee-for-service structures, and diffused strategic planning and strategy responsibilities, appears to reduce its effectiveness.

The Lynn, Heinrich, and Hill (1999) governance framework guided the design of this chapter. Their hypothesized linkage of program outcomes to organizational structure, managerial roles, client characteristics, environmental factors, and interactions of these factors was confirmed.

There are lessons for both the study of governance and the study of policy implementation. First, the hierarchical models with all client-level and site-level variables performed fairly well in explaining variance in earnings. Although there is significant unexplained variation in earnings outcomes, most of it is at the client level, which is to be expected in studies of social programs that serve the poor (Heinrich and Lynn 2000). Between 74 and 81 percent of the variation in earnings between sites was explained by the models. As important, this study shows that organizational structure and managerial arrangements clearly matter.

Some important qualifications, however, must be noted. First, as is the case with most welfare earnings studies, the impact of structure and management on earnings estimated in this study—while statistically and substantially significant—is at best measured in the short term, and at worst still not enough to materially improve a given client's well-being. Only jobs that pay a living wage can do that. Second, as noted above, the hierarchical models do not explain variance in individual level outcomes particularly well. Thus, although the average effects across sites discussed here are important and contribute to a better understanding of linkages between governance and performance, the models are not appropriate for inferring the impact of network structure and managerial arrangements on any individual client.

Finally, the "churning" nature of welfare participation, in which clients move on and off the program for a variety of reasons that may or may not have to do with program treatments, can confound policy studies. For this reason, studies that consider the longer-term earnings of *former* welfare recipients and link those outcomes to particular structural and managerial arrangements will be most effective at opening the black box of governance.

Notes

1. See Kaboolian (1998) for a description of reform movements in the public sector that collectively comprise NPM. I adopt her definition of NPM as a series of innovations that—considered collectively—embody public choice approaches, transaction-cost relationships, and preferences for efficiency over equity.

2. It should be noted that, more recently, Kentucky has followed other states in seeing caseloads increase and decrease sporadically. During the time period under study, however, caseloads in Kentucky and all other states were falling.

3. The Center for the Study of Social Policy (1998) defines a "governance partnership" as the decision-making process by which a community takes responsibility for developing and implementing broadly supported strategies to achieve better outcomes for children, youth, families, and communities.

4. Conversation with Wanda Faircloth, LexLinc executive director, October 17, 2000.

5. Conversation with Joe Spaulding, Jefferson County human resources director, November 10, 2000.

6. Each level 1 explanatory variable is centered on its grand mean value. The intercept is thus the adjusted average outcome, controlling for differences in client characteristics across offices (Bryk and Raudenbush 1992).

7. All continuous variables in the level 2 model were centered on their grand means.

References

Agranoff, R., and M. McGuire. 1998. "Multinetwork Management." *Journal of Public Administration Research and Theory* 8:67–91.

Alexander, E. 1995. *How Organizations Act Together: Interorganizational Coordination in Theory and Practice.* Amsterdam: Gordon and Breach.

Alter, C., and J. Hage. 1993. *Organizations Working Together.* Sage Library of Social Research 191. Newbury Park, Calif.: Sage.

Barnow, B., and J. Trutko. 1997. *Inventory of Employment and Rehabilitation Programs and Approaches for the Severely Disabled.* Washington, D.C.: Urban Institute.

Bryk, A., and S. Raudenbush. 1992. *Hierarchical Linear Models: Applications and Data Analysis Methods.* Newbury Park, Calif.: Sage.

Center for the Study of Social Policy. 1998. *Setting a Community Agenda: A Case Study of the Local Investment Commission.* Washington, D.C.: Center for the Study of Social Policy.

Danziger, S., M. Corcoran, S. Danziger, C. Heflin, A. Kalil, J. Levine, D. Rosen, K. Siefert, and R. Tolman. 1998. *Barriers to the Employment of Welfare Recipients.* Ann Arbor: University of Michigan Poverty Research and Training Center.

Edin, K., and L. Lein. 1997. *Making Ends Meet: How Single Mothers Survive Welfare and Low-Wage Work.* New York: Russell Sage Foundation.

Ewalt, J. 1998. An Analysis of the Job Opportunities and Basic Skills Program in Kentucky: Determinants of Component Choice. Ph.D. diss., University of Kentucky.

Federle, K. 1999. "Juvenile Courts May Face Higher Caseloads Due to Welfare Reform." [Ohio State University] *Research News.*

Frederickson, H. G. 1996. "Comparing the Reinventing Government Movement with the New Public Administration." *Public Administration Review* 56:263–70.

Glazer, N. 1995. "Making Work Work: Welfare Reform in the 1990s." In D. S. Nightingale and R. H. Haveman, eds., *The Work Alternative: Welfare Reform and the Realities of the Job Market.* Washington, D.C.: Urban Institute Press.

Goldstein, H. 1995. *Multilevel Statistical Models,* 2d ed. New York: Halstead Press.

Goldstein, H., J. Rashbash, M. Yang, G. Woodhouse, H. Pan, D. Nuttall, and S. Thomas. 1993. "A Multilevel Analysis of School Examination Results." *Oxford Review of Education* 19:425–33.

Grubb, W., N. Badway, D. Bell, B. Chi, C. King, J. Herr, H. Prince, R. Kazis, L. Hicks, and J. Taylor. 1999. *Toward Order from Chaos: State Efforts to Reform Workforce Development Systems.* Berkeley, Calif.: National Center for Research in Vocational Education.

Hasenfeld, Y. 2000. "Social Services and Welfare-to-Work: Prospects for the Social Work Profession." *Administration in Social Work* 23:185–200.

Heinrich, C., and L. Lynn, Jr. 2001. "Means and Ends: A Comparative Study of Empirical Methods for Investigating Governance and Performance." *Journal of Public Administration Research and Theory* 11:109–38.

———. 2000. *Governance and Performance: New Perspectives.* Washington, D.C.: Georgetown University Press.

Hjern, B., and D. Porter. 1981. "Implementation Structures: A New Unit of Administrative Analysis." *Organization Studies* 2:211–27.

Hobbs, G. 1996. "Welfare to Work: The Kansas City Experiment and Experience." *Public Welfare* 54 (4):6–12.

Hood, C. 1991. "A Public Management for All Seasons." *Public Administration* 69:3–19.

Jefferson County Department of Human Resources. 2000. *A Plan for Reforming Welfare in Jefferson County with State's Responses.* Louisville, Ky.: Jefferson County Department of Human Resources.

Kaboolian, L. 1998. "The New Public Management: Challenging the Boundaries of the Management vs. Administration Debate." *Public Administration Review* 58:189–93.

Kamensky, J. M. 1996. "The Role of the 'Reinventing Government' Movement in Federal Management Reform." *Public Administration Review* 56:247–55.

Kettl, D. F. 1997. "The Global Revolution in Public Management: Driving Themes, Missing Links." *Journal of Policy Analysis and Management* 16:446–62.

———. 1995. "Building Lasting Reform: Enduring Questions, Missing Answers." In D. F. Kettl and J. J. DiIulio, eds., *Inside the Reinvention Machine: Appraising Governmental Reform*. Washington, D.C.: Brookings Institution Press, 239–46.

Leonard, P. 1999. *Welfare to Work Block Grants: Are They Working?* Washington, D.C.: Brookings Institution Press.

Local Investment Commission. 2000. *Local Investment Commission: Caring Communities Plan for Jackson County/Kansas City, 1999–2000*. Kansas City, Mo.: Local Investment Commission.

Lynn, L., Jr., C. Heinrich, and C. Hill. 1999. "The Empirical Study of Governance: Theories, Models and Methods." Paper presented at the Workshop on Models and Methods for the Empirical Study of Governance, University of Arizona, Tucson, April 29–May 1.

Martinson, K. 1999. *Literature Review on Service Coordination and Integration in the Welfare and Workforce Development Systems*. Washington, D.C.: Urban Institute.

Mathiasen, D. 1996. "The New Public Management and Its Critics." Paper presented at the Conference on the New Public Management in International Perspective, St. Gallen, Switzerland, July 11–13.

Meier, K., and L. O'Toole. 2001. "Managerial Strategies and Behavior in Networks: A Model with Evidence from U.S. Public Education." *Journal of Public Administration Research and Theory* 11:271–92.

Meyers, J., J. Gornick, and L. Peck. 2001. "Packaging Support for Low-Income Families: Policy Variation across the United States." *Journal of Policy Analysis and Management* 20:457–83.

Meyers, J., N. Riccucci, and I. Lurie. 2001. "Achieving Goal Congruence in Complex Environments: The Case of Welfare Reform." *Journal of Public Administration Research and Theory* 11:165–201.

Milward, H. B., and K. Provan. 2000. "How Networks Are Governed." In C. Heinrich and L. Lynn, eds., *Governance and Performance: New Perspectives*. Washington, D.C.: Georgetown University Press, 238–62.

Mintzberg, H. 1996. "Managing Government, Governing Management." *Harvard Business Review* (May–June):75–83.

Nightingale, D., J. Trutko, and B. Barnow. 1999. *Status of the Welfare-to-Work Grants Program after One Year*. Washington, D.C.: Urban Institute.

Ostrom, V. 1973. *The Intellectual Crisis in American Public Administration*. Tuscaloosa: University of Alabama Press.

O'Toole, L. J., Jr. 1996. "Hollowing the Infrastructure: Revolving Loan Programs and Network Dynamics in the American States." *Journal of Public Administration Research and Theory* 6:225–42.

O'Toole, L. J., Jr., and K. J. Meier. 2000. "Networks, Hierarchies, and Public Management: Modeling the Nonlinearities." In C. Heinrich and L. Lynn, eds., *Governance and Performance: New Perspectives*. Washington, D.C.: Georgetown University Press, 239–91.

Peters, B. G., and J. Pierre. 1998. "Governance without Government? Rethinking Public Administration." *Journal of Public Administration Research and Theory* 8:223–43.

Pindus, N., R. Koralek, K. Martinson, and J. Trutko. 2000. *Coordination and Integration of Welfare and Workforce Development Systems*. Washington, D.C.: Urban Institute.

Provan, K., and H. B. Milward. 1995. "A Preliminary Theory of Interorganizational Network Effectiveness." *Administrative Science Quarterly* 40:1–33.

Singer, J. 1998. "Using SAS PROC MIXED to Fit Multilevel Models, Hierarchical Models, and Individual Growth Models." *Journal of Educational and Behavioral Statistics* 24:323–55.

Smith, M. 1999. "Making a Connection: LexLinc Strives to Unite Clients With What They Need to Get Jobs." *Lexington* [Kentucky] *Herald-Leader*, August 28, C1.

Stoker, G. 1998. "Governance as Theory: Five Propositions." *International Social Science Journal* 50:17–28.

Trutko, J., N. Pindus, B. Barnow, and D. Nighingale. 1999. *Early Implementation of the Welfare-to-Work Grants Program.* Washington, D.C.: Urban Institute.

U.S. Department of Health and Human Services. 2002. "Agency for Families and Children Data and Statistics: U.S. Welfare Caseload Information." Available at www.acf.dhhs.gov /news/stats/recipients.htm.

U.S. General Accounting Office. 1998. *Grant Programs: Design Features Shape Flexibility, Accountability, and Performance.* Report GAO/GGD-98137. Washington, D.C.: U.S. Government Printing Office.

Four

Governance, Evidence-Based Practice, and Performance in Substance Abuse Treatment Programs

Carolyn J. Heinrich

The recently formed Coalition for Evidence-Based Policy, sponsored by the Council for Excellence in Government and including distinguished scholars and former government officials, aims to elevate the role of empirical research in improving government performance.[1] The coalition advocates the use of rigorous, scientific evidence of program effectiveness (e.g., deduced from studies with experimental controls) to improve policymaking and program outcomes. Advances in medicine and health are attributed, for example, to the promulgation of clinical evidence among health professionals who draw directly upon this evidence to determine effective treatments for patients. The mission of the coalition is to promote and extend the use of evidence-based policymaking in social and economic policy arenas, with the expectation of bringing similar improvements to education, economic development, poverty reduction, and health care financing and delivery.

Efforts to promote evidence-based policymaking or practices in social welfare programs will fade, however, without the contributions of public administration theories and research to identifying linkages among structure, administration, and practice in these programs and their outcomes or performance. Unlike the field of medicine, it is not common practice for public managers to regularly consult field journals to determine how to operate their programs or treat clients. And even the more scientific- or academically minded managers would not find a correspondingly large body of experimental evidence that identifies or prescribes the "right treatments" or best approaches to social services delivery. To the extent that there exists a consensus in a given social policy arena about the effectiveness of a particular practice in improving program outcomes, successful advocacy of this practice will demand a thorough understanding of the political, organizational, and administrative impediments or supports to its implementation.

This discussion motivates the larger question addressed in this chapter: as more rigorous evidence about effective program treatments or practices is produced in social science research, what political, structural or administrative barriers are likely to impede public managers' use of this evidence to improve program performance? This is an important governance question and could be rephrased using the definition of public sector governance offered by Lynn, Heinrich, and Hill (2001, 7): What "regimes of laws, rules, judicial decisions, and administrative practices . . . constrain, prescribe, and enable the [effective] provision of publicly supported goods and services" through formal and informal relationships in the public and private sectors? In this study, I pursue this question in a specific policy area—substance abuse treatment.

Unlike many other areas of social welfare policy, the field of substance abuse treatment has a fairly strong base of rigorous (clinical and other) research intended to inform effective treatment practices. Yet, despite the decades of accumulating evidence in this field, recent publications criticize the continuing gap between research and substance abuse treatment practice and call for more studies that identify governance—or policy and administrative factors— that are facilitators or barriers to the implementation of evidence-based practices. This study specifically responds to this call to link governance, evidence-based practice, and performance in substance abuse treatment organizations.

The chapter begins with a brief description of the progress of substance abuse treatment research over time toward the identification of evidence-based practices and the program-level factors that influence their implementation. The integration of public management theories to develop a conceptual framework for the analysis of linkages between politics, program administration, treatment practice, and program outcomes is discussed next. An important contribution of this chapter is the presentation of research findings based on the use of this framework and newly available data to empirically link structural and administrative factors to treatment practice and, ultimately, to client outcomes. The chapter concludes with a discussion of the policy relevance of these findings and insights for future research that might extend this research approach to other policy areas.

Progress in Substance Abuse Treatment Research

There is good reason for the public to have a serious interest in the governance and performance of substance abuse treatment programs. The government bears the major burden of substance abuse treatment costs (i.e., three-fourths of total expenditures), and all bear the failure of public policy to effectively address substance abuse problems. In fact, for more than three decades, the government has invested significantly in research—including large-scale, multisite studies and smaller clinical investigations—to determine the most effective approaches to substance abuse treatment. The first large-scale studies of substance abuse treatment effectiveness—the Drug Abuse Reporting Program (DARP) in the late 1960s and the Treatment Outcome Prospective Study (TOPS) of the late 1970s—were undertaken primarily to describe basic characteristics of treatment programs (e.g., services provided) and to address the fundamental question, Does treatment work? Nonexperimental analyses of these data collected from 44,000 and 11,000 patients, respectively, produced early evidence of patients' positive posttreatment outcomes (Gerstein and Harwood 1990). The dearth of information collected about the organization or administration of treatment programs in these studies, however, impeded efforts to predict or understand how evolving differences in program structure, size, setting, funding, and philosophy were likely to influence substance abuse treatment practice and patient outcomes (Hubbard et al. 1997). This limitation became particularly important as the 1980s brought new problems to managers of substance abuse treatment programs, including reduced federal funding for treatment, different patterns of drug use (e.g., crack cocaine use), and AIDS. And although clinical research continued to be useful in identifying effective treatment approaches for specific drug addictions (e.g., heroin, cocaine) targeted to particular segments of the drug-abusing population (e.g., pregnant women, veterans, adolescents, HIV-positive patients), these narrow, compartmentalized studies offered little information to program managers about how to integrate these practices into broader treatment strategies or to manage tradeoffs in service provision demanded by limited funding.

At the same time, one of the seminal case studies in substance abuse treatment confirmed the important roles of politics, organization, and administration in determining treatment practices. Attewell and Gerstein (1979) investigated managerial responses at the program level to government (Food and Drug Administration) policy and institutional regulation (embodied in state laws) of methadone maintenance therapy. They described how federal protocols, shaped by politics and competing medical and public interests, were integrated into state laws, which then became the bases for site inspections of program quality and compliance. At the local level, conflicts seethed between supporters of methadone maintenance and drug-free treatment approaches both within treatment programs and in the public view. In their rich analysis, Attewell and Gerstein described bureaucratic-administrative conflicts, goal displacement, and staff confrontations over treatment approaches and compliance and qualitatively linked these management problems to ineffective treatment practice and poor outcomes for patients.

The growing need to address these more complex substance abuse treatment policy and management issues led to the support of other large-scale studies that included the collection of data from program administrators and more information characterizing substance abuse treatment programs and their environments. Research using the Outpatient Drug Abuse Treatment Systems (ODATS) study data and the Drug Abuse Treatment Outcomes Study (DATOS) data in the early to late 1990s confirmed that substance abuse treatment programs in the same major treatment modalities and with similar treatment goals varied substantially in their implementation of treatment practices. D'Aunno, Sutton, and Price (1991) attributed differences in treatment approaches observed in ODATS in part to the sometimes-unpredictable influence of environmental factors, such as new patterns of drug use or health care policy changes, and to discordant perspectives within mental health and substance abuse treatment sectors about how to manage treatment programs. Others saw the problem as more inherent in the internal organization of the programs. In their DATOS study of the relationship of counseling and self-help participation to patient outcomes, for example, Etheridge et al. (1999) attributed the reported ineffectiveness of some self-help services to differences in the structure and philosophy of practice in the ineffective programs. They subsequently urged more investigation of program factors that influence the implementation of drug abuse treatment and patient outcomes.

The data used in this research are from the National Treatment Improvement Evaluation Study (NTIES), a 1992–97 national evaluation of the effectiveness of substance abuse treatment services delivered in treatment programs supported by the Center for Substance Abuse Treatment (CSAT). To date, it is the largest single study of substance abuse treatment outcomes, with data from 519 substance abuse treatment service delivery units (SDUs) and 6,593 patients. Although a purposive rather than random sample, the program-level data are rich in information about the structure, setting, administration, financial and human resources, philosophy, goals, and treatment practices in the SDUs and have been linked to patient-level data for a subset of programs (62 SDUs) that served 4,149 patients. In fact, the wealth of information about treatment programs in NTIES presents researchers with a daunting task of how to organize the analysis of literally thousands of program- and patient-level variables to produce knowledge that will inform more effective delivery of treatment services and lead to improved treatment outcomes.

The contributions of theories of governance and public administration to the study of substance abuse treatment program effectiveness enter importantly here. Those long engaged in the field of substance abuse treatment research have expressed frustration over the lack of a useful organizing framework for modeling substance abuse treatment systems and synthesizing study findings dispersed across multidisciplinary literatures (Etheridge and Hubbard 2000). In the next section, I present a theoretical framework, based on the more general theory of governance framed by Lynn, Heinrich, and Hill (2001), that has guided the empirical analysis of NTIES data presented in this and other works and that might also be employed in other social policy research efforts.

A Theoretical Framework for the Empirical Study of Substance Abuse Treatment Effectiveness

Etheridge and Hubbard (2000) have led the substance abuse treatment literature in developing a theoretical framework to guide the empirical analysis of substance abuse treatment program management and effectiveness. They present a "multilevel conceptual framework" that includes seven levels of variables: (1) the external policy environment, (2) treatment and service systems, (3) structural and operational features of programs, (4) treatment/service interventions, (5) patient characteristics, (6) patient social environment, and (7) patient outcomes. They specifically urged researchers to apply their model with the goal of establishing "evidence-based standards for clinical practice and valid guidelines and criteria for determining the quality and effectiveness of treatment" (Etheridge and Hubbard 2000, 1758).

The major components in Etheridge and Hubbard's framework for substance abuse treatment research—e.g., policy environment (including fiscal constraints), program characteristics such as philosophy, structure and staff training and skill, patient characteristics, treatment, and service interventions—are common to more general models or theories of organizational effectiveness developed by public management researchers. Rainey and Steinbauer's (1999) model of management and organizational performance, for example, describes relationships among organizational culture, mission, leadership, task design, resources, and external stakeholders. In addition, the multilevel framework advanced by Lynn, Heinrich, and Hill (2001) and discussed in chapter 1 of this volume similarly explores the role of managers at different levels of organization and specifies a rich array of organization and management factors, including ownership, centralization of control, administrative rules and incentives, resource allocations, institutional culture/values, contractual arrangements, leadership practices, staff-management relations, monitoring and control mechanisms, and organizational mission.

Synthesizing and simplifying among the levels of analysis and pertinent factors in these models, figure 4.1 presents a basic two-level model of the substance abuse treatment system in a governance framework and indicates probable relationships among these general categories of variables at program and patient levels. Substance abuse treatment research findings that elaborate on the nature of these relationships are described further in the next section and also in greater detail in Heinrich and Lynn (2002) and Heinrich and Fournier (2004). For example, the research of Goldman et al. (2001), Marinelli-Casey, Domier, and Rawson (2002), Simpson (2002), Drake et al. (2001), and others highlights the importance of the financing of treatment in determining services made available and treatment practice. The financing of treatment is also entangled with the ownership of substance abuse treatment units, the single aspect of organizational structure that has received the most attention in the substance abuse treatment literature. These research findings suggest that private, for-profit treatment units charge more for their services and do less to facilitate access to care than public and nonprofit units (Rodgers and Barnett 2000; Wheeler and Nahra 2000).

Evidence-based practices are not a component in this model but are shown in bold in figure 4.1 to suggest where the role of research enters into the treatment system, with the expectation of influencing program management and treatment practice. For example, clinical research has shown that, to be effective, methadone dosage levels for heroin addicts should be at least 60 milligrams per dose. This evidence has influenced federal guidelines for methadone treatment and treatment practice, although research has also shown that many treatment programs continue to administer dosages that are below (clinically defined) effective levels (D'Aunno and Vaughn 1992). Achieving consistently positive treatment outcomes, as Goldman et al. (2001) and others note, is the ultimate goal of evidence-based practice. It is precisely due to this disconnect between evidence and practice that substance abuse treatment researchers and policymakers have urged further study of the organization and management of treatment programs and their implications not only for treatment practice, but also for patient outcomes.

Empirical Investigation of the Relationships of Policy and Program Factors to the Implementation of Evidence-Based Practices and Patient Outcomes

The large body of substance abuse treatment research that has accumulated in the last three decades has produced some consistent findings about specific substance abuse treatment practices that facilitate positive posttreatment outcomes (Lennox and Mansfield 2001). Four of these consistent empirical associations between treatment practice and patient outcomes (i.e., that define an *evidence-based practice*) are longer duration or retention in treatment, greater counseling intensity, self-help group participation, and the availability and use of medical services (Lamb, Greenlick, and McCarty 1998; Lennox and Mansfield 2001).

The primary objective of this empirical investigation is to explore the relationships of governance factors to the implementation of this core set of evidence-based practices in substance abuse treatment. More specifically, it is hypothesized that factors originating at policy and organizational/managerial levels influence the implementation of evidence-based treatment practices and patient responses to treatment (or outcomes). For example, treatment duration may be constrained by program financial management factors, and the resulting shorter time in treatment might negatively affect patients' clinical outcomes. Four main categories of policy and program variables are used in the analysis, corresponding to those shown in the model in figure 4.1: financing of service provision, program leadership and staffing, organizational structure, and other aspects of service technology and delivery.

The separate effects of these different factors operating at (and across) the policy or program level to affect patients' treatment experiences and their subsequent treatment outcomes are modeled using hierarchical generalized linear models with cross-level interactions. The partitioning of the variance in treat-

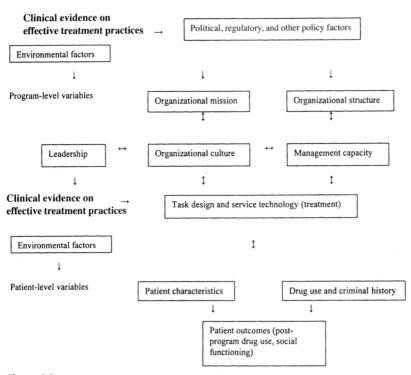

Figure 4.1
Multilevel Model of a Substance Abuse Treatment System

Note: Two-headed arrows represent the possibility of interaction effects among the different program- and patient-level variables, including cross-level effects between program- and patient-level variables.

ment outcomes between the program and patient levels showed that about 25–40 percent of the variation in patient clinical and social functioning outcomes is between programs. The simple random-intercept specification for a generalized hierarchical linear model allows for the exploration of the policy and program factors that contribute significantly toward explaining the between-program variation in patient outcomes. Cross-level effects are modeled with the addition of random coefficients to the models, where the coefficient on a particular evidence-based practice (e.g., length of treatment greater than eighteen weeks) is specified as random and as a function of one or more policy or program factors. Statistically significant cross-level effects indicate the influence of policy and program factors on treatment practice (as measured by patients' treatment experience), and the magnitude and direction of these effects indicate their implications for patients' outcomes. The construction of measures used in the analysis is briefly described next, followed by statistical notation for the estimated models and the findings of the analysis.

Measures of Evidence-Based Practices, Policy and Program Factors, Patient Outcomes, and Other Patient-Level Controls

As noted above, the NTIES program-level data were linked to patient-level data for a subset of sixty-two SDUs serving a total of 4,149 clients. After excluding patients with limited exposure to the hazards measured by clinical and social functioning outcomes (e.g., incarcerated persons who would have limited opportunities for using drugs or becoming employed), 3,543 client-level observations were available for analysis. Appendix A provides additional information about how these data were collected, and appendix B describes in detail the construction of all measures used in the analysis (briefly described below).

Patient-level measures of the four evidence-based practices were developed for the analysis using data from the NTIES Treatment Experience Questionnaire (TEQ).[2] The TEQ data on length of stay were used to construct four categories of treatment retention (0 weeks, 1–12 weeks, 13–18 weeks, and greater than 18 weeks), where treatment greater than 18 weeks is defined as an effective practice. A measure of counseling intensity combines TEQ information on the frequency and duration of individual and group counseling sessions to compute the treatment counseling "dose" in minutes. Greater counseling intensity (or dose) is expected to positively influence patient outcomes. The third evidence-based practice is patients' participation in self-help groups while in treatment (i.e., attendance at any meeting of Cocaine Anonymous [CA], Narcotics Anonymous [NA], or Alcoholics Anonymous). Finally, patients' receipt of medical services during treatment (e.g., medical tests, physical exams, or other ancillary medical services) is also expected to positively affect outcomes.

The policy- and program-level variables are based on data collected in baseline and follow-up questionnaires of program administrators.[3] They include measures of the financing of treatment: revenue per patient; the percentage of total revenues originating from federal, state, and local governments, Medicaid and Medicare, patient fees or private insurance, and so on; and patient insurance (private, public, or unable to pay). Leadership and staffing are another set of program-level measures: program directors' tenure and education; total full-time staff equivalents (per patient); contract staff; percentage of total staff who were in recovery from alcohol or drug dependence; and other standardized measures of personnel.

Organizational structure measures include treatment modality, program affiliation, CSAT grant type, ownership, and accreditation and licensing. Modality describes the provision of services in a residential (long-term or short-term) setting or outpatient program, and whether treatment is "drug-free" or methadone based (i.e., four variables indicating short-term residential, long-term residential, outpatient nonmethadone, and outpatient methadone.) Among the standard program affiliations are a community mental health center, general hospital, halfway house, or freestanding nonresidential facility. The CSAT grants consisted of four main types: centralized grant programs with a range of incentives and priorities in the largest cities ("Target Cities"); smaller, more individualized grants with priorities to serve high-risk, disadvantaged groups ("Critical Populations"); grants to correctional facilities; and those to units providing treatment to adolescent/juvenile justice populations. Ownership is defined by legal status (private for-profit, nonprofit, or public unit). In addition, accreditation and licensing are studied because they have been proposed as a policy instrument to encourage the adoption of evidenced-based treatment practices (Carpinello et al. 2002). Finally, a number of variables describe other aspects of service technology or delivery, including patient referrals, the provision of supportive services in on-site or off-site locations, and measures indicating the extent to which programs tailored or matched services to specific target populations.

The other key patient-level variables, based on patient intake, discharge, and follow-up interviews, are four measures of patient outcomes, including two clinical outcomes and two measures of social functioning.[4] The two clinical measures are indicators of no postprogram drug use (abstinence) and a decrease in the frequency of drug use (compared to drug use levels at intake). The social functioning measures are indicators of continued or began work and continued or began full-time work. Each of these outcome measures is a dichotomous dependent variable indicating a positive treatment outcome. Other patient-level variables included as controls in the analysis are age, gender, race/ethnicity, education level, work status at program intake, drug and alcohol treatment history/participation prior to intake, treatment goals defined for/with patient (clinical or social functioning), patient involvement in treatment planning, and an indicator of whether the patient completed treatment.

Models Estimated

As indicated earlier, a random intercept–random coefficient (or intercepts and slopes as outcomes) specification of the hierarchical generalized linear model is used to estimate the effects of policy and program factors on the implementation of evidence-based practices.[5] The level one submodel in this specification for a given (binomial) outcome (η_{ij}) is

$$\eta_{ij} = \beta_{0j} + \beta_{1j}X_{1ij} + \ldots + \beta_{nj}X_{nij} + r_{ij}, \qquad [1]$$

where patient characteristics and treatment experiences (X_{1ij} to X_{nij}) are included as controls at the patient level.[6] The intercept of the level one submodel (β_{0j}) is specified as random and modeled as a function of the various program and policy factors in the level-two submodel. In addition, the coefficient on a given evidence-based practice (e.g., length of treatment greater than eighteen weeks, counseling intensity, participation in self-help services, or receipt of medical services) is also specified as random and as a function of one or more policy/program factors. The level-two submodel is specified as follows:

$$\beta_{0j} = \gamma_{00} + \gamma_{01}\mathbf{W}_{1j} + \cdots + \gamma_{0n}\mathbf{W}_{nj} + \mathbf{u}_{0j}$$ [2]
$$\beta_{1j} = \gamma_{10} + \gamma_{11}\mathbf{W}_{1j} + \cdots + \gamma_{1n}\mathbf{W}_{nj} + \mathbf{v}_{0j}$$
$$\beta_{2j} = \gamma_{10}, \dots, \beta_{nj} = \gamma_{n0}.$$

The second equation line in [2] shows the coefficient (β_{1j}) of a particular evidence-based practice specified as random (a function of a given set of policy or program factors), and the other β_{2j} to β_{nj} coefficients defined as fixed.

Because of the limited degrees of freedom available in the analysis, separate models are estimated with each of the four evidence-based practices specified as random and with the particular practice as a function of only one type or set of the different measures of policy and program factors in the level-two submodel (for each of the four patient outcomes). Thus, this approach involves the estimation of a very large number of models, in light of the many alternative specifications possible with the large number of policy and program variables, four different evidence-based practices, and four dependent variables. The direct effects of the core set of policy and program factors on outcomes are estimated with the random intercept function. Statistically significant cross-level effects indicate the policy and program factors that are likely to facilitate or constrain the implementation of evidence-based practices and their effects on patient outcomes.

Effects of Policy and Program Factors on the Implementation of Evidence-Based Practices and Patient Outcomes

The findings of the empirical analysis are presented in two summary tables (tables 4.1 and 4.2) and an additional table (table 4.3) that presents the full results on estimated effects for two models (one clinical outcome and one social functioning outcome) to aid readers' understanding of the empirical findings. Table 4.1 summarizes the *statistically significant* direct effects of governance or policy and program factors in explaining the variation in patients' clinical and social functioning outcomes between programs (as estimated with the random intercept equation in the model). Table 4.2 summarizes the statistically significant findings of the models testing for different cross-level effects of the program and policy factors on the implementation of evidence-based practices.[7]

The direct effects of policy and program factors on patient outcomes are generally consistent for each of the two measures of clinical outcomes and for the two measures of social functioning, but were different across these two types of outcomes. For example, Medicaid financing has been described as critical to substance abuse treatment programs' financial capacity to make ser-

Table 4.1

Summary of Findings on Direct Effects of Policy and Program Variables on Patient Clinical and Social Functioning Outcomes

	Patient Clinical or Social Functioning Outcomes			
Policy and Program Variable[a]	Abstinence	Reduced Drug Use	Work	Full-Time Work
Funding sources (%)				
Medicare/Medicaid	+	+	0	–
Federal revenues	0	0	0	+
Patient insurance (%)				
Privately insured	0	0	+	+
Treatment modality				
Methadone	–	–	–	–
Affiliation/location				
General hospital	–	–	0	0
Ownership				
Private for-profit	0	–	0	+
Private nonprofit	–	–	0	+
Accreditation				
City agency	0	0	0	+
Referral source (%)				
From other SDU, physician, other				
health agency, school, employer	+	+	0	0
Medical services available				
On-site	+	+	0	0
Off-site	0	0	0	+
Treatment experience				
Patient involved in goals/plan	+	+	0	0
Completed treatment	+	+	0	0
Treatment >18 weeks	+	+	0	–
Patient characteristics				
Age (years)				
<18	–	–	0	0
30–39	+	+	0	0
40 and over	+	+	–	–
Gender (male = 1)	0	0	+	+
Race/ethnicity				
Black, non-Hispanic	0	0	–	–
Hispanic	0	0	–	0
High school/GED	0	0	+	0
Employed at intake	+	+	+	0
Prior drug treatment	–	–	0	+
Prior alcohol treatment	+	+	0	0

Note: +, positive, statistically significant relationship; –, negative, statistically significant relationship; 0, not significant relationship at $\alpha < .05$.

[a] The effects of policy and program factors, treatment experience variables, and patient characteristics are only shown in this table if they were statistically significant in at least one model of patient outcomes.

Table 4.2

Summary of Findings on Cross-Level Effects of Policy and Program Variables on Evidence-Based Treatment Practices and Patient Clinical and Social Functioning Outcomes

Policy or Program Variable	Clinical Outcome (abstinence, reduced drug use)				Social Functioning (work, full-time work)			
	Length of treatment	Counseling intensity	Medical care	Self-help	Length of treatment	Counseling intensity	Medical care	Self-help
Revenue sources	0	+ (Medicaid/ Medicare)	0	0	0	+ (federal government)	+ (federal, local government)	– (Medicaid/ Medicare)
Patient insurance	0	0	0	0	0	0	0	0
Ownership	0	– (for profit)	0	0	0	0	0	0
Affiliation	0	0	0	0	0	0	+ (halfway house)	0
Accreditation	0	0	+ (JCAHO) – (city agency)	0	0	0	0	0
Full-time staff	0	+	0	0	0	0	0	0
Contract staff	–	0	0	0	–	0	0	–
Percent staff in recovery	0	0	0	0	0	0	0	0
Case management	0	0	0	0	0	0	0	0
Medical care on-site provision	+	+	+	n.a.	0	0	0	n.a.
Medical care off-site provision	0	0	0	n.a.	0	0	0	n.a.
Patients with treatment required (%)	–	0	0	0	0	0	0	0

Note: +, positive, statistically significant relationship; –, negative, statistically significant relationship; 0, no significant relationship at $\alpha < 0.05$; n.a., not estimated.

vices available (Gerstein et al. 1997). Medicaid programs, however, vary substantially from state to state in the types of services they fund, and localities frequently fear that they will lose the money necessary to cover treatment. Table 4.1 shows that a higher percentage of Medicaid and Medicare funding is positively related to abstinence and reduced drug use among patients. On the contrary, a higher percentage of Medicaid and Medicare financing is negatively related to the social functioning outcome of full-time work, while the percent of patients privately insured is positively related to work and full-time work outcomes. These latter relationships might reflect an association between patients' labor force attachment and access to private insurance that aids their progress toward higher levels of social functioning. At the same time, a higher proportion of funding from federal sources (other than patient-generated Medicaid/Medicare funds) is positively associated with full-time work outcomes, which suggests that federal support for treatment programs is importantly linked to improving both clinical and social functioning outcomes.

In table 4.2, the results show that, in addition to the direct effects of financing on outcomes, there are also some statistically significant cross-level effects on treatment practice. Substance abuse treatment programs with higher proportions of Medicaid and Medicare funding delivered more counseling services (i.e., higher intensity/doses) that had positive effects on clinical outcomes. In addition, consistent with the direct effect findings, higher proportions of funding from the federal government contributed to greater intensity of counseling services and medical care provision, both of which improved social functioning outcomes (see the details of this model in table 4.3, column 2). Higher proportions of Medicaid and Medicare funding were related to lower levels of patient participation in self-help services, however, with negative implications for social functioning outcomes.

Other program and policy factors with statistically significant direct effects on patient outcomes include measures of organization and treatment structure. The provision of outpatient methadone treatment, for example, is negatively related to all four patient outcomes. This result was not unexpected, in light of the fact that these programs serve a high proportion of heroin addicts and aim to achieve maintenance of drug problems, not necessarily a drug-free state within the short follow-up period of one year. Treatment programs' affiliation with or location in a general hospital is also negatively associated with abstinence and reduced drug use, which might again reflect these programs' intermediate treatment objectives for a patient population with greater severity of substance abuse problems. Programs based in a general hospital are also likely to have different sources of funding than those in a freestanding nonresidential facility and thus may face different regulatory and compliance or reporting burdens. Table 4.3 shows that affiliation/location in a halfway house is positively associated with increased medical service provision that has a positive effect on work/full-time work outcomes. It is possible that those patients in halfway houses who are focusing on reentering so-

Table 4.3

Full Model Examples

Predictor Variable	Patient Outcome	
	Reduced Drug Use	Full-Time Work
Level-1 variables (n = 3,543 patients)		
Intercept	1.705*	-2.509**
Demographics:		
<18 years of age	-0.690**	-0.162
30–39 years of age	0.168	-0.217
40 years of age and over	0.266**	-0.594**
Gender (male = 1)	-0.089	0.257*
Black, non-Hispanic	-0.074	-0.190
Hispanic	0.080	0.030
High school/GED	0.042	0.143
Employed at intake	0.298*	-0.998*
Prior drug treatment	-0.462**	0.373**
Prior alcohol treatment	0.071	0.033
Three or more prior treatments	-0.192	-0.202
Treatment experience:		
Set health-related treatment goals	-0.092	n.a.
Set social functioning treatment goals	n.a.	0.092
Patient involved in goals/plan	0.224	-0.083
Completed treatment	0.041	-0.036
Mental health services provided	0.021	-0.087
Evidence-based practices:		
Treatment >18 weeks	0.600**	-0.300*
Counseling dose/intensity($\div$100)	-0.018	0.003
Medical services provided	-0.093	-0.892
Participated in self-help services	-0.285	-0.032
Level-2 variables (n = 62 SDUs)		
Treatment modality and CSAT grant type:		
Residential long-term	0.041	-0.230
Methadone	-1.012*	-0.931**
Outpatient drug-free	0.187	0.192
Critical populations	0.288	-0.640*
Criminal populations	0.270	0.188
% patients with treatment required	0.243	-0.671
Affiliation:		
General hospital	-0.928	0.470
Halfway house	-0.161	0.473
Free-standing nonresidential facility	0.210	0.105
Private for-profit ownership	-0.727*	0.986**
Private nonprofit ownership	-0.641*	0.535*
Funding sources:		
% Medicare/Medicaid	1.082*	-1.024*
% federal revenues	-0.323	0.114
% state revenues	-0.739	-0.160
% local government revenues	-0.041	-1.063

Table 4.3
Full Model Examples (*continued*)

Predictor Variable	Patient Outcome	
	Reduced Drug Use	Full-Time Work
Patient insurance: % unable to pay	−0.0001	0.004*
City/county accreditation	−0.266	0.652*
Medical services available on site	0.032	0.286
Medical services available off site	−0.251	0.618**
Psychological services available on site	−0.193	0.022
Psychological services available off site	0.024	−0.065
Counseling intensity (÷100) * Medical services Available on site	0.054**	n.a.
Counseling intensity (÷100) * Medical services Available off site	0.017	n.a.
Medical services provided * % Medicare/Medicaid	n.a.	−0.043
Medical services provided * % federal revenues	n.a.	1.073*
Medical services provided * % state revenues	n.a.	0.715
Medical services provided * % local government revenues	n.a.	1.230*
% of explainable variation between SDUs explained by the model	82.7	93.5

Note: Statistically significant * $\alpha < .05$; ** $\alpha < .01$.

ciety (social functioning goals) benefit from having medical services accessible in a setting that simultaneously facilitates their participation in the labor force.

The ownership of service delivery units also has both direct and cross-level effects on patient outcomes that differ by the type of outcome. Relative to publicly owned programs, private for-profit and nonprofit units are less effective in reducing drug use or promoting abstinence among patients, whereas private for-profit and nonprofit ownership are positively related to patients' full-time work outcomes (see table 4.1). The single, statistically significant result (cross-level effect) for ownership in table 4.2 suggests that for-profit treatment units provide less intensive counseling services, with negative implications for abstinence and reduced drug use. Other research has found that, compared to public programs, private (particularly for-profit) units are more likely to provide specialized treatment services and to cater to patients who are able to pay for treatment or who rely on private insurance (Rodgers and Barnett 2000; Wheeler and Nahra 2000). These patients may also be more likely to have social functioning as their primary treatment goal. In a more in-depth exploration of the implications of ownership and related dimensions of organizational form, Heinrich and Fournier (2004) also speculate that private sector programs may develop more linkages with private sector businesses and employers than public treatment units that facilitate patient connections with employment opportunities.

A program's accreditation has differing effects on clinical versus social functioning outcomes as well. The only main effect observed on patient outcomes of the different types of accreditation (Joint Commission on the Accreditation of Health Care Organizations [JCAHO], U.S. Food and Drug Administration [FDA], state, or city/county) is a positive association of local (city/county) accreditation with patients' full-time work (see table 4.1). The results in table 4.2 also show, however, that JCAHO accreditation is positively associated with the provision of medical services that has positive effects on clinical outcomes, whereas local accreditation is negatively associated with medical services provision and clinical outcomes. Friedman, Alexander, and D'Aunno (1999) have associated JCAHO-accredited treatment programs with better access to services such as primary care and mental health services. They also identified for-profit units, which are more likely to be locally accredited, as less likely to deliver these types of medical services.

Although SDU staffing (full-time, contract, medical personnel, percent in recovery, etc.) did not have any direct effects on patient outcomes in this analysis, the number of full-time staff per patient and the percent of contracted staff did have statistically significant effects on the implementation of three of the four evidence-based practices. Table 4.2 shows that a higher ratio of full-time staff to patients increases the intensity of counseling services provided and improves clinical outcomes. On the contrary, a higher proportion of contracted staff reduces the length of substance abuse treatment, which has negative implications for both clinical and social functioning outcomes. A higher proportion of contracted staff also reduces patients' participation in self-help services and, ultimately, patients' work and full-time work participation.

The final set of policy and program direct and cross-level effects that emerge in this analysis relate to on-site versus off-site provision of critical medical and supportive services to patients. Table 4.1 shows that on-site provision of medical services has direct, positive effects on clinical outcomes (i.e., reducing drug use and promoting abstinence). This finding is consistent with that of Friedmann et al. (2003), who found that on-site primary medical care improves patients' addiction-related outcomes. Furthermore, table 4.2 presents some clear findings about how the availability of on-site medical care might improve clinical outcomes. The availability of on-site medical care is significantly related to longer time in treatment, greater counseling intensity, and higher levels of receipt of medical services, all of which promote improved clinical outcomes (see the details of this model in column 1 of table 4.3). It is interesting, though, that the availability of off-site medical services has a direct, positive effect on full-time work outcomes (table 4.1). Intuitively, these results make sense. Patients who are in treatment and working toward abstinence benefit more from on-site availability of medical services, while those making the effort to work full-time will benefit from services that they can access in off-site locations.

Looking to the other results presented in table 4.1 on the relationship of patients' treatment experiences and characteristics to treatment outcomes, one also sees differences in these effects by the two types of outcomes, clinical and social functioning. For example, patients' involvement in setting treatment goals and plans, completion of treatment, and length of treatment all have statistically significant positive effects on clinical outcomes, but only length of treatment is a significant predictor of work/full-time work outcomes, and that effect is negative. This latter result is not unexpected, as a longer time in treatment (and time out of the labor force) is certain to limit labor force participation opportunities. In addition, age, gender, ethnicity, education and prior drug or alcohol treatment all have differing effects on patients' clinical and social functioning outcomes. For example, consistent with labor research findings, older patients (forty years and over), minorities, and females are significantly less likely to be employed or working full-time at follow-up, whereas older patients are more likely to achieve successful clinical outcomes, and gender and race/ethnicity are not significantly related to reduced drug use or abstinence. Substance abuse treatment programs that attempt to tailor program services to patient needs and work with patients toward multiple treatment goals should be aware of these differing effects of patient characteristics, treatment experiences, and program characteristics (e.g., on-site versus off-site location of medical and supportive services) on alternative treatment objectives and outcomes (clinical, social functioning, or other).

The results shown in table 4.3 for a model of reduced drug use and a model of full-time work outcomes illustrate in greater detail some of the findings that have been discussed in this section. The parameter estimates are not presented in terms of log-odds ratios, because this capability has not yet been developed for hierarchical generalized linear models, yet the interpretation of the coefficients is still fairly straightforward, and their sign and significance are clear. For example, length of treatment greater than eighteen weeks increases the probability by 60 percent that a patient will reduce drug use in the postprogram period (compared to those in treatment eighteen weeks or less), whereas treatment greater than eighteen weeks has a negative effect on full-time work outcomes, reducing by 30 percent the probability that a patient is employed full-time at follow-up. The percent of funding from Medicaid and Medicare also has substantial direct effects on treatment outcomes, although these effects are interpreted as follows. On average, 20 percent of SDU funding comes from Medicare/Medicaid. Thus, for the average unit, patients in these programs would be $1.082 \times 0.20 = 0.216$, or about 22 percent more likely to reduce drug use in the postprogram period; however, the negative coefficient in the full-time work model indicates that they would be $-1.024 * 0.20 = .205$, or 20.5 percent, less likely to become employed in a full-time job relative to those patients in SDUs with no Medicaid/Medicare funding.

The interpretation of the cross-level effects in table 4.3 also requires some calculations. For example, patients receiving the average level of counseling dose or intensity (755 hours) that are in SDUs that also provide *on-site* medical services will have an increased probability of reduced drug use of about 41 percent—i.e., $.054 \times (755/100) = .408$, compared to those in SDUs without on-site medical services provision. In addition, patients in SDUs with the average percent of federal revenues (38 percent) who also receive medical services are about 41 percent more likely to become employed in a full-time job— i.e., $1.073 \times 0.38 = 0.407$. In the many models estimated, of which only these two are shown, the cross-level effects (summarized in table 4.2) provide the key information about how policy/program factors influence the implementation of the evidence-based practices and mediate their effects on patient outcomes.

Conclusion

The findings of this research constitute an important contribution to understanding how governance—or the organization and administration of substance abuse treatment programs—influences the use of evidence-based practices and their implications for patient outcomes. The theories of governance discussed in this chapter and earlier in the volume provide a framework for organizing an abundance of detailed information on the programs and the patients served, and the analyses break new ground in terms of the policy/ program and patient interaction effects explored. At the same time, the research findings are consistent with the store of knowledge (or evidence) that has been built from many individual studies about factors that are critical to patient outcomes and treatment improvement. For example, like other studies, these analyses demonstrate that the availability of medical services on-site in programs improves patients' clinical outcomes. By linking program structure and management to treatment practice, however, this work further shows that it is the availability of medical services on-site that increases the length of treatment for patients, contributes to higher levels of counseling intensity, and increases their receipt of medical services, all of which increase the probability of abstinence and reduced drug use in the postprogram period.

This work should help to begin to fill the gap in knowledge that frustrates substance abuse treatment researchers and, in particular, the policymakers and program administrators who endeavor daily to manipulate a wide range of factors that might influence program success. For example, although it has been reported before that Medicaid is critical to service availability, this research confirms the importance of Medicaid and other federal revenue sources in increasing the intensity (or dose) of counseling services provided to patients, which in turn is positively linked to both clinical and social functioning posttreatment outcomes. This type of information is particularly important in light of proposed Medicaid reforms that would convert federal Medicaid dollars to state block grants and thereby shift responsibility from the federal government to the states for determining Medicaid spending priorities. Having research evidence that links Medicaid funding to positive posttreatment outcomes could be critical to substance abuse treatment program administrators' efforts to maintain or increase Medicaid funding for their programs. A number of other statistically significant findings discussed in the preceding section have practical implications for the way substance abuse treatment programs are managed and services delivered.

This work also suggests that the agenda supported by the Coalition for Evidence-Based Policy to promote the role of empirical research in improving government performance should fundamentally focus on the links between policy and program governance and service delivery (or receipt of services by clients) that ultimately impact outcomes. The case history of substance abuse treatment programs is a prime example of how the existence of a large body of experimental or other rigorous evidence about effective practices does not readily translate into clear guidelines for program implementation and achievements. A number of the chapters in this volume are moving this more ambitious empirical research agenda forward in a variety of policy areas, and it is my hope that this is only the beginning of broader and enduring research enterprise.

Appendix A
Background Information on the National Treatment Improvement Evaluation Study

The National Opinion Research Center (NORC), at the University of Chicago, and its subcontractor, the Research Triangle Institute (RTI), were responsible for the design, collection of data, and analysis of data in NTIES, a multisite evaluation of CSAT grantees. The program-level data used in this research come from the NTIES baseline administrative report, June 1992 through May 1993. The unit of analysis is a SDU, defined as "one treatment modality provided by a single site." A total of 519 service delivery units completed the baseline questionnaire (82% of the 792 grantees).

A purposive sample of the CSAT grantee "universe" of SDUs was selected to provide clinical outcomes data. Admissions to these 65 SDUs were randomly sampled for the clinical-outcomes data collection, resulting in an enrollment of 6,593 treatment clients. Two rounds of administrative data (baseline and follow-up) on staffing, clinical organization, patient flows, costs, and revenues were collected from each program's chief financial officer and chief executive officer, and questionnaires were also administered to all clinicians in each program. Administrative data collection began in July 1993 and continued through November 1994. These data are also described in depth in the NTIES final report (Gerstein et al. 1997).

All clients enrolled as randomly sampled admissions completed an interview at intake to determine recent and lifetime drug use and impairments or problems across a panel of domains including mental health, crime, employment, family situations, housing, and so forth; 5,274 (80 percent) completed the treatment experience questionnaire at discharge. Follow-up interviews (and, in parallel, a urine specimen and collection of arrest record information), conducted eleven months (on average) after discharge from treatment, were completed for 83 percent of the original 6,593 treatment clients. The administration of patient intake questionnaires began in July 1993 and continued through November 1994. Discharge questionnaires were administered between July 1993 and April 1995. Follow-up questionnaires were fielded between August 1994 and November 1995. Measures of treatment experience and of change from pre- to post-treatment are essential to the analyses presented in this chapter. Only subjects who completed all three questionnaires (4,149 clients in sixty-two SDUs) were eligible. Thus, the multilevel analysis focuses on sixty-two treatment programs in sixteen cities, counties, or institutions with statewide catchment areas, in which more than 4,000 patients were included in the final analytical sample used to study patient outcomes. A comparison of the subsample of sixty-two treatment programs with the full sample of NTIES SDUs by CSAT program type and treatment modality showed some differences in these two samples, such as the overrepresentation of adult correctional facilities and short-term residential programs, although they were fairly comparable across other measures.

Further exclusion from the analysis was also necessary because of the limited exposure of continuously incarcerated patients to the hazards measured as outcome; 606 cases were dropped from the analysis because they were incarcerated at the time of follow-up and reported the length of that incarceration as either "more than one year" or "incarcerated since last interview."

Appendix B
Construction of Measures Used in the Models

I. Client Characteristics

Demographics

Age   Age of respondents, from the date of birth collected at intake. We created four categories: aged 17 or less, 18–29, 30–39, 40 and over.

Gender   Gender of the respondent (a dummy variable) is coded 1 for males.

Race/Ethnicity   Information on the race/ethnicity of the respondent includes three categories (non-Hispanic black, Hispanic, nonblack), coded as dummy variables.

Diploma or Equivalent   High school education status is coded 1 if the respondent reported having at least a high school diploma or a GED.

Intake Characteristics

Mandatory Treatment   Dummy variable coded 1 for respondents whose treatment was required or recommended by the criminal justice system.

Prior Substance Abuse Treatment   Three measures of respondent's prior exposure to substance abuse treatment for alcohol and drug problems: treated for alcohol problems (1/0), treated for drug problems (1/0), and how many times entered treatment.

Referral Sources Dummy variables indicating respondent's sources of referral to the treatment episode: drug treatment staff; criminal justice persons; medical, psychiatric/mental health, or other health agency staff; school teachers, counselors, or school administrators; other public service agency staff; an employer, supervisor, union official, or employee assistance program; spouse, partner, or family member; friend, coworker, acquaintance, or fellow inmate; self-referral.

Treatment Descriptors

Treatment Completion Dummy variable coded 1 for "completed treatment plan/graduated from program" as main reason treatment was stopped.

Length of Treatment Four mutually exclusive categories for length of treatment period: no treatment, 1–12 weeks, 13–18 weeks, and more than18 weeks.

Mental Health Services Dummy variable indicating the receipt of mental health counseling services or treatment.

Counseling Intensity Information on counseling frequency and length of sessions was used to construct a measure of counseling intensity or "dose" (in minutes).

Self-Help Meetings Dummy variable coded 1 if the respondent reported attending any meetings of three self-help groups (Alcoholics Anonymous, Cocaine Anonymous, or Narcotics Anonymous).

Received Medical Services Dummy variable coded 1 if the respondent reported receiving medical services during treatment.

Patient Involvement in Treatment Plan Dummy variable coded 1 if the respondent reported that s/he helped to decide the treatment plan or treatment goals.

Treatment Goals Treatment goals are described using four dummy variables: reducing/abstaining from substance use, improving (mental or physical) health, improving behaviors related to social interactions, and reducing criminal activity or legal problems.

II. Treatment Outcomes

Clinical Outcomes

Abstinence The NTIES measure of abstinence is use of a substance five times or less during the twelve-month follow-up period. This information was collected for each substance; our measure is a dummy variable coded 1 to account for use of *any* substance.

Decreased Substance Use during the Follow-Up Period NTIES collected drug use information at intake and at follow-up approximately 12 months postdischarge. To measure a *change in the frequency* of use, we constructed substance-specific measures coded 1 to indicate no increase or a decrease in the frequency of use. The outcome measure is a composite of the substance-specific measures and is coded 1 to indicate no increase in frequency for *any* substance.

Social Functioning

Work   The NTIES work question items record at intake and follow-up whether the respondent is currently receiving income through legal activity. The dummy outcome variable is coded 1 for respondents who continued to be employed or who become employed in legal activity.

Full-Time Work   Full-time work in the NTIES data collection instruments is recorded as thirty-five hours or more in a week at a job that did not involve illegal activity. The full-time work dummy variable is coded 1 for respondents who continued to be employed full time or who became employed full time in legal activity at follow-up.

III. Program Characteristics

Financing

Patient Insurance   Percentage of the programs' patients with private insurance, public insurance, or who were unable to pay for treatment.

Revenue Sources   Percentage of the programs' *total receipts* from each of the following sources over the reference year: patient fees, private insurance, Medicaid, Medicare, CSAT support, other federal support, direct state support, direct local government support, interest income, charitable contributions, and other sources.

Ownership   Three dummy variables indicating whether the program was a private for-profit, private nonprofit, or public unit.

Leadership

Director Tenure   Program director's tenure with the treatment organization in years.
Director Education   Nine dummy variables indicating the program directors' educational degrees and professional credentials (BA/BS, MA/MS, MSW/MPH/MSPH/MPA, PhD/ScD/EdD/DSW/DrPH, MBA, MD, CAC, RN/LPN, and other).

Treatment Approach/Standardization

Modality   Four dummy variables (mutually exclusive) identify the modality of treatment programs: residential long-term, outpatient drug free, methadone, and short-term inpatient.

Accreditation   Six dummy variables indicating programs' accreditation or licensure by: JCAHO, Commission on the Accreditation of Rehabilitation Facilities (CARF), FDA, a state agency, a city or county agency. Another dummy variable was created to indicate whether a program had *any* accreditation or licensure.

Grant Type   Dummy variables indicating four program types: centralized grant programs in the largest cities ("Target Cities"); smaller, more individualized grants serving high-risk, disadvantaged groups ("Critical Populations"); substance abuse treatment services for correctional (incarcerated) populations; and programs for the adolescent/juvenile justice population.

Notes

1. See the program description of the Coalition for Evidence-Based Policy at www.excelgov.org.

2. These measures correspond to the treatment (T) variables in Lynn, Heinrich, and Hill's (2001) reduced-form expression that is also presented in chapter 1:

$O = f(E, C, T, S, M)$, where O = outputs/outcomes (individual or organizational); E = environmental factors (political, economic, and so on); C = client or consumer characteristics; T = treatments (primary work, core processes, or technology); S = structures (administrative or organizational); and M = managerial roles, strategies, or actions.

3. The policy and program-level measures used in this study correspond to the structures (S) and managerial (M) factors in the reduced-form governance model expression.

4. The substance abuse treatment client outcome measures (O) and client characteristic (C) variables are individual-level measures in the reduced-form model.

5. See Bryk and Raudenbush (1992).

6. η_{ij} is the log of the odds of success for a binomial outcome variable (the logit link function), defined as $\log(N_{ij}/1 - N_{ij})$.

7. The full set of model results for all specifications is available upon request from the author.

References

Attewell, P., and D. Gerstein. 1979. "Government Policy and Local Practice." *American Sociological Review* 44:311–27.

Bryk, A. S., and S. W. Raudenbush. 1992. *Hierarchical Linear Models: Applications and Data Analysis Methods*. London: Sage.

Carpinello, S. E., L. Rosenberg, J. Stone, M. Schwager, and C. J. Felton. 2002. "New York State's Campaign to Implement Evidence-Based Practices for People with Serious Mental Disorders." *Psychiatric Services* 53:153–55.

D'Aunno, T., R. I. Sutton, and R. H. Price. 1991. "Isomorphism and External Support in Conflicting Institutional Environments: A Study of Drug Abuse Treatment Units." *Academy of Management Journal* 34:636–61.

D'Aunno, T., and T. E. Vaughn. 1992. "Variations in Methadone Treatment Practices." *Journal of American Medical Association* 267:253–58.

Drake, R., S. M. Essock, A. Shaner, K. B. Carey, K. Minkoff, L. Kola, D. Lynde, F. C. Osher, R. E. Clark, and L. Richards. 2001. "Implementing Dual Diagnosis Services for Clients with Severe Mental Illness." *Psychiatric Services* 52:469–76.

Etheridge, R. M., S. G. Craddock, R. L. Hubbard, and J. L. Rounds-Bryant. 1999. "The Relationship of Counseling and Self-Help Participation to Patient Outcomes in D.A.T.O.S." *Drug and Alcohol Dependence* 57:99–112.

Etheridge, R. M., and R. L. Hubbard. 2000. "Conceptualizing and Assessing Treatment Structure and Process in Community-Based Drug Dependency Treatment Programs." *Substance Use and Misuse* 55:1757–95.

Friedmann, P. D., J. A. Alexander, and T. A. D'Aunno. 1999. "Organizational Correlates of Access to Primary Care and Mental Health Services in Drug Abuse Treatment Units." *Journal of Substance Abuse Treatment* 16:71–80.

Friedmann, P. D., Z. Zhang, J. Hendrickson, M. D. Stein, and D. R. Gerstein. 2003. "Effect of Primary Medical Care on Addiction and Medical Severity in Substance Abuse Treatment Programs." *Journal of General Internal Medicine* 18:1–8.

Gerstein, D. R., A. R. Datta, J. S. Ingels, R. A. Johnson, K. A. Rasinski, S. Schildhaus, K. Talley, K. Jordan, D. B. Phillips, D. W. Anderson, W. G. Condelli, and J. S. Collins. 1997. *The National Treatment Improvement Evaluation Study: Final Report*. Chicago: National Opinion Research Center.

Gerstein, D. R., and H. J. Harwood, eds. 1990. *Treating Drug Problems: A Study of the Evolution, Effectiveness, and Financing of Public and Private Drug Treatment Systems*. Washington, D.C.: National Academy Press.

Goldman, H. H., V. Ganju, R. Drake, P. Gorman, M. Hogan, P. S. Hyde, and O. Morgan. 2001. "Policy Implications for Implementing Evidence-Based Practices." *Psychiatric Services* 52:1591–97.

Heinrich, C. J., and E. Fournier. 2004. "Dimensions of Publicness and Performance in Substance Abuse Treatment Organizations: A Multilevel Investigation." *Journal of Policy Analysis and Management* 23:49–70.

Heinrich, C. J., and L. E. Lynn, Jr. 2002. "Improving the Organization, Management, and Outcomes of Substance Abuse Treatment Programs." *American Journal of Drug and Alcohol Abuse* 28:601–22.

Hubbard, R. L., S. G. Craddock, P. M. Flynn, J. Anderson, and R. M. Etheridge. 1997. "Overview of 1-Year Follow-Up Outcomes in the Drug Abuse Treatment Outcomes Study (DATOS)." *Psychology of Addictive Behaviors* 11:261–78.

Lamb, S., M. R. Greenlick, and D. McCarty. 1998. *Bridging the Gap between Practice and Research: Forging Partnerships with Community-Based Drug and Alcohol Treatment*. Washington, D.C.: Institute of Medicine, National Academy Press.

Lennox, R. D., and A. J. Mansfield. 2001. "A Latent Variable Model of Evidence-Based Quality Improvement for Substance Abuse Treatment." *Journal of Behavioral Health Services and Research* 28:164–76.

Lynn, L. E., Jr., C. J. Heinrich, and C. J. Hill. 2001. *Improving Governance: A New Logic for Empirical Research*. Washington, D.C.: Georgetown University Press.

Marinelli-Casey, P., C. P. Domier, and R. A. Rawson. 2002. "The Gap between Research and Practice in Substance Abuse Treatment." *Psychiatric Services* 53:984–87.

Rainey, H. G., and P. Steinbauer. 1999. "Galloping Elephants: Developing Elements of a Theory of Effective Government Organizations." *Journal of Public Administration Research and Theory* 9:1–32.

Rodgers, J. H., and P. G. Barnett. 2000. "Two Separate Tracks? A National Multivariate Analysis of Differences between Public and Private Substance Abuse Treatment Programs." *American Journal of Drug and Alcohol Abuse* 26:429–42.

Simpson, D. D. 2002. "A Conceptual Framework for Transferring Research to Practice." *Journal of Substance Abuse Treatment* 22:171–82.

Wheeler, J. R. C., and T. A. Nahra. 2000. "Private and Public Ownership in Outpatient Substance Abuse Treatment: Do We Have a Two-Tiered System?" *Administration and Policy in Mental Health* 27:197–209.

Five

Can Casework Design Choices Improve Outcomes for Clients Who Are Difficult to Employ?

Evidence from Welfare-to-Work Offices

Carolyn J. Hill

The Personal Responsibility and Work Opportunity Reconciliation Act (PRWORA) of 1996 gave states flexibility to administer programs and imposed new work expectations and time-limited benefits on welfare recipients. Under the new regime, concern is often focused on the most disadvantaged among the welfare population—those recipients who face relatively more severe barriers to attaining and maintaining employment and to moving off welfare. Are particular aspects of welfare-to-work programs differentially effective for different types of clients? If so, are these aspects of programs under the control of managers or program designers? Such issues are ongoing concerns for the design and evaluation of welfare and work policies.

Research has shown that welfare-to-work programs can be effective for some types of recipients, especially for those who were neither the most nor the least employable (Friedlander and Burtless 1995; Gueron and Pauly 1991; Heckman, LaLonde, and Smith 2000). Furthermore, the fact that client success (measured by increased earnings and reduced Aid to Families with Dependent Children [AFDC] receipt) varies across program delivery locations suggests that site-level decisions concerning program design and management may affect the success of welfare-to-work programs (Gueron and Pauly 1991; Blank 1997). Recent work begins to shed light on the specific factors that influence local office effectiveness (e.g., Bloom, Hill, and Riccio 2001, 2003), but many factors remain unexplored.

Reference to a logic of governance (Lynn, Heinrich, and Hill 2001; see also Heinrich, Hill, and Lynn, present volume) underscores the fact that variations in effectiveness across offices may arise from many different factors: the characteristics of clients served, local economic or political environments, the formal structures or rules of programs, organizational relationships or features, managers' discretionary actions, the service technologies employed, or other factors that vary across administrative units or sites. Thus, understanding what drives the effectiveness of welfare-to-work offices—and whether public managers have control over those factors that can make a difference—represent potential opportunities for governance, that is, how "public-sector regimes, agencies, programs, and activities [can] be authorized, organized, and managed to perform at high levels in achieving public purposes" (Lynn, Heinrich, and Hill 2001, 2).

In particular, the issue of how to divide tasks among caseworkers (the street-level bureaucrats engaged in the primary work of the program) and whether different divisions are differentially effective are concerns for public managers in a wide variety of settings. For example, even in welfare-to-work programs in states with a strong central state role, local program managers may have discretion over how to assign staff to different casework tasks (Kemple and Haimson 1994). Thus, the questions focus on discretionary managerial decisions and primary work (levels d and e in the logic of governance) and relate these factors to client outcomes (level f in the logic) (Lynn, Heinrich, and Hill 2001; Heinrich, Hill, and Lynn, this volume).

In this chapter, I extend previous work (Hill 2001; in press) to examine whether the effects of factors linked to work barriers vary across offices and whether casework configurations can explain these variations. In other words, do the discretionary decisions of local administrators influence whether offices are differentially effective in addressing the needs of hard-to-employ welfare recipients, for whom getting and keeping a job, and moving off welfare, is most difficult?

To identify the influence of case management and specialists on client outcomes, the analysis takes advantage of the natural variation in client and office characteristics across local welfare-to-work offices. A randomized experiment was not used to isolate these effects. Thus, it remains a possibility that the findings are subject to omitted variable bias. This concern is mitigated (but not eliminated) by the use of an extensive set of controls for individual client characteristics, local office characteristics, and characteristics of the local economy and states—all factors that the logic of governance suggests should be taken into account.

Consistent with previous findings, I find that factors over which local program administrators have control—the design of casework—can have effects on overall client outcomes. I find little evidence, however, that particular kinds of casework increase or decrease the average earnings of clients who face barriers to working (where these barriers are a function of race, education, or recent work experience). Further, I find little evidence that the structure of casework differentially affects AFDC benefits received by clients for whom leaving the welfare rolls may be difficult: those with a young child less than six years old, those who received welfare consistently in the recent past, and those who do not have a high school diploma or GED.

The chapter proceeds as follows. First, I provide additional details about the configuration of casework tasks, specify hypotheses, and discuss characteristics of welfare recipients who face special challenges in moving from welfare to work. The sections that follow describe the data, variable definitions, methods, and findings. The final section concludes.

Casework Job Design and Public Management

How casework is structured affects clients' interactions and experiences with the welfare system and work programs. Furthermore, the discretionary decisions of case managers may influence clients' experiences in the program (Lipsky 1980; Doolittle and Riccio 1992; Hagen and Lurie 1994a, 1994b; Meyers, Glaser, and McDonald 1998).

Three basic models characterize the possible division of casework tasks in an office. First, under *case management,* a caseworker is involved in all core aspects of casework—assessing the client's need for services, working with the client to develop an employability plan, arranging and coordinating services, and monitoring client progress (Hagen and Lurie 1994a; Rothman 1991). Second, under *categorical services,* a caseworker may be involved in only one or a subset of these activities (e.g., monitoring); clients thus receive sequential or parallel services from different caseworkers. Third, *coordinated services* combines case management and categorical services models, where caseworkers specialize but maintain communication and work as a team to address a client's needs.[1]

Caseworkers do not directly influence a welfare recipient's job experience, but these line staff are "policy makers" whose interactions with clients can determine the "range of behavioral actions from which clients may choose their responses" (Lipsky 1980, 61). Casework job design thus structures interactions between caseworkers and clients, introducing boundaries within which the caseworker can exercise discretion.

Each casework configuration holds potential advantages as well as drawbacks (Doolittle and Riccio 1992; Hagen and Lurie 1994a, 1994b; Brown 1997). With case management, a caseworker is the primary contact with the client throughout her involvement in the program. This case manager is positioned to obtain a holistic view of clients' needs and to respond accordingly. Case managers manage access to other specialized services, leading to duplication of work across case managers in a single office. For example, multiple case managers may contact the same service providers to monitor clients or to locate childcare services.

By contrast, caseworkers in categorical services delivery specialize in particular stages or processes of the welfare-to-work program. A caseworker thus develops expertise that can be used for clients' benefit. Line staff who specialize in certain tasks lack direct control or knowledge of other specialties that may affect the client. "Specialization permits street-level bureaucrats to avoid seeing their work as a whole. . . . Specialists tend to perceive the client and his or her problems in terms of the methodologies and previously established processing categories that their training dictates" (Lipsky 1980, 147).

Guidance for managers on how to configure casework effectively has emphasized the various advantages and disadvantages of different task configurations, but effectiveness of case management or specialists has not been directly tested. Furthermore, a theoretical basis for testing the effectiveness of different configurations has not been emphasized.

Principal-agent theories and organizational theories together provide insight into expectations regarding configurations of casework tasks and produce some testable hypotheses. Principal-agent theories indicate that the range and type of agents' tasks, and the grouping of tasks into jobs, affect individual effort and (by extension) organizational performance. Holmstrom and Milgrom (1991) are concerned specifically with a single agent's work on multiple tasks. When it is difficult to observe this work, they argue, a principal can direct the agent's attention to tasks that are relatively more difficult to measure by constraining the tasks the agent is responsible for. Thus, tasks that are easily measured and those that are more difficult to measure should be assigned to different workers.

In the context of welfare-to-work programs, for example, the core casework tasks (assessing needs, developing plans, assigning to activities, and monitoring progress) involve interactions between caseworkers, clients, and external parties that are difficult for managers to observe because of the very nature of frontline work in human services (Lipsky 1980; Hasenfeld 1983). By contrast, tasks such as client job development are more easily measured— for example, by number of contacts with potential employees or by number of positions developed in a specified amount of time.

Casework tasks in an office may be characterized further according to their degree of interdependence. The core tasks of casework (those bundled in case management) reflect sequential and reciprocal interdependence (Thompson 1967). For example, a client must receive a job or program component assignment before caseworkers can monitor her participation (sequential interdependence), and assessment of client needs, assignment to program components, and monitoring may require adjustments throughout participation in the program as more information about the client is obtained and as her needs change (reciprocal interdependence). Other tasks, such as developing job contacts or conducting specific kinds of services (for example, job skills workshops), are clearly delineated as sequential elements of the welfare-to-work program. As noted above, these functions are also relatively easier for managers to observe. Elsewhere (Hill in press), I draw on these ideas of multiple tasks and interdependence to develop the following testable hypotheses:

H1: Local welfare-to-work offices that combine the core tasks of casework into a single job (i.e., case management) will have better client outcomes than offices that do not combine these tasks.

H2: Local welfare-to-work offices that use specialists for relatively easily measured tasks such as job development or conducting services will have better client outcomes than offices that do not have at least one employee focusing on such activities.

Welfare Recipients Who Face Barriers to Employment

Whether and how welfare-to-work programs are differentially effective for different types of clients are ongoing concerns for the design and evaluation of these programs. For example, subgroup analyses are a standard component of random assignment evaluations, and controls for client characteristics are standard in nonexperimental quantitative studies.

Are specific aspects of welfare-to-work programs more or less effective for serving different kinds of clients? Two types of concerns are relevant for answering this question: the first concern is conceptual, and the second is methodological. First, what groups should be focused on? That is, which groups are difficult to employ? Second, does sufficient variation exist across offices to explore whether the relationships between these characteristics and the outcomes of interest vary according to office or program characteristics?

A fair amount of consensus exists regarding the characteristics of persons who find it most difficult to find and hold on to jobs that pay anything more than a meager wage. Most employers that supply low-skill jobs prefer or require the applicant to have at least a high school diploma (or equivalent) and some work experience or training (Holzer 1996; Danziger et al. 2000). Furthermore, discrimination and skill requirements for jobs often disproportionately affect blacks and Hispanics (Holzer 1996; Blank 1997; Moss and Tilly 2001). Hiring decisions may be based on employers' beliefs about racial and ethnic groups, which "consist in part of fallacious stereotypes, in part of cultural gaps, and in part of accurate perceptions of performance differences" (Moss and Tilly 2001, 247).

Regarding AFDC dependency, Bane and Ellwood (1994) found that blacks, Hispanics, older persons, and those with limited work experience and long-term dependence on AFDC were the most difficult to move off welfare. They conclude that earnings capacity as well as other factors (such as marriage) mostly influence exits from AFDC. In fact, "the major predictors are marital status, age of youngest child, and number of children" (Bane and Ellwood 1994, 97).

In this chapter, I focus on these characteristics that indicate potential difficulty in increasing employment and earnings, and reducing receipt of AFDC. In the case of earnings and employment outcomes, I focus on clients who are black, who did not have a high school degree or GED, or who did not work in the year prior to random assignment. For AFDC outcomes, I focus on clients who have young children (less than six years old), who did not have a high school degree or GED, or who received AFDC in all twelve months prior to random assignment.

Having identified key characteristics of clients who tend to be difficult to employ, the next step in an empirical analysis is to investigate whether the effects of each of these characteristics show statistically significant variation across offices in the sample. Such variation did exist, and thus it was reasonable to pursue the question of what explained this variation (this process is described in the "Methods" section).[2]

Focusing on the client characteristics noted above, I apply the following hypotheses to test the relative effectiveness of casework configurations:

H3: Offices that use case management will be relatively more effective for difficult-to-employ welfare clients, and

H4: Offices that use specialists for relatively easily measured tasks (such as job development or conducting services) will be relatively more effective for difficult-to-employ welfare clients.

These hypotheses, extended from the more general hypotheses described earlier, can be applied to a range of possible outcome variables. Results will show whether service technology factors that managers can influence (that is, casework design) can make a difference for welfare-to-work clients who face barriers to work.

Data

Data in this study are merged from three evaluations of welfare-to-work programs conducted by MDRC:[3] Greater Avenues for Independence (GAIN) in California, Project Independence (PI) in Florida, and the National Evaluation of Welfare-to-Work Strategies (NEWWS) in six states.[4] These evaluations aimed to determine whether the programs increased client labor force participation and earnings, and decreased welfare receipt, compared to a control group of persons who did not receive program services; to provide information about implementation conditions; and to provide an analysis of benefits and costs of the program.

These random assignment experiments examined the states' JOBS programs. Though implemented prior to the PRWORA, these programs were mandatory welfare-to-work programs and thus provide a comparable setting for examining decisions that local office managers face under current program rules. This chapter measures client outcomes over a two-year period after their random assignment date. Because random assignment ranged from March 1998 for some GAIN offices to December 1994 for some NEWWS offices, the follow-up period for clients ranges over a period from the late 1980s through the mid-1990s.[5]

Two different types of data are used in this analysis: (1) individual-level data on welfare-to-work female clients who were randomly assigned to the treatment (or program) component of the evaluation and (2) office-level data on casework configurations and other organizational characteristics.[6] By pooling these data, information is available on 47,115 treatment group members (14,645 from GAIN, 7,111 from PI, and 25,359 from NEWWS) in seventy-five offices in fifteen counties in seven states.

Administrative data provide information about each treatment group member for the individual-level data: information about labor force participation and earnings from state unemployment insurance (UI) systems, receipt of AFDC from county and state records, and personal characteristics from administrative data intake forms.

Approximately 1,600 staff in the seventy-five offices were surveyed regarding casework practices and relationships with clients and supervisors. The surveys were administered during a period that generally corresponded to clients' follow-up periods.[7] Survey coverage was high (more than 90 percent), and response rates were high (also greater than 90 percent in most offices). Office supervisors' survey responses ($n = 218$) are excluded, which resulted in a sample that ranges from one to eighty-three staff respondents per office, with a mean of eighteen and a median of ten staff respondents.

Measures

A range of measures of program performance or client success might be considered (for discussion, see Friedlander and Burtless 1995; Riccio, Bloom, and Hill 2000). In this chapter, I focus on earnings and AFDC client outcomes over a two-year period, but also report findings for a number of other earnings, employment, and AFDC measures.[8] Increasing earnings and decreasing AFDC receipt are two visible and widely acknowledged goals of welfare-to-work programs, and a two-year follow-up period provides time for most persons to have completed training or education. Average earnings for all clients over the two-year follow-up period were $6,042, with a standard deviation of $10,220; and average AFDC benefits received over the eight quarters was $7,818 with a standard deviation of $6,358.[9]

The key primary work variables in this chapter are the measures of casework job design. Unfortunately, it was not possible to match each staff respondent with the individual clients they served. Therefore, *offices* are characterized by the kinds of casework service technologies they use. These configurations are captured through four indicator variables (which are *not* mutually exclusive), each equal to one if the following conditions held:

- At least half of the line staff were case managers—that is, involved in all four core tasks of casework (twenty-seven offices);

- At least one specialist was used in a core casework task (forty offices);
- At least one specialist was used for job development (thirteen offices);
- At least one specialist was used to conduct services, such as orientation or job club (twenty-nine offices).

Staff survey responses regarding involvement in a variety of tasks provided the information needed to construct these measures. Further information on variable construction and sensitivity tests using alternative definitions of each measure are described in greater detail elsewhere (Hill 2001). Individual client- and office-level controls are also included in the analysis.

Individual-Level Measures

Individual-level client characteristics included as controls are standard in welfare-to-work and job training studies: age, number of children, age of youngest child, race/ethnicity, AFDC receipt history, earnings history, and education level. The *ceteris paribus* effects of such variables on earnings and

Table 5.1
Descriptive Statistics: Individual-Level Measures

Individual-Level Variables (n = 47,115 clients)	Mean	Standard Deviation	Minimum	Maximum
Total earnings in eight quarters after random assignment (1996$)	6,042	10,220	0	160,000
Total AFDC in eight quarters after random assignment (1996$)	7,818	6,358	0	55,940
Client age (years):				
<25	0.17		0	1
25–34	0.49		0	1
35–44	0.27		0	1
>44	0.07		0	1
Race/ethnicity:				
White, non-Hispanic	0.42		0	1
Black, non-Hispanic	0.38		0	1
Hispanic	0.16		0	1
Native American	0.01		0	1
Asian	0.02		0	1
Other race/ethnicity, nonwhite	0.01		0	1
Number of children	1.92	1.05	0	10
Youngest child <6 years of age	0.42		0	1
Did not have a high school diploma or GED at random assignment	0.44		0	1
Received AFDC all twelve months prior to random assignment	0.41		0	1
Earnings in year prior to random assignment (1996$)	2,231	4,589	0	80,000
Never employed in year prior to random assignment	0.55		0	1

Table 5.2
Descriptive Statistics: Office-Level Measures

Office-Level Variables (n = 75 offices):	Mean	Standard Deviation	Minimum	Maximum
At least half of line staff were case managers	0.36		0	1
At least one specialist in core casework tasks	0.53		0	1
At least one specialist in job development	0.17		0	1
At least one specialist in conducting services	0.39		0	1
Staff emphasis on moving clients into jobs	0.00	1.00	–1.91	2.65
Caseload per caseworker	151	73	63	367
Staff with education beyond a college degree (%)	26	21	0	100
Staff work experience in welfare-to-work programs (%)	42	24	0	100
Tenure (years)	2.76	1.58	0.49	7.67
Number of line staff	18	18	1	83
Average unemployment rate during follow-up period	7.57	2.85	3.51	14.29

AFDC receipt are the focus of this chapter. Table 5.1 shows descriptive statistics for the full sample: At the time of random assignment, on average, sample members were thirty-two years old and had two children. Thirty-eight percent were black (non-Hispanic), 42 percent had a child younger than six years old, 44 percent did not have a high school degree or GED, and 41 percent had received AFDC for all twelve months prior to their random assignment. Fifty-five percent of clients had not worked at any point in the previous year, and average total earnings in the year prior to random assignment (including zero earnings) were $2,231.

Office-Level Measures

Table 5.2 provides descriptive statistics for office-level controls included in the analysis (appendix A describes the creation of these variables). The first set of measures are office characteristics that may be associated with both casework task organization and average client outcomes. These variables are caseload size, quick job emphasis, caseworker professional characteristics, and office size. The second set of measures attempts to account for the economic and political environment within which the office operates.

Local Office and Caseworker Characteristics. *Average caseload size* is included as a control because large caseloads may prevent case managers or specialists from being able to spend time with clients; it has been found to be a significant predictor of differences in performance across offices (Gueron and Pauly 1991; Bloom, Hill, and Riccio 2003). In addition, caseload size may reflect the level of resources available to the office.

Emphasis that staff place on moving clients quickly into jobs (instead of building basic skills) was also included as a control. This emphasis is an important aspect of service technology in successful welfare-to-work programs (e.g., Riccio, Friedlander, and Freeman 1994; Hotz, Imbens, and Klerman 2000; Bloom, Hill, and Riccio 2003). It is likely associated with local managers' decisions about how to structure casework (especially whether to employ a staff person who specializes in job development).

Tenure and *welfare-to-work experience* of caseworkers were included as controls for experience and turnover in the office. It is possible that less-experienced caseworkers are assigned to a subset of the full range of possible tasks or that they are more likely to fill case management roles. Similarly, more experienced workers might fill either specialist or case management positions. Furthermore, "learning by doing" is an important part of gaining expertise.

Education beyond a college degree was included as a proxy for professional training. As Scott (1998, 255) notes, "One way to manage greater task complexity is not to divide the work and parcel it out among differentiated groups or departments, but to confront the complexity with more highly qualified and flexible performers—with professionals." Finally, I control for the *number of caseworkers* in each office: larger offices may be more likely to use specialists than smaller offices, because complexity of structure increases with larger organizational size (Scott 1998, 260–61).

Economic and Political Environment. The *average local unemployment rate* was included to measure the weakness or strength of the local economy. In an analysis that pools local offices across a wide range of geographic areas to examine client outcomes associated with the labor market, including such a measure of local economic conditions is especially important.

An indicator variable for each state (California GAIN is the excluded category) was also included. Ideally, additional information would be available about the economic and political environment of the state within which each of these local offices operated. That information could be used to further specify program and management decisions made at the local level. In lieu of such information, however, adding these state-fixed effects to the model absorbs effects specific to each state. This approach, by necessity, combines the myriad state-specific factors that may influence local decision making. Such factors raise interesting governance questions (representing issues at the *c* and *d* levels of analysis in the logic of governance). Sufficient information, however, was not available to include specific measures in the empirical model. Thus, a conservative strategy includes the state fixed effects: it controls for possible correlations between decisions made at the state level (e.g., AFDC benefit levels) and local area decisions regarding casework task configurations.

Other aspects of interactions between clients and staff that may be associated with clients' earnings are *not* controlled for. These include the level of trust, frequency of interaction, counseling intensity or frequency, or client participation in activities (Hasenfeld 1983; Gueron and Pauly 1991; Riccio and Orenstein 1996). Such factors may be correlated with particular casework configurations: for example, trust may be greater between clients and case managers who interact more often than between clients and caseworkers who specialize in only one part of the process. Including such factors in the model, however, would risk overcontrolling, leaving the casework variables stripped of their characteristic features and thus difficult to interpret. Furthermore, personalized attention, trust, and other such factors may be influenced by the casework task configuration in an office, but the reverse is likely not true (e.g., trusting relationships between clients and caseworkers are unlikely to precede an office selecting a case management model).[10]

Methods

The individual-level data and the office-level measures are utilized simultaneously in the analysis, by use of hierarchical linear modeling (HLM) to estimate effects at each level (Raudenbush and Bryk 2002). Such multilevel models (also known as mixed, random coefficient, or variance component models) can be particularly useful in governance research, where levels of variation and influence may occur at multiple hierarchical levels (see also Heinrich and Lynn 2001). The level 1 model uses individual client level data:

$$Y_{ij} = \beta_{0j} + \beta_{1j}X_{1ij} + \beta_{2j}X_{2ij} + \ldots + \beta_{nj}X_{nij} + \varepsilon_{ij}, \qquad [1]$$

where Y_{ij} = outcome measure Y for client i in office j, β_{0j} = average outcome for clients in office j, adjusted for observable differences in clients across offices, $X_{1ij} \ldots X_{nij}$ = n individual client characteristics for client i in office j, $\beta_{1j} \ldots \beta_{nj}$ = average effect of $X_1 \ldots X_n$ on Y, and ε_{ij} = individual-level error.[11] The variation in the adjusted average outcome for each office, β_{0j}, can be modeled using information from the 75 offices:

$$\beta_{0j} = \gamma_{00} + \gamma_{01}W_{1j} + \gamma_{02}W_{2j} + \ldots + \gamma_{0k}W_{kj} + \mu_{0j}, \qquad [2]$$

where β_{0j} = adjusted average outcome in office j, γ_{00} = overall average outcome, $W_{1j} \ldots W_{kj}$ = k office-level characteristics for office j, and $\gamma_{01} \ldots \gamma_{0k}$ = effect of office-level characteristic $W_1 \ldots W_k$ on β_{0j}, and μ_{0j} = office-level component of error.[12] Furthermore, it is possible to allow effects for each of the client characteristics $X_1 \ldots X_n$ to vary across offices. In Hill (2001; in press), the estimated models constrained these effects to be fixed across offices. In the current chapter, I investigate further the variation in these factors across offices. Using results from the literature discussed earlier regarding clients who face barriers to working, and also checking each of the effects for statistically significant variation across offices, the effects of clients' race, education, and prior work experience are modeled as varying randomly across offices in regressions that explain earnings and employment outcomes. The effects of education, prior AFDC history, and presence of a young child in the household are modeled as varying randomly across offices in regressions that explain AFDC receipt. The remainder of the client characteristics are modeled as fixed across offices, thus $\beta_{1j} \ldots \beta_{nj} = \beta_1 \ldots \beta_n$ for $m \neq n$. The random effects are modeled at level 2 (the office level) as:

$$\beta_{mj} = \gamma_{m0} + \gamma_{m1} W_{1j} + \gamma_{m2} W_{2j} + \ldots + \gamma_{mk} W_{kj} + \eta_{mj}, \qquad [3]$$

where β_{mj} = adjusted average influence of client characteristic m in office j, γ_{m0} = overall average effect of client characteristic m on Y, $W_{1j} \ldots W_{kj}$ = k office-level characteristics for office j, $\gamma_{m1} \ldots \gamma_{mk}$ = effect of office-level characteristic $W_1 \ldots W_k$ on β_{mj}, and η_{mj} = office-level component of error.[13]

Equations [1], [2], and [3] are estimated simultaneously using restricted maximum likelihood. Model selection and specification were guided by theory and prior studies discussed earlier, as well as by the use of model-based statistics (especially deviance statistics) using full maximum likelihood.[14]

Results

The conditional variation across offices in both total earnings, and total AFDC receipt, during the two-year period following random assignment is statistically significant. That is, with all client characteristics included as controls at level 1, but no controls for any effect at level 2, the randomly varying components of the model each showed real variation across offices. After controlling for client characteristics, this remaining statistically significant variation may be due to economic or environmental factors, office characteristics, or other unobservable factors. As expected, most of the total variation is at the individual client level, whereas a smaller proportion of the total variance is at the office level.

Effects on Total Earnings in Two Years after Random Assignment

Table 5.3 shows coefficient estimates from models with different sets of level 2 covariates (all models contain the same set of individual covariates at level 1), where the outcome variable is total earnings in the two years after random assignment. The individual- and office-level coefficient estimates shown here are estimated simultaneously by use of HLM. Model A includes four office-level job design variables to explain the four randomly varying coefficients at level 2; model B includes these variables plus other office-level control variables; and model C includes the job design variables, office-level control variables, and state fixed effects.

The top panel of the table shows coefficient estimates for the client characteristics whose effects are held fixed across offices. The middle panel shows overall average estimates for the intercept and for each of the client characteristics that varies randomly at level 2. The intercepts (adjusted grand mean estimates) are shown in rows with the variable names in italics. Below each of these intercepts is a set of coefficient estimates for the office-level casework variables. For example, the estimates from model A show that the overall average effect on total two-year earnings for clients without a high school degree or GED is –$1,890 (controlling for the other client characteristics and job design variables). This overall average is substantively and statistically significant; however, once other aspects of the local office are controlled for, and state fixed effects are included (model C), none of the casework variables is statistically significant: earnings of clients without high school diplomas are no different, on average, when they receive services through welfare-to-work offices with these characteristics (the case management variable does approach significance at the 0.10 level). The bottom panel of the table reports the percent variation explained in each randomly varying level 2 factor.[15]

The changing pattern of coefficients and standard errors for the casework variables across rows of the table indicates that it is important to control for organizational factors and state fixed effects before interpreting the findings regarding casework. Adding these additional control variables reduces the degrees of freedom available to estimate the parameters (and thus affects statistical significance); however, the inclusion of these variables is crucial to mitigate concerns about omitted variable bias on the casework coefficients. The following section discusses each of the sets of estimates. Although not always explicitly stated, all estimates are interpreted as holding constant the other level 1 and level 2 variables in the model.

Casework Job Design and Overall Average Earnings. Equation 2 specified how a random intercept for each office, adjusted for client characteristics across offices, could be further modeled at level 2. The casework results for this equation are shown in the middle section of the table. The indicator variables in level 2 are entered as 0/1 values, but all other level 2 variables are grand-mean centered. Thus, the constant ($6,380 in model C) is the overall adjusted mean for offices that do not primarily use case management, do not use specialists in the core tasks of case work, do not use a job development specialist, do not have specialists conducting services, and have the mean value on all other level 2 variables. In addition, because of the use of state fixed effects in model C, the intercept conveys these values for offices in the California GAIN evaluation (the omitted state fixed effect).

Table 5.3

Individual- and Office-Level HLM Estimates: Dependent Variable Total Earnings in Two Years after Random Assignment (in 1996 dollars)

Independent Variable	Model A Coefficient	Model A Standard Error	Model B Coefficient	Model B Standard Error	Model C Coefficient	Model C Standard Error
Level 1 (Fixed Effects)						
Age 24 or younger	−50	108	−43	111	−42	134
Age 35–44	190**	84	190**	84	190	104
Age older than 44	−920†	165	−912†	166	−903†	179
Hispanic	436***	142	471***	146	479***	145
Asian	−233	402	−217	413	−265	343
Native American	−985***	329	−985***	339	−966***	385
Other race/ethnicity (nonwhite)	321	624	370	626	354	572
Number of children	−38	39	−42	39	−42	43
Youngest child less than 6 years old	−151	120	−191*	116	−182*	108
Received AFDC all 12 months before random assignment	36	171	46	169	41	106
AFDC applicant	−159	149	−104	150	−23	142
Earnings year prior to random assignment	0.9	0.04	895†	42	898†	11
Level 2 (Random Effects)						
Overall average (intercept):	5,422†	265	5,322†	226	6,380†	291
At least half of line staff were case managers	6	257	385*	199	343	222
At least one specialist in core casework tasks	82	277	−67	224	−167	194
At least one specialist for job development	907***	312	917†	205	496**	221
At least one specialist for conducting services	351	289	386*	212	140	186
Black, non-Hispanic:	−14	192	40	191	484	489
At least half of line staff were case managers	468*	245	305	256	398	369
At least one specialist in core casework tasks	266	214	208	248	206	320
At least one specialist for job development	437	324	296	315	246	340
At least one specialist for conducting services	−429*	227	−579***	221	−649**	285
Did not have high school diploma or GED:	−1,890†	298	−1,855†	256	−3,047†	463
At least half of line staff were case managers	−290	341	−619**	295	−607	371
At least one specialist in core casework tasks	−76	330	−2	308	−18	317
At least one specialist for job development	−577*	333	−636**	321	−246	358

Table 5.3. Continued

Independent Variable	Model A Coefficient	Model A Standard Error	Model B Coefficient	Model B Standard Error	Model C Coefficient	Model C Standard Error
At least one specialist for conducting services	−223	311	−160	261	−84	295
Never employed in year prior to random assignment:	933***	348	610*	313	−147	424
At least half of line staff were case managers	−797**	344	−777***	298	−822**	337
At least one specialist in core casework tasks	−701**	347	−232	305	−83	286
At least one specialist for job development	−200	364	−157	293	130	321
At least one specialist for conducting services	−867***	326	−646**	322	−205	263
Other office-level controls included	No		Yes		Yes	
State indicator variables included	No		No		Yes	
Percent variance explained in:						
Level 2 variance in intercept	9		54		81	
Level 2 variance in *Black, non-Hispanic*	17		2		42	
Level 2 variance in *Did not have a high school diploma or GED*	1		37		57	
Level 2 variance in *Never employed in year prior to random assignment*	26		40		81	

*P < .10; **P < .05; ***P < .01; †P < .001.

The results show mixed support for the hypotheses regarding case management and specialization. In support of the hypotheses, the results from model C (the preferred model that includes all controls for client- and office-level characteristics) indicate that average total client earnings in offices where at least half of all line staff are case managers are $343 higher over the two years following random assignment than earnings in offices where the majority of line staff are not case managers (this estimate just misses statistical significance). Furthermore, average client earnings in offices with at least one line staff specialist in job development are $496 higher over the two years following random assignment than in offices without such a specialist. These point estimates are substantively significant when compared to average total earnings: the $343 higher average earnings in offices that primarily use case management (marginally statistically significant) represents about 6 percent of average total two-year earnings, and the $496 job development specialist estimate represents about 9 percent of average total earnings. Estimates for other job design variables do not provide support for the hypotheses developed earlier.

Casework Configuration and Average Earnings for Blacks. Clients who are black, on average, do not earn more or less during the two years after random assignment, compared to clients who are not black. Even though the main effect for this coefficient was not statistically significant, it exhibited statistically significant variation across offices. Thus, it was appropriate to let it randomly vary and attempt to explain this variation with office characteristics. The results from model C indicate that, on average, blacks served in welfare-to-work offices that use specialists to conduct services such orientation and job search workshops tend to have lower earnings than blacks served in offices that do not have such specialists (the coefficient estimate is –$649 and statistically significant at the $P < .05$ level). Though the other casework coefficients are all positive, they are not statistically significant; on average, then, blacks served in offices that primarily use case management, or at least one specialist for core casework tasks, or at least one specialist for job development, earn no more (and no less) than blacks served in offices without these casework configurations, holding the other variables in the model constant.

The last panel of the table indicates that only 42 percent of the across-office variation in the black slope coefficient is explained by model C—which indicates a specification with relatively weak explanatory power despite the full set of controls.

Casework Configuration and Average Earnings for Clients Lacking a High School Diploma. On average, clients without a high school diploma or GED earn substantially less over the two-year follow-up period than those with a high school diploma, no matter which specification is used to estimate the effect (–$1,890 for model A; –$1,855 for model B; and –$3,047 for model C). These estimates are highly statistically significant. None of the casework variables, however, attains statistical significance in model C. Thus, on average, clients who do not have a high school diploma or GED do not seem to benefit from, or be harmed by, casework design choices. (The case management coefficient approaches statistical significance at the 0.10 level. If interpreted, the estimated coefficient would indicate that clients who do not have a high school diploma and are served in offices that primarily use case management earn even less, on average, than do clients without a high school diploma who are *not* served in such offices.) The explanatory power of this model is slightly greater than in the previous case: model C explains 57 percent of the variation across offices in the effects of clients who are not high school graduates; but explanatory power remains relatively weak.

Casework Configuration and Average Earnings for Clients Not Employed in the Prior Year. Explanatory power is the highest for the level 2 model that explains across-office variation in the effects of never being employed in the year prior to random assignment: Model C explains 81 percent of this variation. The intercept estimate of −$147 is not statistically significant: thus, on average, clients who were never employed in the year prior to random assignment earned no more or less in the two-year follow-up period compared to clients who had worked in the previous year (controlling for the other level 1 and level 2 factors). The model indicates, however, that predicted earnings would be $822 less, on average, for such clients who were served in welfare-to-work offices that primarily used case management. This finding is contrary to the hypothesis.

Another way to state these results is to say that clients who *were* employed in the year prior to random assignment make no more or less than clients not employed, on average; however, when those previously employed clients are served in welfare-to-work offices that primarily use case management, we expect their earnings to increase by $822, on average, compared to previously employed clients who are not served in such offices. None of the other casework configuration effects are statistically significant (possible reasons for this finding are discussed later in the chapter).

Effects on Total AFDC Benefits Received in Two Years after Random Assignment

The second type of outcome examined in this chapter is total AFDC benefits in the two years after random assignment (table 5.4). Scanning the model C estimates in this table shows that each of the main effects (except for the overall intercept) is statistically and substantively significant. The casework variables show substantive and statistical significance in explaining variation across offices for whether clients have a young child in the household. The estimates for this model show that clients who have a young child receive $374 less in AFDC benefits over the two-year period when they are served in offices that have at least one specialist in the core tasks of casework compared to clients with a young child not in these offices. Further, the coefficient on the job development specialist variable is statistically and substantively significant.

For the other indicators of whether clients are difficult to employ, the casework variables are not generally useful in explaining the variation in these effects across offices: all the casework measures are statistically insignificant in level 2 models for the intercept and the randomly varying effects of whether clients had received AFDC in all previous twelve months or did not have a high school diploma or GED.

Other Outcome Measures

In addition to these two-year total measures for earnings and AFDC benefits, I examined a number of other outcome measures, such as total earnings in each of the two years, total earnings in the last quarter of follow-up, earnings per quarter worked, total quarters employed, percent ever employed,

Table 5.4

Individual- and Office-Level HLM Estimates: Dependent Variable Total AFDC Benefits Received after Random Assignment (1996 dollars)

Independent Variable	Model A Coefficient	Standard Error	Model B Coefficient	Standard Error	Model C Coefficient	Standard Error
Level 1 (Fixed Effects):						
Age 24 or younger	483†	72	484†	72	475†	72
Age 35 to 44	−567†	55	−566†	55	−571†	55
Age older than 44	−1,009†	96	1,007†	96	−1,011†	96
Black, non-Hispanic	795†	60	793†	61	811†	60
Hispanic	451†	76	452†	77	443†	76
Asian	96	182	91	182	92	182
Native American	111	205	108	205	115	205
Other race/ethnicity (nonwhite)	−285	305	−270	305	−272	305
No. of children	1,531†	23	1,532†	23	1,532†	23
AFDC applicant	−340†	76	−366†	76	−356†	79
Earnings year prior to random assignment	−0.05†	0.006	−0.05†	0.006	−0.05†	0.006
Level 2 (Random Effects)						
Overall average (intercept):	6,270†	589	7,582†	472	11,541	207
At least half of line staff were case managers	−204	666	−401	493	−146	157
At least one specialist in core casework tasks	1,027	672	−175	531	47	138
At least one specialist for job development	1,492*	833	1,143*	625	169	165
At least one specialist for conducting services	1,990†	676	531	528	−21	134
Has a child younger than 6 years of age:	284*	171	372**	184	509*	278
At least half of line staff were case managers	−329*	189	−228	193	252	208
At least one specialist in core casework tasks	−226	186	−440**	208	−374**	180
At least one specialist for job development	303	219	303	231	403*	209
At least one specialist for conducting services	304*	183	152	196	96	169
Received AFDC in all previous twelve months:	1,639†	362	2,427†	293	4,333†	79
At least half of line staff were case managers	281	398	171	293	101	224
At least one specialist in core casework tasks	671*	398	−257	313	−49	183
At least one specialist for job development	492	481	213	358	−192	206

Table 5.4. *Continued*

Independent Variable	Model A		Model B		Model C	
	Coefficient	Standard Error	Coefficient	Standard Error	Coefficient	Standard Error
At least one specialist for conducting services	1,009**	394	344	299	109	165
Did not have high school diploma or GED:	414***	140	535†	145	1,013†	241
At least half of line staff were case managers	34	153	−3	152	153	194
At least one specialist in core casework tasks	187	153	87	166	115	165
At least one specialist for job development	144	174	66	177	4	186
At least one specialist for conducting services	175	147	−5	152	−23	153
Other office-level controls included	No		Yes		Yes	
State indicator variables included	No		No		Yes	
Percent variance explained in:						
Level 2 variance in intercept	18		59		98	
Level 2 variance in *Has a child younger than 6 years of age*	10		13		58	
Level 2 variance in *Received AFDC in all previous twelve months*	12		64		96	
Level 2 variance in *Did not have a high school diploma or GED*	4		22		34	

$P < .10$; **$P < .05$; ***$P < .01$; †$P < .001$.

total AFDC received in each of the last two years of follow-up and in the last quarter, AFDC benefits per quarter benefits were received, total quarters received AFDC, and percent who ever received AFDC benefits over different periods of time. I used the specification for each of these outcomes that included a full set of controls for client characteristics at level 1 and the full set of casework variables, office-level controls, and state fixed effects at level 2.

In general, all the casework configuration variables were statistically insignificant in the level 2 models for the randomly varying slope coefficients.[16] There were three exceptions to this pattern, and each mirrors the findings reported above for the two-year earnings results. First, in almost all the earnings regressions, the coefficient on a specialist that conducted services was negative, and statistically and substantively significant, for blacks. That is, blacks who were served in offices with at least one specialist that conducted services earned less, on average, than blacks not served in these offices. It is not immediately clear why this would be the case: it is possible that, after coming into contact with specialists in these sessions, the black dropout rate from the program is relatively greater than the dropout rate in offices without these specialists. This is, however, speculation.

Second, earnings and employment are statistically and substantively lower, on average for clients who never worked in the previous year when they are served in offices that use case management than clients without work experience in the previous year who are not served in these kinds of offices. It *may* be the case that the more personal interactions that characterize the case management model are less effective, on average, for these clients without recent work experience: one possibility is that the increased scrutiny or attention by a single case manager prompts clients to drop out. Or perhaps clients without recent work experience who are served in offices with case managers are placed relatively more often in education and training programs, which decreases their earnings in the short run relative to others who enter the labor market more quickly (but who may not be as successful in the longer run).

Third, clients with children younger than six years of age tend to have lower AFDC benefits when they are served in offices with specialists in the core tasks of casework and higher AFDC benefits when they are served in offices with job development specialists compared to those with young children who are not served in these kinds of offices.

Except for these three cases, however, the results do not show a relationship between the structure of casework in welfare-to-work offices and differential effects for groups of clients who traditionally find it difficult to find and maintain a job or to move off welfare. Although the intercept model (overall adjusted average earnings) for AFDC benefits did not show statistically significant effects of the casework variables, the intercept model for earnings did show a positive effect of offices that use case management and job development specialists. These results indicate that factors over which local program administrators have control—the design of casework—can have effects on overall client outcomes. I find, however, only limited evidence that particular kinds of casework help boost—or depress—the earnings of clients who may be considered difficult to employ.

Conclusion

To develop effective programs that raise welfare recipients' long-term earnings, policy designers and managers need to know why certain programs or offices are more successful than others, what roles or practices of frontline workers are associated with greater effectiveness, and how managers influence program success, controlling for observable characteristics of clients and environments that vary across sites. Viewing this question through a logic of governance underscores the importance of taking factors such as client and local characteristics into account when one attempts to model the relationships between local office practices and client outcomes.

This chapter examines casework job design in JOBS welfare-to-work programs, but the job design issues continue to be relevant in the PRWORA era as program designers and managers consider how best to structure the work of line staff (Brown 1997). The uses of case management and of specialists in designing these and other human service programs are elements of program structure that have been assumed to influence client outcomes but that have not been submitted to rigorous tests.

In this chapter, I pool data on clients and staff in seventy-five offices and control for a number of potentially confounding variables in a multilevel regression model. I focus on case management and the use of specialists, and find that average total client earnings over a two-year period and in the eighth quarter after random assignment are higher in offices that use case management and in offices that have at least one job development specialist. Further, I find little evidence that the organization of casework differentially affects (either positively or negatively) clients who may be considered difficult to employ or to move off welfare. These findings suggest that local decisions regarding how casework is structured may benefit all clients in an office, on average, but are unlikely to be powerful levers for targeting clients with particular characteristics (especially those who are traditionally difficult to employ).

This analysis uses natural variation in casework job designs across offices to identify the effects of different configurations of casework tasks. One qualification in interpreting these findings is that the analysis does not measure factors that led to the use of certain casework task configurations. In terms of the logic of governance, the choice of casework configuration could itself be considered a dependent variable, modeled as some function of discretionary management choices or other factors. If such factors are also correlated with client outcomes, the findings reported in this chapter regarding job design and client outcomes absorb these influences. Ideally, the relationship between casework task division and client outcomes could be examined using an experiment that randomizes casework task divisions within office and across a number of offices (e.g., Brock and Harknett 1998) and that can link caseworkers and clients. In lieu of such ideal data, in this analysis I control for a number of characteristics of individual clients, caseworkers, office characteristics, and the local economic environment. The full model uses a set of state indicator variables, and has considerable explanatory power.

The analysis in this chapter is part of a larger research effort to explore implementation factors that may influence performance across human services offices and to better understand how "management matters" in these offices (Hill 2001; Bloom, Hill, and Riccio 2003). If program designers and managers are to plan and implement welfare-to-work programs—or any program carried out in units across dispersed locations—there is a need for analysis that can explore the variations in performance across offices in a rigorous way, controlling for observable characteristics of clients and environments that may vary across sites, and identifying implementation practices, governance mechanisms, or management actions that are related to better performance. My analysis complements and extends existing studies that find cross-office differences but that do not address the question of why performance varies and studies that examine implementation in depth but that are unable explicitly to link these findings to outcomes. This research is one strategy for understanding management and service technology in welfare-to-work programs and, thus, is a piece of the governance puzzle.

Appendix A
Construction of Dependent and Independent Variables

Outcome Variables—Individual Client Level

Total earnings in two years following random assignment:
    Source: State UI administrative data. Sum of earnings in eight calendar quarters, where the first quarter is the quarter after random assignment. All dollar amounts were converted to constant dollars (1996 base) using the Consumer Price Index for Urban Consumers (CPI-U). Maximum earnings in each quarter were top-coded at $20,000.
    Total AFDC benefits received in two years following random assignment:
    Source: AFDC administrative data. Sum of AFDC benefits in eight calendar quarters, where the first quarter is the quarter following the quarter of random assignment. All dollar amounts were converted to constant dollars (1996 base) using the CPI-U.

Explanatory Variables—Individual Client Level

Note on missing information: To maintain as many observations as possible, I imputed the office-level mean value for an observation when a variable value was missing.
Note on transformation of variables in level 1 of HLM model: I centered each individual's value on the following variables around the overall average value (i.e., grand-mean centering). With this transformation, the level 1 intercept for each office is interpreted as an estimate of the office-level average outcome, adjusted for client differences across offices (Raudenbush and Bryk 2002).
    Age of client at random assignment (omitted category is age 25–34 years old):
    Client age less than 25 (indicator variable)
    Client age between 35 and 44 (indicator variable)
    Client age 45 or older (indicator variable)
    Race/ethnicity (omitted category is white, non-Hispanic):
    Asian (indicator variable)
    Black, non-Hispanic (indicator variable)
    Hispanic (indicator variable)
    Native American (indicator variable)
    Other race/ethnicity, nonwhite (indicator variable)
    Total number of children (continuous variable)
    Youngest child is younger than age 6 (indicator variable)

Not a high school graduate or GED recipient (indicator variable)
Received AFDC continuously for all twelve months prior to random assignment (indicator variable)
AFDC applicant (instead of ongoing recipient) at time of random assignment (indicator variable)
Never employed in twelve months prior to random assignment (indicator variable)
Total earnings in twelve months prior to random assignment (1996 dollars)

Explanatory Variables—Office Level

Job design (for a full description of the creation of these variables, see Hill 2001):
Used primarily case management model
Used at least one specialist for core casework tasks
Used at least one specialist for job development
Used at least one specialist for conducting services
Staff emphasis on moving clients into jobs, versus building skill levels:

- Used staff responses to four questions on staff survey (the response scale is listed in parentheses after each question):

1. Based on the practices in your unit, what would you say is the more important goal: to help clients get jobs as quickly as possible or to raise the education or skill levels of clients so that they can get jobs in the future? (1 = skills . . . 7 = jobs)
2. In your opinion, which should be the more important goal of your unit: to help clients get jobs as quickly as possible or to raise the education or skill levels of clients so that they can get jobs in the future? (1 = skills . . . 7 = jobs)
3. After a short time in the program, an average welfare mother is offered a low-skill, low-paying job that would make her slightly better off financially. Assume she has two choices: either to take the job and leave welfare OR to stay on welfare and wait for a better opportunity. If you were asked, what would your personal advice to this client be? (1 = welfare . . . 7 = jobs)
4. What advice would your supervisor want you to give to a client of this type? (1 = welfare . . . 7 = jobs)

- Calculated the average of available responses for each line staff person.
- Calculating the average line staff response in the office created an office-level measure, which was standardized to have a mean equal to 0 and standard deviation equal to 1.

Caseload: Average caseload per line staff (based on line staff survey self-reports).
Postcollege education: Percentage of line staff that completed at least some graduate work, beyond college.
Previous work experience in welfare-to-work programs: Percentage of line staff that have prior experience in a JTPA program or WIN program or as an employment counselor.

Tenure: Average number of years that line staff have been in their current jobs.
Total number of line staff in the office.

Average unemployment rate during two-year period following random assignment:
First, constructed at the individual client level using monthly county-level data, covering the twenty-four-month follow-up period after random assignment (Sources: U.S. Bureau of Labor Statistics, Local Area Unemployment Statistics; and California Employment Development Department). Second, computed the office-level average of individual-level values.

State indicator variables: For California GAIN (the omitted category), California NEWWS, Florida, Georgia, Michigan, Oregon, Oklahoma, and Ohio.

Notes

1. It will not be possible in the current analysis to examine this third type of casework division.

2. Also of potential interest are questions such as whether Hispanic clients benefit differentially from different configurations of casework. Preliminary analyses showed, however, that the effects of these factors did not vary significantly across offices. Thus, explaining variation that does not, in fact, exist was not relevant for the clients and offices in this data set. Furthermore, clients may have other barriers to employment such as psychiatric disorders or transportation problems (Danziger et al. 2000), but information on such factors was not available, so these questions could not be pursued in the present analysis.

3. The findings and conclusions presented in this chapter do not necessarily represent the official positions or policies of MDRC or its funders.

4. MDRC reports describe the evaluations and findings for GAIN (Riccio and Friedlander 1992; Friedlander, Riccio, and Freedman 1993; Riccio, Friedlander, and Freedman 1994), for PI (Kemple and Haimson 1994; Kemple, Friedlander, and Fellerath 1995), and for NEWWS (Hamilton and Brock 1994; Hamilton et al. 2001).

5. Random assignment ranged from March 1998 to June 1990 for GAIN; from January to August 1991 for PI; and from June 1991 to December 1994 for NEWWS. The PI evaluation included random assignment of clients throughout 1991, however, because of program changes in 1991, the sample is restricted in this chapter (see Kemple and Haimson 1994; Kemple, Friedlander, and Fellerath 1995).

6. The restriction to females improves model specification. Dropping males from the analysis has little effect on the sample size: females constitute more than 90 percent of all persons in the full sample.

7. GAIN staff surveys were administered in two waves between mid-1989 and mid-1991; PI staff surveys were administered in September and October 1991; NEWWS staff surveys were administered in August through December 1993.

8. Longer periods of follow-up data are available for the GAIN and NEWWS offices. For consistency and ease of interpretation in this chapter, however, I examine client outcomes over eight quarters following random assignment for GAIN, PI, and NEWWS.

9. All earnings and AFDC benefit amounts are in 1996 dollars. 1996 was the last year for which two-year follow-up data were available in NEWWS.

10. In addition, participation data are not available for sixteen of the seventy-five offices. Sensitivity analyses that include office-level controls for program participation for clients in these fifty-nine offices indicate that the substantive findings are not altered substantially.

11. When estimating the model, I center each level 1 explanatory variable on its grand mean value; thus, the intercept can be interpreted as the adjusted average outcome, con-

trolling for differences in client mix across offices (Raudenbush and Bryk 2002). To simplify the presentation, I do not show the centering notation in equation [1].

12. All continuous variables in the level 2 model were centered on their grand means. All indicator variables were entered in 0, 1 form.

13. All continuous variables in the level 2 model were centered on their grand means. All indicator variables were entered in 0, 1 form.

14. For further information on the use of deviance statistics for model testing, see Raudenbush and Bryk (2002), Singer and Willett (2003), and Snijders and Bosker (1999).

15. Coefficient estimates for these other control variables are available from the author.

16. That is, the slope coefficients allowed to randomly vary at level 2 for the earnings and employment models were the coefficients on black, did not have a high school diploma, or never worked in the year prior to random assignment; and for the AFDC models, the coefficients on young child less than six years old received AFDC all prior twelve months; or did not have a high school diploma.

References

Bane, Mary Jo, and David T. Ellwood. 1994. *Welfare Realities: From Rhetoric to Reform.* Cambridge, Mass.: Harvard University Press.

Blank, Rebecca M. 1997. *It Takes a Nation: A New Agenda for Fighting Poverty.* New York: Russell Sage Foundation.

Bloom, Howard S., Carolyn J. Hill, and James Riccio. 2003. "Linking Program Implementation and Effectiveness: Lessons from a Pooled Sample of Welfare-to-Work Experiments." *Journal of Policy Analysis and Management* 22:551–75.

———. 2001. *Modeling the Performance of Welfare-to-Work Programs: The Effects of Program Management and Services, Economic Environment, and Client Characteristics.* New York: MDRC.

Brock, Thomas, and Kristen Harknett. 1998. "A Comparison of Two Welfare-to-Work Case Management Models." *Social Service Review* 72:493–520.

Brown, Amy. 1997. *Work First: How to Implement an Employment-Focused Approach to Welfare Reform.* New York: MDRC.

Danziger, Sandra, Mary Corcoran, Sheldon Danziger, Colleen Heflin, Ariel Kalil, Judith Levine, Daniel Rosen, Kristin Seefeldt, Kristine Siefert, and Richard Tolman. 2000. *Barriers to the Employment of Welfare Recipients.* Ann Arbor: University of Michigan Poverty Research and Training Center.

Doolittle, Fred, and James Riccio. 1992. "Case Management in Welfare Employment Programs." In Charles F. Manski and Irwin Garfinkel, eds., *Evaluating Welfare and Training Programs.* Cambridge, Mass.: Harvard University Press, 310–43.

Friedlander, Daniel, and Gary Burtless. 1995. *Five Years After: The Long-Term Effects of Welfare-to-Work Programs.* New York: Russell Sage Foundation.

Friedlander, Daniel, James Riccio, and Stephen Freedman. 1993. *GAIN: Two-Year Impacts in Six Counties.* New York: MDRC.

Gueron, Judith M., and Edward Pauly. 1991. *From Welfare to Work.* New York: Russell Sage Foundation.

Hagen, Jan L., and Irene Lurie. 1994a. *Implementing JOBS: Case Management Services.* Albany, N.Y.: Nelson A. Rockefeller Institute of Government.

———. 1994b. *Implementing JOBS: Progress and Promise.* Albany, N.Y.: Nelson A. Rockefeller Institute of Government.

Hamilton, Gayle, and Thomas Brock. 1994. *The JOBS Evaluation: Early Lessons from Seven Sites.* Washington, D.C.: U.S. Department of Health and Human Services, Administration for Children and Families, Office of the Assistant Secretary for Planning and

Evaluation, and U.S. Department of Education, Office of the Under Secretary, Office of Vocational and Adult Education.

Hamilton, Gayle, Stephen Freedman, Lisa Gennetian, Charles Michalopoulos, Johanna Walter, Diana Adams-Ciardullo, Anna Gassman-Pines, Sharon McGroder, Martha Zaslow, Jennifer Brooks, and Surjeet Ahluwalia. 2001. *National Evaluation of Welfare-to-Work Strategies: How Effective Are Different Welfare-to-Work Approaches? Five-Year Adult and Child Impacts for Eleven Programs.* Washington, D.C.: U.S. Department of Health and Human Services, Administration for Children and Families, Office of the Assistant Secretary for Planning and Evaluation, and U.S. Department of Education, Office of the Under Secretary, Office of Vocational and Adult Education.

Hasenfeld, Yeheskel. 1983. *Human Service Organizations.* Englewood Cliffs, N.J.: Prentice Hall.

Heckman, James J., Robert J. LaLonde, and Jeffrey A. Smith. 2000. "The Economics and Econometrics of Active Labor Market Programs." In Orley Ashenfelter and David Card, eds., *Handbook of Labor Economics.* Amsterdam: Elsevier Science.

Heinrich, Carolyn J., and Laurence E. Lynn, Jr. 2001. "Means and Ends: A Comparative Study of Empirical Methods for Investigating Governance and Performance." *Journal of Public Administration Research and Theory* 11:109–38.

Hill, Carolyn J. In press. "Casework Job Design and Client Outcomes in Welfare-to-Work Offices." Accepted with minor revisions to *Journal of Public Administration Research and Theory.*

———. 2001. Implementation and Governance in Welfare-to-Work Programs. Ph.D. diss., University of Chicago.

Holmstrom, Bengt, and Paul Milgrom. 1991. "Multitask Principal-Agent Analyses: Incentive Contracts, Asset Ownership, and Job Design." *Journal of Law, Economics, and Organization* 7 (special issue):24–52.

Holzer, Harry J. 1996. *What Employers Want: Job Prospects for Less-Educated Workers.* New York: Russell Sage Foundation.

Hotz, V. Joseph, Guido W. Imbens, and Jacob A. Klerman. 2000. "The Long-Term Gains from G.A.I.N.: A Re-Analysis of the Impacts of the California GAIN Program." National Bureau of Economic Research Working Paper no. W8007.

Kemple, James, Daniel Friedlander, and Veronica Fellerath. 1995. *Florida's Project Independence: Benefits, Costs, and Two-Year Impacts of Florida's JOBS Program.* New York: MDRC.

Kemple, James, and Joshua Haimson. 1994. *Florida's Project Independence: Program Implementation, Participation Patterns, and First-Year Impacts.* New York: MDRC.

Lipsky, Michael. 1980. *Street-Level Bureaucracy.* New York: Russell Sage Foundation.

Lynn, Laurence E., Jr., Carolyn J. Heinrich, and Carolyn J. Hill. 2001. *Improving Governance: A New Logic for Empirical Research.* Washington, D.C.: Georgetown University Press.

Meyers, Marcia K., Bonnie Glaser, and Karin MacDonald. 1998. "On the Front Lines of Welfare Delivery: Are Workers Implementing Policy Reforms?" *Journal of Policy Analysis and Management* 17:1–22.

Moss, Philip, and Chris Tilly. 2001. *Stories Employers Tell: Race, Skill, and Hiring in America.* New York: Russell Sage Foundation.

Raudenbush, Stephen W., and Anthony S. Bryk. 2002. *Hierarchical Linear Models: Applications and Data Analysis Methods,* 2d ed. Thousand Oaks, Calif.: Sage.

Riccio, James, Howard Bloom, and Carolyn J. Hill. 2000. "Management, Organizational Characteristics, and Performance: The Case of Welfare-to-Work Programs." In Carolyn J. Heinrich and Laurence E. Lynn, Jr., eds., *Governance and Performance: New Perspectives.* Washington, D.C.: Georgetown University Press, 166–98.

Riccio, James, and Daniel Friedlander. 1992. *GAIN: Program Strategies, Participation Patterns, and First-Year Impacts in Six Counties.* New York: MDRC.

Riccio, James, Daniel Friedlander, and Stephen Freedman. 1994. *GAIN: Benefits, Costs, and Three-Year Impacts of a Welfare-to-Work Program.* New York: MDRC.

Riccio, James, and Alan Orenstein. 1996. "Understanding Best Practices for Operating Welfare-to-Work Programs." *Evaluation Review* 20:3–28.

Rothman, Jack. 1991. "A Model of Case Management: Toward Empirically Based Practice." *Social Work* 36:520–28.

Scott, W. Richard. 1998. *Organizations: Rational, Natural, and Open Systems,* 4th ed. Upper Saddle River, N.J.: Prentice Hall.

Singer, Judith D., and John B. Willett. 2003. *Applied Longitudinal Data Analysis: Modeling Change and Event Occurrence.* New York: Oxford University Press.

Snijders, Tom A. B., and Roel J. Bosker. 1999. *Multilevel Analysis: An Introduction to Basic and Advanced Multilevel Modeling.* London: Sage.

Thompson, James D. 1967. *Organizations in Action: Social Science Bases of Administrative Theory.* New York: McGraw-Hill.

Part III

Government Organizations:
Identifying the Linkages in Diverse Settings

Six

Management and Performance Outcomes in State Government

Amy K. Donahue • Willow S. Jacobson • Mark D. Robbins
Ellen V. Rubin • Sally C. Selden

As the preface to this volume explains, the role of government managers in policymaking and their influence on performance are issues of continuing significance for the fields of public administration and policy analysis. Most public managers and contemporary scholars of public management assume that effective management is positively related to effective performance (Kettl and Milward 1996; Lynn 1997; Ingraham and Kneedler 2000a); most definitions of management make reference to the purpose of promoting positive outcomes. Swiss (1991), for example, defines management as the coordination of people and resources to achieve policy outcomes. As Lynn (1997) points out, though, these claims are largely putative and unproven.

In recent years, however, empirical evidence around the governance of public organizations and programs, specifically the relationship between management and performance, has gained momentum. The policy analysis literature has considered the scope of administrative discretion and influence (see, for example, Schneider 1988; Carnevale 1995; Bowling and Wright 1998) and has sought to reveal how administrative actions and structures relate to measurable differences in public programs and policies (Milward and Provan 1995, 2000; Sandfort 1998; Heinrich, 2000; Lynn, Heinrich, and Hill 2000a; Heinrich and Lynn 2001).[1] Other work has sought to characterize the components and competencies of effective management (Ingraham, Joyce, and Donahue 2003). In addition, researchers have examined external organizational relationships as levers of performance. As this body of work has evolved, the notions of networks and network behavior, both as a means of arranging and coordinating service provision and as a deeper concept that describes the nature of operational, managerial, political, and social linkages within and between organizations, have become better specified (Mandell 1990; Milward and Provan 1995; O'Toole 1996; Provan and Milward 1998, 2001). Many authors assert that the job of the manager in an interdependent setting is to shield the technical core of the organization from disruption by external actors and environmental forces (Thompson 1967; Peters and Waterman 1982; Schein 1992). Some note that organizational environments may pose both threats and opportunities and that the job of the manager is to buffer the organization in the former case but exploit the environment in the latter (O'Toole and Meier 1999 and 2000; Rainey and Steinbauer 1999).

In this chapter, we address how the governance of key management functions affects the quality and outcomes of those functions. Here, we consider "governance" to include policies, practices, procedures, structures, and managerial activities and behaviors. O'Toole and Meier (1999, 2000; see also chapter 9, present volume) have developed a formal model that specifies the relationship between management and outcomes along two dimensions: the influence of managerial activities, designed to create and maintain organizational structures, and the influence of managers' interactions with stakeholders in the organizational environment. We test their model for two important functions: human resources management and financial management. We have chosen to examine these core areas because they have been targeted by significant efforts to prescribe best practices.[2] Insights into the nature of management in these areas thus capture the interest of researchers and public managers alike. And, although various management functions receive some attention in the literature, careful explication of how to measure and evaluate public human resources and financial management systems is scarce and presents a compelling research opportunity.

We make three contributions with the work presented here. First, we better illuminate management practices and quantify their ramifications. Second, we provide additional tests of some aspects of the O'Toole and Meier framework, which has so far been subject to relatively limited analysis (see Meier and O'Toole 2001a, 2001b). Third, we extend O'Toole and Meier's work in a novel way by applying their model to examine management functions rather than examine units of government. To accomplish these objectives, we use ordinary least squares (OLS) regression to analyze survey data about the character of human resources and debt management policies and practices in state governments. The work presented here is an exploratory attempt to compare the nature of management systems across states and to measure the impact of managerial behavior on management quality and functional area outcomes. Our early findings demonstrate that management can be quantified and does have an independent impact on government performance, which lends empirical support to our logic of governance.

This chapter is organized as follows: We first orient the reader to the particular aspects of the human resources and financial management functions we focus on in this study. Next, we describe the framework for this analysis, state our research questions, and explain our methods. Finally, we present and discuss our findings, draw some inferences for public management theory, and conclude with an agenda for further work.

The Human Resources Management Function

Personnel represent one of the largest expenditures of state governments, with funds spent on salaries, benefits, recruiting, training, and supervision. According to the U.S. Census Bureau, in 2001 the fifty states spent about $13 billion per month in salaries alone. At the state level, human resources issues are essential to an agency's ability to deliver services to the public, but the scope of human resources management varies tremendously across governments, with some incorporating the full spectrum of human resources practices, others utilizing a narrower set of practices aimed at monitoring and controlling, and a few paying limited attention to human resources management centrally.

A well-designed system will have an impact on the ability of state government to respond to stakeholder concerns and needs. Successful implementation of a state's human resources management system, however, is contingent on having a capable, motivated, and dedicated workforce. Studies have shown that modern human resource management practices in training and compensation have improved human resource management and organizational performance (Snell and Dean 1992; Arthur 1994; Huselid 1995; Delaney and Huselid 1996). Research has shown that organizations committed to their employees typically invest more in progressive human resources management practices and see an economic benefit as a result (Arthur 1994; Huselid 1995; Becker, Huselid, and Ulrich 2001).

In the past decade, considerable energy has been directed in many states—such as Oklahoma, Georgia, Florida, Maryland, and New York—toward reforming or transforming civil service (Selden, Ingraham, and Jacobson 2001). The approach to human resource management in state government is shifting in some places from a culture of regulatory watchdog to strategic partner who adds value to the state (Selden, Ingraham, and Jacobson 2001). Some human resources practices, such as strategic and workforce planning, can be used to foster an organizational culture that is forward looking—that is, focused on anticipating future challenges or shortfalls so that the potential performance or knowledge gaps can be filled (Becker, Huselid, and Ulrich 2001). Others, such as training and performance evaluations, can be used to communicate the important goals of an agency and also are tools for empowering employees and managers and holding staff accountable for programmatic results.

Human resource management is central to the operation of every agency and department in the state. As mentioned previously, the structure of the human resources management functions vary from state to state. On one extreme is Texas, which operates a largely decentralized system that pushes responsibility for most strategic and technical human resource management practices to state agencies. Rhode Island, by contrast, centrally manages most of its human resources management practices. Still others integrate services by sharing responsibility between agencies and the central office. Recent research suggests that the operational linkages, interactions, and interrelationships of human resource management systems in state governments are multifaceted and more complex than typically modeled in the literature (Selden et al. 2000).

Likewise, the development and growth of human resource management networks in state government are directly influenced by structural decisions about the foci and loci of responsibility for human resources management functions. As a result, the nature of a director's networking relationships with other stakeholders in states is likely to vary because of decisions about functional responsibilities, strategic objectives of the agency, management characteristics, the demand for services, and the degree to which human resources are viewed as a strategic asset. The state human resources management director works with multiple stakeholders, including but not limited to the governor and staff, the legislature and staff, citizen groups, directors, managers, human resources management professionals in state agencies and departments, and other human resources management professionals.

The Debt Administration Function

Government financial management encompasses a broad spectrum of activities and objectives. To permit meaningful empirical tests of the influence of management on outcomes, we have chosen to narrow our focus to one important aspect of the financial management—debt administration. State governments borrow substantial amounts of money, typically to purchase long-life physical assets, giving rise to a large and complex municipal debt market (Hildreth 1993; Stone 1994). In 1999, state governments and their authorities borrowed $102 billion (Thompson Financial Corporation), and owed more than $510 billion in outstanding debt (U.S. Census Bureau 2001). At the state level, this function is typically the responsibility of a treasury department or other central financial management office.

The legitimate public expectation of accountability for public resources has prompted financial management systems to develop detailed control mechanisms to guard against waste, fraud, and abuse. One of the major criticisms leveled against financial management systems is that these controls are sometimes counterproductive to the adaptability and flexibility needed to pursue the goals and objectives of the government. This has led to a general trend that favors holding managers accountable for results, but providing them with additional discretion in the allocation and management of resources to achieve those results (Holmes and Shand 1995). The tradeoff between flexibility and control is delicate, however, and discretion that is decoupled from accountability is an invitation to abuse.

The policy exigencies and implications of debt administration have prompted public finance researchers and professional associations to search for better techniques to manage money and ensure predictable financing flows, including appropriate guidelines for borrowing.[3] These norms are given traction by the responses of other institutions that interact in debt markets. For example, bond rating agencies routinely track the debt practices and capacity of state governments that issue debt and incorporate these factors into decisions concerning the creditworthiness of state and local governments.[4] We take our cue from this approach and use key debt administration choices as measures of management outcomes, because they have predictable economic consequences and are known indicators of a government's ability to maintain its fiscal health (Bland 1985; Robbins, Simonsen, and Jump 2001).

Debt managers must also be facile at interacting with the array of institutions and actors that populate capital markets and the financial management profession more broadly. Public financial managers have responsibilities in one or more networks where many actors are in positions to significantly influence outcomes but control of these actors is limited. The implications of these arrangements and their complexity have received limited attention in the literature. Measures of network behavior that embrace the full complexity of these arrangements have not been developed and applied, but researchers have recognized both the networked nature of financial management (Miller 1993) and the significant potential for agency problems arising from reliance on outside actors with information advantages (Simonsen and Hill 1999). In this work, we couple extant empirical research regarding the interdependent nature of municipal debt systems with O'Toole and Meier's (1999, 2000) theoretical model to explicitly incorporate network behavior into our exploration of the influence of management in debt administration.

Conceptual Framework

In a recent review of the literature surrounding governance and performance, and as explained in greater detail in chapter 1 of this volume, Lynn, Heinrich, and Hill (2000c) assert that consensus on the logic of governance has emerged and can be expressed with the function:

$$O = f(E, C, T, S, M), \qquad [1]$$

where O = individual-level and/or organization-level outputs or outcomes, E = environmental contingencies, C = client characteristics, T = primary work or core processes or technology, S = structures, and M = managerial roles and actions. Lynn, Heinrich, and Hill acknowledge, however, that the simple appearance of this function belies the complex set of causal relationships and interdependencies likely to exist among these variables. O'Toole and Meier (1999, 2000) move from this foundation to specify a model of the relationship between public management and program performance that attempts to address these complexities. They make the important point that the literature does not generally characterize management as simply another input to performance. Rather, its relationship to performance is presumed to be interactive and nonlinear. To represent this notion, their general model is

$$O_t = \beta_1(H + M_1)O_{t-1} + \beta_2(X_t/H)M_2 + \varepsilon_1,$$ [2]

where O is public program output or performance, H is a measure of hierarchy, X is a set of environmental factors, and M is management, which has two components. M_1 comprises internal managerial activity that contributes to program stability, and M_2 is network management.[5] Meier and O'Toole have tested a simplified version of this model that focuses on the effects of M_2, using data about public education systems in Texas (2001a). They find that organizations in which managers engage in more network interactions perform better.

We build on this theoretical foundation by defining and applying measures of the discretionary procedural choices (M_1) and the network behavior (M_2) of managers in state governments to determine the relationship between management and performance for the functions of human resources management and debt administration. This is an extension of O'Toole and Meier's work, which has so far focused on organizations as the unit of analysis, and the influences on organizations' ability to deliver program performance.

Why look at a management function rather than at a specific agency or organization? Management of a government's production technologies is commonly facilitated by the systematic arrangement and application of common management functions. A management function is a distinct set of administrative procedures that supports managerial decision making across programs to collect information on organizational performance, to coordinate routine activities, and to control the use of resources. Ingraham and Kneedler (2000b) argue that a government's ability to marshal its resources is housed within its core administrative functions, such as financial management, human resources management, capital management, and information technology management, which are frequently identified in the public management literature. These activities, immersed in a context rich in political exigencies, interact in highly complex ways to influence a government's performance across all of its programs, rather than for a particular program. Thus, understanding the levers of performance for a management function has implications for policy outcomes government-wide.

Applying O'Toole and Meier's framework to a function raises an additional question. What do M_1 and M_2 mean for a function? Fundamentally, management functions constitute the building blocks of a government's infrastructure for garnering, allocating, and maintaining its human, financial, capital, and information resources across its programs and agencies. Managers' M_1 activities serve much the same purpose for a function as for an agency. That is, managers must define performance standards, prescribe practices, and create procedures that promote stable and predictable flows of government resources. Thus, just as managers contribute to structures in an organizational or agency setting, as O'Toole and Meier describe, they stabilize systems in a government-wide or functional setting.

At the same time, Meier and O'Toole (2001b) explain that managers leverage their ability to achieve programmatic outcomes by cooperating in joint implementation activities with other actors who expect to receive complementary performance benefits. This behavior constitutes M_2, which involves the activities managers undertake to buffer shocks and exploit opportunities presented by the environment. Like organizations, functions operate in an environment that poses contingencies. The boundaries of a management function are harder to discern than the boundaries of an agency, so the concept of environment is not as sharp, but the environment of a function may be thought of as the set of actors and conditions that affect the stream of resources a management function is designed to handle. In directing a function, managers interrelate with actors and monitor conditions with a view toward garnering, sustaining, and deploying public resources in support of public programs.

Finally, why look at financial and human resources management, in particular? As a glance at the tables of contents of most public management textbooks demonstrates, financial and human resources management are arguably the two most important functions of government managers because of their profound effect on the level and quality of the main inputs to public production, labor, and capital. Moreover, the policies, processes, and practices in these areas are worthy of examination because they affect policy results government-wide both directly and indirectly. We also find these areas interesting to study because their activities transcend agency and organizational boundaries. In short, these are areas in which multiple institutions and actors, arranged in a variety of networks, influence outcomes. This operational complexity necessitates both M_1 and M_2 functions, facets of financial and human resources management often neglected in empirical work. Recent research suggests, however, that the development and growth of management capacity in state government are directly influenced by structural decisions about the foci and loci of responsibility and that the operational linkages, interactions, and interrelationships of management systems in state government are multifaceted and more complex than typically modeled in the literature (Selden et al. 2000). We propose to explore these propositions empirically.

Thus, as O'Toole and Meier examine how maintenance of organizational structures and network management contribute to the outcomes of a program, we analogously seek to examine how maintenance of management systems and network management contribute to the quality and outcomes of a management function. Specifically, our primary research questions concern how the contributions managers make to functional stability, and the level of interaction managers have with other actors, affect management quality and functional outcomes in state governments. We begin to explore this question for human resources management and debt administration below.

Table 6.1

Descriptive Statistics for Human Resources Management

Variable	N	Mean	Standard Deviation	Minimum	Maximum
Voluntary turnover, 1999	48	8.079	3.603	1.56	19.64
Voluntary turnover, 1998	48	8.084	3.872	1.37	18.99
Quality of hires	49	7.776	1.137	4.00	10.00
Decentralization	49	19.714	7.624	.00	34.00
Formal reporting	44	.091	.291	.00	1.00
Workforce planning	50	2.320	1.115	1.00	5.00
Frequency of contact	44	4.538	1.142	1.93	6.87
Reciprocality	44	5.614	3.052	.00	15.00
Responding	44	6.750	3.307	.00	15.00
Diversity of training	50	25.820	2.027	18.00	28.00
Average salary ($)	49	29,095.716	12,554.322	15.80	54,278.00
Right-to-work	50	.440	.501	.00	1.00
Unemployment	50	4.114	1.013	2.50	6.60

Measures, Data, and Methods

A central challenge in this work was to operationalize measures of management behavior, quality, and outcomes for the human resources management and debt administration functions. This section describes our data collection effort, explains the rationale for the measures we defined, and identifies our estimating equations and analytic approach. Descriptive statistics for the variables in our human resources and debt administration models, as defined below, are reported in tables 6.1 and 6.2, respectively. For reference, the variable names are included parenthetically in the text in bold. Also, the appendix describes the construction of the human resources variables.

Data. This research uses data collected from three surveys of state government managers conducted over the past three years, as well as data from the U.S. Bureau of the Census and the Securities Data Corporation. Some of the human resources data were collected from a telephone survey of state human resources directors conducted in 2001. In this survey, respondents were asked to specify the frequency of their contact with an array of actors within and outside their state government and to identify whether they or the other parties more often initiated these interactions. Human resources directors were faxed a copy of the survey ahead of the telephone interview to promote more careful assessments of these interactions. Additional human resources data were derived from a written survey of state human resources managers conducted in 2000 as part of the Government Performance Project.[6] In this survey, respondents were asked 104 multipart open- and closed-ended questions about a broad array of human resources activities. Germane to the present re-

Table 6.2
Descriptive Statistics for Debt Administration

Variable	Mean	Standard Deviation	Minimum	Maximum
Competitive sales (%)	17.38	17.66	0.00	75.00
Request for proposal (%)	36.17	19.45	0.00	50.00
Capital improvement plan	0.489	0.505	0	1
Debt capacity	0.383	0.491	0	1
Proceed limits	0.149	0.360	0	1
Credit quality	0.489	0.505	0	1
Repayment life	0.681	0.471	0	1
Negotiated sales	0.617	0.491	0	1
Use of financial advisors	0.872	0.337	0	1
Underwriter training	0.638	1.241	0	4
Internal control	0.511	0.505	0	1
Population	5,483,366	6,003,576	589,000	32,300,000
Number of bond sales	45.021	34.173	8	172
State tax rate	5.56	3.114	0	12

search were questions about the extent to which the state engages in work-force planning, the degree to which various human resources activities are centralized or decentralized, the level of turnover in the workforce, and the nature of training offered to state employees. The survey data were combined with unemployment data from the U.S. Census Bureau.

The debt administration portion of this study uses data collected from a 1999 survey of state debt managers. Survey respondents were asked to answer questions about twenty-four different policy elements. When choosing the policy elements to include in the survey instrument we incorporated the elements recommended by the GFOA for state and local governments. We supplemented these with elements found in existing polices and identified as important or in use by survey pretest respondents.[7] The survey was pretested by officials from two states and two universities, and several format and content changes were made. The first surveys were mailed in June 1999, with follow-up mailings in July, August, and September. Follow-up phone calls were placed in attempts to secure completed surveys from the state governments. Forty-seven states ultimately returned completed surveys. In cases where states do not issue debt directly, we surveyed the largest issuing state authority in 1998 according to Moody's Municipals and Securities Data Corporation.

The resulting population included forty-two state treasury or central debt management officials and eight state authorities and agencies. The results for the agencies and authorities represent the same statutory and constitutional constraints controlling all state level issues but stand only for each specific organization's rules and practices. These data were combined with those from the U.S. Census Bureau (population and debt measures) and from Securities Data Corporation (debt issuance statistics), to form a complete picture of each state's policies and practices. The resulting dataset contains the type of policy control across twenty-four different policy elements for each of the forty-seven participating states, coupled with the observed patterns of issuance within those states during the same year.

Measures of M_1

O'Toole and Meier (1999) define M_1 as "maintenance," or managers' efforts to contribute to program stability. As part of their responsibility for upholding organizational performance, managers have a central role in defining the essence of what the organization is designed to achieve. That is, they help define the organization's purpose and mission and determine how the organization will meet these over time. This is the essence of strategic planning and goal setting reserved for policymakers under traditional models; under contemporary conceptualizations, the boundary between policy planning and operational planning is permeable. Management thus includes the exercise of strategic judgment to ascertain the organization's current performance (Cohen 1993; Cohen and Eimicke 1995), devise operational plans to meet those goals (Allison 1983), monitor achievement of goals (Lynn 1997), and impose remedial strategies to improve performance (Lynn 1997). Managers are, however, granted varying degrees of control over these areas. Because managers have more discretion to define the substance of plans, procedures, and policies, the function can be viewed as decentralized.

Human Resources Management. For human resources management, we include two measures that characterize the locus of responsibility for human resources management tasks and procedures. The first (*decentralization*) is the number of such tasks that are decentralized to the agency level, based on a list of thirty-five common and well-established core human resources activities in areas such as bargaining, recruiting, testing, candidate assessment, hiring, performance evaluation, job classification, and training. The second measure is whether there is a direct reporting relationship between the agency and central human resources offices (*formal reporting*). We also capture managers' contributions to stability by evaluating the extent to which formal statewide human resources plans exist (*workforce planning*).

Debt Administration. We include several measures to capture managers' ability to control the activities inherent in debt administration. These are a set of dummy variables that identify whether state debt managers pursue policies that directly affect the bond sale process. Managers may assure that projects align with the larger capital improvement plan of the state (*capital improvement plan*) and may assess the ability of the state to absorb additional debt (*debt capacity*). Managers may exert control over or enforce provisions regarding the appropriate use of bond funds (*proceed limits*) as a way to assure that project funds are used for their intended purposes (typically capital infrastructure) and not diverted to other uses (such as for operations). The same normative supposition applies to control over the repayment life of the state's issues (*repayment life*), which is exerted in order to assure that the maturity length of securities does not exceed the useful life of the financed capital assets. In some cases debt managers, rather than senior state officials, are considered to be responsible for maximizing the state's credit rating. Our measure (*credit quality*) indicates whether this responsibility is explicitly assigned to management through a debt policy.

Measures of M_2

Meier and O'Toole (2001b) define M_2 as "network management," or the extent to which managers exert skill and effort to tap opportunities presented by actors in the environment. In their first empirical test of the impact of M_2, they base their measure of network management on the frequency of contact a manager has with various sets of external actors. This is a rudimentary view of network management that omits many dimensions of the nature of network interactions, but it does indicate the level of effort managers make with respect to external relationships. We pursue a similar strategy.

Human Resources Management. We define and examine two structural properties of human resources management networks: network density and network interaction. Density describes the overall level of interchange reported by the human resources management director. We measure this as the frequency with which the human resources director has contact with governmental stakeholders, including the governor and his staff, legislators and their staffs, and agencies (*frequency of contact*).

Interaction describes how interchanges are initiated; interactions can be initiated by the director, a stakeholder, or both. We consider three types of network interaction: responding, reciprocal, and initiating. The responding type captures interactions between the director and stakeholders that are initiated by the stakeholder. We measure this as the extent to which other parties tend to initiate contact with the human resources director (*responding*). The reciprocal type represents the extent to which human resources management directors consult, collaborate, and interact with other stakeholders. A high level of collaboration exists when human resources management directors frequently communicate with other stakeholders and when both the director and stakeholders initiate contacts. We measure this as the extent to which the relationships between the human resources director and other parties are initiated about as often by the director as by the other party (what we term *reciprocality*). The initiating type represents interactions between the director and stakeholders that are initiated by the director. This type of interaction may reflect a human resources management director who is predominantly scanning and analyzing the state government environment to identify its threats, opportunities, and options. We measure this as the extent to which the human resources director tends to initiate contact with other parties (*initiating*). This type is used as the reference group in our models.

Debt Administration. For the financial management function we have selected measures of management interaction with networks that are expressed in a variety of ways. The measures capture the method of bond sales and the source and amount of the training that state debt managers receive. Each exposes government actors to networks with different qualities.

The first measure is the use of financial advisors (*use of financial advisors*), which captures efforts to avoid appearances of impropriety and access cost savings through the use of an outside expert whose advice can influence and legitimize the choices the debt manager makes. State debt managers often hire expert financial advisors to work on their behalf to help them to obtain the most favorable borrowing terms, but state governments may also invoke the option of issuing debt without using a financial advisor. We view the use of this particular set of professionals as normatively superior in both appearance and fact, particularly in light of research associating advisor use with lower borrowing costs (Robbins and Simonsen 2001).

State government agencies and authorities typically choose to sell their bonds in one of two ways, through either competition or negotiation. When states sell bonds through negotiation, debt management staff interactions are primarily with the underwriter, which involves network interactions with a particular character. In some states, debt managers receive no policy guidance and have no control over how underwriters are selected for negotiated sales. We include a variable here (*negotiated sales*) to indicate whether debt managers have policies in place that indicate how such selections will be made.

Managers and staff interact with networks not only in the sales process but also in the training process. Training creates interactions among peers of similar professionals and interactions with the providers of the training. We asked debt managers to identify the number of topical areas of training (of five) in which state debt management staff attended training provided by municipal bond underwriters. Underwriters are the professionals involved most often in bond transactions and are likely to be most familiar with the nuances of the issuance process. Training interactions expose debt management staff to the knowledge and also the interpretations of the firms that ultimately purchase bonds from municipalities. Although these interactions may provide qualitative improvements in the understanding and judgments of debt managers, they may also create a greater likelihood of pursuing actions that favor underwriters. Our measure (*underwriter training*) counts the number of topical areas in which staff attended training from underwriters.

Finally, we have included an overall measure of the degree to which managers have control over the debt issuance function. Our measure (*internal con-*

trol) counts the instances in which they indicated that they possessed "complete control" over this function, which suggests less network influence than in instances where external actors also exert control.

Measures of Outcomes

Policy analysis generally examines programs, their implementation, and their outputs and outcomes. In this chapter, our focus on management functions as the unit of analysis alters the nature of the results of interest. Rather than final results of *programs*, we seek indicators of the outcomes of *functions*—what might be thought of as intermediate outcomes—as well as of the quality of the administration of those functions.[8] The human resources management literature has begun to specify the characteristics of good personnel systems. Likewise, the literature on municipal bond issuance offers some evidence about the characteristics of well-managed debt finance processes. We use these to define outcome measures for this study. Quality of program or in this case function is a commonly used measure of performance (Campbell 1977; Cummings 1977). Indicators of quality can be used to assess how well the function is utilizing its resources to produce the desired impact.

Human Resources Management. One of the primary concerns of stakeholders in the late 1990s was competing for talent in a tight labor market (Ingraham, Selden, and Moynihan 2000). As a result, we focus on two important human resources management outcomes—one that focuses on obtaining quality human capital and the other that considers retaining such individuals. To ascertain the quality of a hire, we included a subjective probe to human resources directors regarding their 1999 hires (*quality of hires*). For retention, we looked at turnover, specifically voluntary turnover. Voluntary turnover is a more appropriate measure than total turnover because involuntary turnover and retirements may be used to ensure that poorly performing employees are separated and that state government can acquire new skills through its new hires. Voluntary turnover typically involves employees whom the government wants to retain but who subsequently reduce the skill base of the state workforce. Low voluntary turnover is viewed as a successful indicator of the human resource management function (Tsui and Gomez-Mejia 1988). We measure the percent of employees who left the state workforce voluntarily, excluding by retirement, in both 1999 and 1998 (*voluntary turnover*).

Debt Administration. As mentioned above, state government agencies and authorities typically choose to sell their bonds in one of two ways. One method is through competitive bidding, in which groups of underwriters compete to win the right to purchase and resell the bonds by pledging the highest price (lowest interest cost) for the securities. Using a competition assures the appearance of a fair and open process in the awarding of potentially lucrative state bond sales. Evidence from previous research also indicates that such choices assure the lowest borrowing costs for issuers (Simonsen and Robbins 1996). We apply these lessons to create a measure of management quality (*competitive sales %*) based on the proportion of each state's bond issuance (in 1999) conducted through a competitive sales process.

A second indicator of management quality relates to the manner in which contracts are let. Governments hire an assortment of consultants and contractors (such as legal counsel, insurance firms, rating agencies, financial advisors, paying agents, and so forth) to assist in the completion of the bond sales process. This selection process is often dominated by inertial factors. Such is often the case when persisting with an existing contractor. In other cases, managers request qualifications prior to awarding such work. Another option is to issue a request for proposals (RFPs). This approach potentially invokes some market forces under the presumption that the superior proposal obtains the work. Although it may be possible to solicit competitive bids for such services, our survey results suggest that such is almost never the case. The choice most commensurate with normative conceptions of good government, on grounds of market efficiency and the transparency of management decisions, is consequently the use of the RFP. We create and apply a proportional measure of RFP use indicating the degree to which managers award work on this basis across the aforementioned contracting areas (*request for proposal %*).

Environmental Variables

Many authors have noted the contingent nature of management and management outcomes. Environmental factors embody a broad array of influences, including both properties of the larger context within which the government operates and properties of the government's jurisdiction. Examples of environmental factors likely to be significant include characteristics of the constituent populations and socioeconomic conditions. Most of the implementation literature, for example, recognizes the dramatic effect that local environmental conditions can have on the character of programs and their outcomes and, thus, policy performance (Pressman and Wildavsky 1984; Linder and Peters 1987; Mazmanian and Sabatier 1989).

Human Resources Management. In our human resources models, we have included two types of control variables: externally focused variables to control for the contingencies of the labor environment, and internally focused variables to control for the nature of the existing human resources policy regime. The external environment is captured by two factors that are known to affect the supply of labor: whether the state has right-to-work laws (*right-to-work*) and the state unemployment rate in 1999 (*unemployment*).[9] We also measure the nature of the existing workforce management culture within the state government by including two important factors known to affect how employees feel about their workplace: professional development opportunities and compensation. Specifically, we measure the diversity of training courses and programs offered to state government employees (*diversity of training*) and the average full-time classified salary (*average salary*).

Debt Administration. We include variables that capture three different components of the environment in which state bond sales are conducted. The first, the amount of debt activity in each state (*number of bond sales*), controls for the portion of the variations in performance that may be associated with experience (Bland 1985). Variations in after-tax returns on municipal securities relative to other investments have the potential to drive performance and outcomes. A greater demand for the bonds of a state may decrease its cost of debt in a manner that stimulates more borrowing or creating pressures for municipalities to move issues to the market more rapidly than would otherwise be the case. Because higher interest rates increase demand for bonds and lower rates tend to increase supply pressures, we include a measure (*state tax rates*) that differentiates between each state on the basis of the tax savings available from holding its bonds. For states with an income tax and a state bond interest exemption, this rate is the highest marginal tax rate in the state income tax structure. For states without the exemption (Illinois, Iowa, Kansas, Oklahoma, and Wisconsin) this rate is 0.396 (the highest federal income tax rate in 1999) multiplied by the highest marginal tax rate in the state income tax structure. (This represents the fact that state taxes are deductible from the income used to calculate the federal tax liability.) For states without an income tax, the savings rate is 0. For states with interactive tax rate structures (Rhode Island and Vermont), the rate is that state's interactive rate multiplied by 0.396. Highest marginal rates are for married individuals filing jointly. Because larger populations place greater pressures on debt management teams for larger and more complex issues, we control for the number of persons in each state (*population*).

Methods

Our models of government outcomes in the domain of human resources management are

$$O_1 = \beta_0 + \beta_1 M_1 + \beta_2 M_2 + \beta_3 P + \beta_4 E + \varepsilon_1 \qquad [3]$$

$$O_2 = \beta_0 + \beta_1 O_{2_{t-1}} + \beta_2 M_1 + \beta_3 M_2 + \beta_4 P + \beta_5 E + \varepsilon_3, \qquad [4]$$

where O_1 is the quality of hires made by the government in 1999, O_2 is the proportion of the state's workforce that left voluntarily in 1999, $O_{2_{t-1}}$ is a lagged dependent variable (the proportion of the state's workforce that left voluntarily in 1998),[10] β_0 is a constant, M_1 is a vector of choices and

Table 6.3

Regression Results for Human Resources Management

Variable	Quality of Employees Hired			Voluntary Turnover		
	Coefficient	Standard Error	t Value	Coefficient	Standard Error	t Value
Contributions to Stability (M_1):						
Decentralization	.045	.022	2.049**	-.027	.035	-.786
Formal reporting	-.567	.602	-.942	-2.046	.928	-2.206**
Workforce planning	.437	.425	2.724*	.002	.249	.006
Network factors (M_2):						
Frequency of contact	-.158	.166	-.951	.456	.262	1.739***
Reciprocality	.161	.073	2.212**	-.344	.113	-3.038*
Responding	.133	.071	1.879***	-.212	.110	-1.927***
Environmental Factors:						
Diversity of training	-.132	.088	-1.495†	.039	.144	.272
Average salary	-.000	.000	-.651	.000	.000	.204
Right to work	-.334	.342	-.977	-.267	.560	-.477
Unemployment	-.343	.170	-2.018**	.066	.262	.256
Voluntary turnover, 1998				.863	.072	12.004
Constant	10.073	2.690	3.745*	2.025	4.249	.477
D				2.00		
Number of observations	43			42		
F	2.61			18.92		
Probability > F	.02			.00		
R^2	.45			.87		
Adjusted R^2	.28			.83		

*$P \leq .01$; **$P \leq .05$; ***$P \leq .10$; †$P \leq .15$.

characteristics related to structure (decentralization, reporting, and workforce planning), M_2 is a vector of network interactions (frequency, reciprocality, and responding), P is a vector of human resources management policy characteristics (diversity of training and average salary), E is a vector of environmental factors (right-to-work and unemployment), and ε is an error term.

Our models of government outcomes in the domain of debt management are

$$O_3 = \beta_0 + \beta_1 M_1 + \beta_2 M_2 + \beta_3 E + \varepsilon_4 \qquad [5]$$

$$O_4 = \beta_0 + \beta_1 M_1 + \beta_2 M_2 + \beta_3 E + \varepsilon_4, \qquad [6]$$

where O_3 and O_4 are the percent of sales that are competitive and the percent of sales that use a request for proposal, β_0 is a constant, M_1 is a vector of managerial policies (capital planning, debt capacity, proceed limits, credit quality, and repayment life), M_2 is a vector of network factors (methods of sale, use of independent financial advisors, training by underwriters, and the presence of internal control), E is a vector of environmental factors (state tax rate, population, and number of sales), and ε is an error term. To isolate the effects of management factors and network interactions on outcomes while holding constant environmental factors, we regress the aforementioned outcomes on these determinants by use of OLS.

Findings

For our analysis, we estimated the four models specified above to test the influences on management quality and a functional outcome for both human resources management and debt administration. These are reported in tables 6.3 and 6.4, respectively.

Human Resources Management. Overall, as table 6.2 shows, M_1 and M_2 factors appear to influence both the quality and outcomes of the human resources management function. In the first regression model, in which the quality of employees hired is the dependent variable, two M_1 and two M_2 factors are significant, and all four are positively related to the quality of new hires. The environment also has some impact on the quality of hires. In the second regression model, in which voluntary turnover is the dependent variable, the lagged dependent variable has a highly significant and positive impact. Even controlling for this lagged effect, one M_1 factor and all three M_2 factors are significant. The environmental factors we include have no significant effect on voluntary turnover, however, which is surprising, because we would expect that incentives like salary would affect people's decision to stay in the government workforce, especially when controlling for unemployment. In addition, we tested interactions between network management and environmental factors, but they were not statistically significant in either model.

Table 6.4
Regression Results for Debt Administration

Variable	Competitive Sales (%)			Requests for Proposal (%)		
	Coefficient	Standard Error	t Value	Coefficient	Standard Error	t Value
Contributions to Stability (M_1):						
Capital improvement plan	0.023	0.049	0.47	0.073	0.039	1.87***
Debt capacity	-0.046	0.048	-0.96	-0.153	0.038	-4.00*
Proceed limits	0.014	0.070	0.20	0.118	0.055	2.14**
Credit quality	-0.094	0.054	-1.74***	0.077	0.043	1.80***
Repayment life	0.028	0.055	0.50	0.079	0.044	1.81***
Network Factors (M_2):						
Negotiated sales	0.129	0.051	2.52**	0.048	0.041	1.17
Use of financial advisors	0.143	0.072	1.99***	0.306	0.057	5.33*
Underwriter training	0.018	0.022	0.83	0.044	0.017	2.52**
Internal control	0.093	0.048	1.95***	0.048	0.038	1.27
Environmental Factors:						
State tax rate	-0.004	0.007	-0.47	0.007	0.006	1.24
Number of bond sales	-0.002	0.001	-2.12**	-0.000	0.001	-0.15
Population	0.000	0.000	2.08**	0.000	0.000	0.69
Constant	-0.001	0.109	-0.09	-0.1256	0.0863	-1.46
Number of observations	47			47		
$F(12, 34)$	2.87			8.14		
Prob > F	0.008			0.00		
R^2	0.50			0.75		
Adjusted R^2	0.33			0.65		

* $P \le .01$; ** $P \le .05$; *** $P \le .10$; † $P \le .15$.

More specifically, our findings show that the more human resources tasks and procedures are decentralized to the agency level, the better human resources managers assess their new employees to be. Many human resources tasks (in fact, about half of those we included in this measure) contribute to the hiring function. This result suggests that the more agency-level human resources staff are involved with hiring—as opposed to central government human resources staff—the better the people are who get hired. This may be because the front-line human resources staff have a better sense of what their agencies need. At the same time, states that engage in more formal workforce planning efforts also seem to hire better-quality people. This is not surprising—states that better understand the personnel they require to fulfill their missions, and that have formulated strategies for obtaining them, appear more likely to make better hiring decisions. Thus, both of the M_1 influences have effects that are consistent with the views of government reformers, which advocate shifting discretion downward (the recent efforts National Performance Review are a case in point) and also have long recognized the importance of planning (here the Government Performance and Results Act is an example). These trends are also seen in contemporary work on human resources management (see, for example, Bennett, Ketchen, and Schultz 1998, and the U.S. General Accounting Office's work on human capital (2000, 2001).

With respect to M_2, the quality of new hires increases as the nature of interactions between the human resources director and other actors in government is more reciprocal (that is, initiated by the director or the other actor about equally as often), and it tends to be more often initiated by the other actor (what we have termed "responding"). This suggests that less directive interactions yield better results.

Finally, with respect to the internal and external environment, as the diversity of training courses currently offered to employees falls, the quality of hires rises, but this finding is only marginally significant (at the $P \leq .15$ level). This perhaps indicates that the more limited the opportunities to train employees are, the more human resources managers make an effort to get the best people they can up front. Also, surprisingly, the results show that as unemployment rises, the quality of hires falls. Although we would expect the opposite effect, it may be that our data fail to tease out complex relationships between employment rates, the nature of the labor pool, the nature of applicants for positions in public agencies, and the hires that are ultimately made.

Looking at voluntary turnover, the presence of a formal reporting relationship between the agency human resources staff and the state human resources director reduces turnover. Also, the more frequent the contact between the human resources director and other government actors, the higher turnover rates are. This suggests that a denser network negatively affects outcomes, which, on its face, appears inconsistent with what Meier and O'Toole (2001b) find. It may be that more interactions constrain the discretion of the human resources director and force suboptimal choices with regard to turnover. We also find, however, that the more the human resources director moves toward a mode of responding to contacts initiated by other parties throughout government, the lower the turnover rates; likewise, the more reciprocal the relationship between the director and other parties, the lower the turnover rates. These results suggest that the nature of network interaction mitigates the negative effect of frequency of contact alone. Perhaps frequent contacts from the human resources director tax other government actors and inhibit their ability to facilitate and obtain good outcomes. On the other hand, less directive (more responsive and reciprocal) interaction and fewer demands (fewer contacts) might be more helpful to other government actors, and thus tend to bolster good outcomes.

Debt Administration. The first debt administration regression model (see table 6.4) reports the effects of M_1, M_2, and the environment, on average and all else equal, on the proportion of a state's bond issuance that are sold competitively. This model reveals significant influence from six of the independent variables. The sole M_1 factor of (statistical) significance with respect to sales proportion was policy control over credit quality strategies. The fact that the sign on this coefficient is negative indicates that these policies appear to relate to less reliance upon competitive sales. There is no perfectly unambiguous interpretation for this finding. One of the strategies commonly pursued with respect to credit quality is to purchase credit enhancement in the form of insurance. Underwriters purchase this insurance on behalf of issuers in the case of negotiated sales and (ostensibly) resell it to the issuer. In competitive sales, the issuer buys the insurance directly. The potential for a profit motive in the case of negotiated offering raises one possible explanation for why credit enhancement policies may be associated with more negotiated sales.

Among the M_2 network factors, policies controlling the underwriter selection process for negotiated sales, use of (external) financial advisors, and complete manager control over the debt function were associated with higher proportions of competitive sale use (on average and all else equal). Selection policies and financial advisor use are both practices associated with good government and in accord with guidance from the GFOA. Presumably, managers following one set of desirable practices will also appreciate the value of competitive sales. Managers appear to use their discretion toward the ends of good governance, as those with such control are associated with significantly higher levels of issuance through competition.

Among the environmental variables, the number of bond sales is negatively associated with sales type, although the state population is positively associated with higher competitive proportions. Once controlling for managerial control and indicators of good governance, the effect of the count of bond sales reflects the influence of the states with the highest sales volume. In this context, the three states with the most sales happen to have had the lowest rates of competitive sales (California, Illinois and New York, with 7 percent,

4 percent, and 9 percent, respectively). The positive and statistically significant relationship between population and sales proportion is not surprising. To the degree that population size proxies the ability to recruit larger and more sophisticated teams of debt management staff, we would expect to find larger states associated with higher levels of competitive sales, all else equal.

The second regression reports the effects of these factors, on average and all else equal, on the proportion of a state's bond issuance that use requests for proposal. All of the M_1 variables and two of the four M_2 variables had a statistically significant impact on this outcome measure. Among the M_1 variables the puzzle is the coefficient on debt capacity, the measure used to indicate management use of decision models to gauge the ability of states to absorb additional debt. Here the story may lie with negotiated sales. (In the competitive sales regression the slope of debt capacity coefficient was negative although it was not statistically significant.) Debt managers may view the service underwriter's offer to calculate debt capacity as costless, leading them to prefer negotiated sales in such circumstances. The suboptimal choice of a negotiated sale is likely to covary with a tendency to use RFPs less (a process that removes to a large degree the ability to award sales to underwriters who have provided "free" debt capacity assessments). The remaining M_1 effects resonate with the principals of good governance, the presence of each policy provision being related to higher reliance on RFPs.

The two M_2 variables of statistically significant (and positive) influence on RFP use were financial advisors and underwriter training. Both suggest that the influence of network interactions (on average and all else equal) increases the proportion of contracts awarded with RFPs. Both sets of interactions are poised to improve the education, sophistication, and judgment skills of the debt manager. These factors ought to be associated with good government choices (like RFP use), and this finding has intuitive appeal.

Conclusions and Future Directions

This chapter explores the governance of key government functions, particularly the influence of management behavior on quality. It looks at two aspects of management behavior: contributions to stability and the character of interactions with other actors. And it looks at outcomes of interest for two state government functions: workforce management and debt management. Many of our findings are clearly consistent with O'Toole and Meier's theory that managerial activities that contribute to functional stability and predictability improve (in this case, intermediate) outcomes. Likewise, the level and nature of network interaction are relevant.

Among the factors we examine are various aspects of the characteristics and locus of managerial discretion in the areas of planning, policy, and procedures for these two functions. But why should we look at this kind of discretion when thinking about management activities and outcomes? The answer has to do with the study of public management. Managers are involved with many activities that produce outcomes from our governments that we care about. If managers do not have choice in these areas, how can we justify our concern over management? Stated differently, if managerial influence is confined solely to the implementation of the dictates of others, then managers are relatively unimportant to the management process!

Our findings suggest, among other things, that managerial discretion matters to key outcomes. When exercising discretion over procedural activities, both financial and human resources managers appear to use their expertise to make things as effective as possible in many of the cases we examine. The exercise of administrative discretion appears, in particular, to increase the desirable outcome of using requests for proposals to achieve the optimal performance of their client governments, and of hiring high-quality personnel equipped to meet the needs and demands of their employers. In the domain of human resources management, our finding that planning improves the quality of employees hired is gratifying because it supports the intuition and management prescriptions that planning efforts will improve government performance.

We also have found evidence that network factors matter to results. Among the M_2 network factors, practices in accord with guidance from the GFOA were associated with higher proportions of competitive sale and request for proposal use. And managers appear to exercise discretion toward the ends of good governance, as those with complete control are associated with significantly higher use of competition. In human resources management, network density is significant. This is fundamentally consistent with the work and findings of O'Toole and Meier that network interactions influence key outcomes. We also have preliminary evidence that the nature of the network may be important in addition to the presence of network interactions. Human resources managers who are more responsive and more collaborative realize lower employee turnover and hire better employees, both desirable results. This qualitative distinction between networks bears further examination.

Also of interest for extensions of this work are the exploration and modeling of suspected nonlinearities in the relationships between managerial factors and outcomes. Certainly the relationship between these management configurations and outcomes are unlikely to be constant across, for instance, environmental factors such as labor force size and collective bargaining arrangements for human resources management, and issuance volume and market volatility for debt administration. We hope to extend our work to allow for these kinds of complexities. We also recognize the desirability of developing models that assess the impact of these managerial factors on costs. The difficulty of creating reliable cost measures with state governments as the unit of analysis has prevented us from doing this thus far, but the creation of some average salary range (for human resources management) or borrowing cost (for debt administration) in relation to market benchmarks remains a possibility.

In conclusion, some of the relationships we find are puzzling—although a managerial influence is evident, its complexity eludes our rough measures. Our work is still very much in progress, but we do find significant evidence that managerial factors influence outcomes. Both contributions to stability and network factors seem to matter, even when controlling for key environmental factors. The challenge to extend this work with sets of measures refined to better capture these relationships remains, but we are encouraged in the interim to discover the significant influence of management on outcomes.

Appendix A
Construction of Human Resources Variables Contained in Final Analyses

Decentralization of Human Resources Processes (Theoretical Range, 0–35):
- Summative index of whether the primary responsibility of thirty-five different human resources management (HRM) processes are decentralized to agencies.
- Alpha = .88.

Frequency of Contact (Theoretical Range, 0–35):
- Summative index of the frequency of contacts the HRM director has with sixteen stakeholders.
- Alpha = .84.

Reciprocality (Theoretical Range, 0–16):
- Summative index of frequency with which the interaction between the HRM director and the stakeholder is initiated by both parties (sixteen relationships).
- Alpha = .82.

Responding (Theoretical Range 0–16):
- Summative index of frequency with which the interaction between the HRM director and the stakeholder is initiated by the stakeholder (sixteen relationships).
- Alpha = .84.

Training Diversity (Theoretical Range, 0–30)
- Summative index of whether thirty different types of training are offered by the state.
- Alpha = .69.

Notes

1. For a comprehensive review of this literature, see Heinrich and Lynn (2001) and Lynn, Heinrich, and Hill (2000a, 2000b).

2. For financial management, these are promulgated especially by the Government Accounting Standards Board (GASB) and the Government Financial Officers Association (GFOA), among others.

3. For examples from the empirical literature, see Robbins, Simonsen, and Jump (2001); Robbins and Simonsen (2002); Chan and Miranda (1998); and Simonsen and Robbins (1996). From the field of practice, see Joseph (1994).

4. Standard and Poor's (1986) specifically lists compliance with generally accepted accounting principles (GAAP), which GASB has insisted on, as an important factor in debt ratings.

5. There are two important complexities captured in this model. First, it is autoregressive to represent the tendency for present performance to depend to a large degree on past performance, that is to change incrementally. Second, M_2, loosely defined as network management, is formally specified as M_3/M_4, where the components are defined as efforts to exploit environmental changes (M_3) and efforts to buffer environmental shocks (M_4).

6. Details of Syracuse University's Government Performance Project and its 2000 State Government Management Survey, as well as summary data tables, are available at the project's website: www.maxwell.syr.edu/gpp and are discussed in Ingraham, Joyce, and Donahue (2003).

7. Early in this research we contacted the party responsible for the oversight of debt issuance in each of the state governments in writing or by phone and collected written debt policies or governing statutes where they existed. This yielded thirty-four sets of widely varying documents. During this phase, we conducted informal and open-ended interviews with state debt managers about the prevalence of policy guidance beyond these written documents.

8. The implicit assumption here is that functional outcomes and administrative quality affect program or policy outcomes government-wide. We acknowledge that the relationship between functional and programmatic outcomes, and the behaviors and decisions that generate them, is likely to be more complex than we portray here. Nonetheless, this assumption that management performance influences policy performance is common in the literature.

9. A right-to-work law guarantees that a person cannot be compelled, as a condition of employment, to join, not to join, or to pay dues to a labor union. Section 14(b) of the Taft-Hartley Act affirms the right of state governments to enact right-to-work legislation. The twenty-two states that have done so are Alabama, Arizona, Arkansas, Kansas, Florida, Georgia, Idaho, Iowa, Louisiana, Mississippi, Nebraska, Nevada, North Carolina, North Dakota, Oklahoma, South Carolina, South Dakota, Tennessee, Texas, Utah, Virginia, and Wyoming.

10. Equation [4] is the only model for which we had lagged data available. We include it here for comparison to the Meier and O'Toole (2001b) model and findings. A Durbin-Watson test of this model showed $d \cong 2$, so we conclude that the threat from serial correlation is minimal.

References

Allison, G. T. 1983. "Public and Private Management: Are They Fundamentally Alike in All Unimportant Respects?" In F. S. Lane, ed., *Current Issues in Public Administration*, 5th ed. New York: St. Martin's, 16–32.

Arthur, J. B. 1994. "Effects of Human Resource Systems on Manufacturing Performance and Turnover." *Academy of Management Journal* 37:670–88.

Becker, B. E., M. A. Huselid, and D. Ulrich. 2001. *The HR Scorecard: Linking People, Strategy, and Performance*. Cambridge, Mass.: Harvard Business School Press.

Bennett, N., D. J. Ketchen, Jr., and E. B. Schultz. 1998. "An Examination of Factors Associated with the Integration of Human Resource Management and Strategic Decision Making." *Human Resource Management* 37:3–16.

Bland, R. L. 1985. "The Interest Cost Savings for Experience in the Municipal Bond Market." *Public Administration Review* 45:233–37.

Bowling, C. J., and D. S. Wright. 1998. "Change and Continuity in State Administration: Administrative Leadership across Four Decades." *Public Administration Review* 58:429–45.

Campbell, J. P. 1977. "On the Nature of Organizational Effectiveness." In P. S. Goodman, J. M. Pennings, and associates, eds., *New Perspectives on Organizational Effectiveness*. San Francisco: Jossey-Bass, 13–55.

Carnevale, D. G. 1995. *Merit System Reform in the States: Partnerships for Change*. Norman: University of Oklahoma, Programs in Public Administration.

Chan, J. L., and R. A. Miranda. 1998. "Principles for Designing the Finance Organization: A Guide for Reform Efforts and Leadership Transitions." *Government Finance Review* (June):15–19.

Cohen, S. 1993. "Defining and Measuring Effectiveness in Public Management." *Public Productivity and Management Review* 17:45–57.

Cohen, S., and W. Eimicke. 1995. *The New Effective Public Manager: Achieving Success in a Changing Government*. San Francisco: Jossey-Bass.

Cummings, L. L. 1977. "Emergence of the Instrumental Organization." In *New Perspectives on Organizational Effectiveness*, ed. P. S. Goodman, J. M. Pennings, and associates. San Francisco: Jossey-Bass, 56–62.

Delaney, J. T., and M. A. Huselid. 1996. "The Impact of Human Resource Management Practices on Perceptions of Organizational Performance." *Academy of Management Journal* 39:949–70.

Heinrich, C. J. 2000. "Organizational Form and Performance: An Empirical Investigation of Nonprofit and For-Profit Job-Training Service Providers." *Journal of Policy Analysis and Management* 19:233–61.

Heinrich, C. J., and L. E. Lynn, Jr. 2001. "Means and Ends: A Comparative Study of Empirical Methods for Investigating Governance and Performance." *Journal of Public Administration Research and Theory* 11:109.

Hildreth, W. B. 1993. "State and Local Governments as Borrowers: Strategic Choice and the Capital Market." *Public Administration Review* 53:41–49.

Holmes, M., and D. Shand. 1995. "Management Reform: Some Practitioner Perspectives on the Past Ten Years." *Governance* 8:551–78.

Huselid, M. A. 1995. "The Impact of Human Resource Management Practices on Turnover, Productivity, and Corporate Financial Performance." *Academy of Management Journal* 38:635–73.

Ingraham, P. W., P. G. Joyce, and A. K. Donahue. 2003. *Government Performance: Why Management Matters*. Baltimore: Johns Hopkins University Press.

Ingraham, P. W., and A. E. Kneedler. 2000a. "Dissecting the Black Box: Toward a Model and Measures of Government Management Performance." In J. L. Brudney, L. J. O'Toole, and H. G. Rainey, eds., *Advancing Public Management: New Developments in Theory Methods, and Practice*. Washington, D.C.: Georgetown University Press, 235–52.

———. 2000b. "Dissecting the Black Box Revisited: Characterizing Government Management Capacity. In C. J. Heinrich and L. E. Lynn, Jr., eds., *Models and Methods for the Empirical Study of Governance*. Washington, D.C.: Georgetown University Press, 292–318.

Ingraham, P. W., S. C. Selden, and D. Moynihan. 2000. "People and Performance: Challenges for the Future Public Service." *Public Administration Review* 60:54.

Joseph, J. C. 1994. *Debt Issuance and Management: A Guide for Smaller Governments*. Chicago: Government Finance Officers Association.

Kettl, D. F., and H. B. Milward. 1996. *The State of Public Management*. Baltimore: Johns Hopkins University Press.

Linder, S. H., and B. G. Peters. 1987. "A Design Perspective on Policy Implementation: The Fallacies of Misplaced Prescription." *Policy Studies Review* 6:459–75.

Lynn, L. E., Jr. 1997. "In Government, Does Management Matter? Explain." Panel presented at the Fourth National Public Management Research Conference, University of Georgia, Athens, October 30–November 1.

Lynn, L. E., Jr., C. J. Heinrich, and C. J. Hill. 2000a. "Governance and Performance: The Influence of Program Structure and Management on Job Training Partnership Act Program Outcomes." In C. J. Heinrich and L. E. Lynn, Jr., eds., *Governance and Performance: New Perspectives.* Washington, D.C.: Georgetown University Press, 68–108.

————. 2000b. "Studying Governance and Public Management: Challenges and Prospects." *Journal of Public Administration Research and Theory* 10:233.

————. 2000c. "Studying Governance and Public Management: Why? How?" In C. J. Heinrich and L. E. Lynn, Jr., eds., *Governance and Performance: New Perspectives.* Washington, D.C.: Georgetown University Press, 1–33.

Mandell, M. P. 1990. "Network Management: Strategic Behavior in the Public Sector." In R. W. Gage and M. P. Mandell, eds., *Strategies for Managing Intergovernmental Policies and Networks.* New York: Praeger, 29–51.

Mazmanian, D. A., and P. A. Sabatier. 1989. *Implementation and Public Policy.* Lanham, Md.: University Press of America.

Meier, K. J., and L. J. O'Toole, Jr. 2001a. "Management in Networks: A Market-Based Measure of Managerial Quality." Paper presented at the Sixth National Public Management Research Conference School of Public and Environmental Affairs, Indiana University, Bloomington, October 18–21.

————. 2001b. "Managerial Strategies and Behavior in Networks: A Model with Evidence from U.S. Education." *Journal of Public Administration Research and Theory* 11:271.

Miller, G. J. 1993. "Debt Management Networks." *Public Administration Review* 53:50–58.

Milward, H. B., and K. Provan. 2000. "Governing the Hollow State." *Journal of Public Administration Research and Theory* 10:359.

————. 1995. "A Preliminary Theory of Interorganizational Network Effectiveness: A Comparative Study of Four Community Mental Health Systems." *Administrative Sciences Quarterly* 40:1–33.

O'Toole, L. J., Jr. 1996. "Rational Choice and the Public Management of Interorganizational Networks." In D. F. Kettl and H. B. Milward, eds., *The State of Public Management.* Baltimore: Johns Hopkins University Press, 241–63.

O'Toole, L. J., Jr., and K. J. Meier. 2000. "Networks, Hierarchies, and Public Management: Modeling the Nonlinearities." In C. J. Heinrich and L. E. Lynn, Jr., eds., *Governance and Performance: New Perspectives.* Washington, D.C.: Georgetown University Press, 263–91.

————. 1999. "Modeling the Impact of Public Management: Implications of Structural Context." *Journal of Public Administration Research and Theory* 9:505–26.

Peters, T., and R. Waterman, Jr. 1982. *In Search of Excellence.* New York: Warner Books.

Pressman, J. L., and A. Wildavsky. 1984. *Implementation: How Great Expectations in Washington Are Dashed in Oakland.* Berkeley: University of California Press.

Provan, K., and H. B. Milward. 2001. "Do Networks Really Work? A Framework for Evaluating Public-Sector Organizational Networks." *Public Administration Review* 61:414.

————. 1998. "Principles for Controlling Agents: The Political Economy of Network Structure." *Journal of Public Administration Research and Theory* 8:203–22.

Rainey, H. G., and P. Steinbauer. 1999. "Galloping Elephants: Developing Elements of a Theory of Effective Government Organizations." *Journal of Public Administration Research and Theory* 9:1–32.

Robbins, M. D., and W. Simonsen. 2002. "Measuring Municipal Borrowing Costs: How Missing Cost Information Biases Interest Rate Calculations." *Public Budgeting and Finance* 22:46–59.

Robbins, M. D., W. Simonsen, and B. Jump. 2001. "Is TIC Always the Most Appropriate Cost of Capital Measure?" *Municipal Finance Journal* 22:1–14.

Sandfort J. R. 1998. "The Structural Impediments to Human Service Collaboration: The Case of Welfare Reform." *Social Service Review* 73:314–39.

Schein, E. H. 1992. *Organizational Culture and Leadership*, 2d ed. San Francisco: Jossey-Bass.

Schneider, S. K. 1988. "Intergovernmental Influences on Medicaid Program Expenditures." *Public Administration Review* 48:756–63.

Selden, S. C., S. Ammar, R. Wright, and W. S. Jacobson. 2000. "A New Approach to Assessing Performance of State Human Resource Management Systems: A Multi-Level Fuzzy Rule–Based System." *Review of Public Personnel Administration* 20 (3):58–74.

Selden, S. C., P. W. Ingraham, and W. S. Jacobson. 2001. "Human Resource Practices: Findings from a National Survey." *Public Administration Review* 61:598.

Simonsen, W., and L. Hill. 1999. "Municipal Bond Issuance: Is There Evidence of a Principal-Agent Problem?" *Public Budgeting and Finance* 18:71–100.

Simonsen, W., and M. D. Robbins. 1996. "Does It Make Any Difference Anymore? Competitive versus Negotiated Municipal Bond Issuance." *Public Administration Review* 56:57–64.

Snell, S. A., and J. W. Dean, Jr. 1992. "Integrated Manufacturing and Human Resource Management: A Human Capital Perspective." *Academy of Management Journal* 35:467–505.

Standard and Poor's Corporation. 1986. *Debt Ratings Criteria*. New York: Standard and Poor's Corporation.

Stone, P. M. 1994. "Bonds of Gold." *National Journal* 26:238.

Swiss, J. E. 1991. *Public Management Systems: Monitoring and Managing Government Performance*. Upper Saddle River, N.J.: Prentice Hall.

Thompson, J. D. 1967. *Organizations in Action*. New York: McGraw-Hill.

Thompson Financial Corporation, Thompson Financial SDC Platinum Global Public Finance New Issues Database. (Accessed January 8, 2001.)

Tsui, A. S., and L. R. Gomez-Mejia. 1988. "Evaluating Human Resource Management Effectiveness." In Lee Dyer, ed., *Human Resource Management: Evolving Roles and Responsibilities*. ASPA/BNA Series No. 1. Washington, D.C.: Bureau of National Affairs, 187–227.

U.S. Census Bureau. 2001. "United States State and Local Government Finances, by Level of Government, 1998–99" [http://www.census.gov]. (Accessed February 1, 2001.)

U.S. General Accounting Office. 2001. *Major Management Challenges and Program Risks: A Governmentwide Perspective*. GAO-01-241. Washington, D.C.: General Accounting Office.

———. 2000. *Human Capital: A Self-Assessment Checklist for Agency Leaders*. GAO/OCG-00-14G. Washington, D.C.: General Accounting Office.

Seven

Linking Dimensions of Public Sector Leadership to Performance

Patricia W. Ingraham • Jessica E. Sowa • Donald P. Moynihan

Lynn, Heinrich, and Hill (2000, 233) succinctly pose the key question under-lying the logic of governance: "How can public-sector regimes, agencies, pro-grams, and activities be organized and managed to achieve public purposes?" The issue of leadership features to an advanced degree many of the qualities that make assembling a literature on public governance difficult. That lead-ership matters is a truism attested to by numerous case studies and accepted by the majority of public administration scholars or practitioners. In fact, Behn (1998, 209) argues, "Leadership is not just a right of public managers. It is an obligation." Most recently a summary of empirical public management scholarship on performance identified leadership as an important independ-ent variable (Boyne 2003); however, differences in conceptualization and measurement of leadership means that the cumulative effect of this literature has not provided a clear consensus definition about what "good" or "suc-cessful" leadership really is, nor a consistent understanding of how leadership relates to administrative processes, and ultimately improves performance. In-deed, the study of leadership in public organizations has had something of a tar-pit quality: a great deal of discussion and struggles that sometimes achieve heroic proportion, but are ultimately unable to escape the morass of case de-tail, exceptionalism, and inability to generalize.

This is not to say that past studies have not been useful. They have con-tributed important lessons about individuals who created change and achieved better results for the organizations they led (Kaufman 1981; Lynn 1981; Doig and Hargrove 1990; Riccuci 1995). The insights they provide into leaders' values, strategies, and culture-building activities—as well as the politics of public leadership—are fundamental to understanding leadership. Two prob-lems emerge from these studies, however, problems that we are seeking to ad-dress in this chapter. First, they are personal portraits and describe personal attributes of a single leader. It is difficult to generalize from their conclusions to other public settings and other public leaders. Second, measures of success were—and continue to be—elusive. It might be added that the styles and strategies of the leaders described do not always fit well with the more diverse leadership pools of today. James Webb may have been exemplary in many ways, but his model of twenty-three-hour workdays and failure to balance work life with any semblance of family or other external interests may not be compelling to others, or realistic to some (Lambright 1995; Stivers 1997).

Whatever the difficulties in studying and drawing lessons about leadership might be, current pressures for increased accountability and results in government mandate that attention be focused on developing a more generalized understanding of how leadership operates in the public sector. It is necessary to understand what leaders do and how they do it; how individuals or teams behave to achieve better performance for their agencies and themselves. Linking leadership to performance and linking the performance of public organizations to greater accountability and better governance are concerns for elected officials, members of the public service, and for citizens. These are difficult problems and not easily amenable to systematic scrutiny or measurement. Yet the significance of leadership flows through many of the components of the governance framework underpinning the work in this volume. Lynn, Heinrich, and Hill (2000) explicitly identify leadership practices as falling primarily within the category of managerial roles and actions described in the reduced-form expression of the logic of governance. The model we present here largely follows this approach, by examining how leadership interacts with administrative systems. More broadly, however, we recognize that leadership is involved at other levels of model, dealing with external stakeholders, setting organizational mission, overseeing appropriate treatments, and attempting to shape formal structures and organizational culture. Indeed, it can be argued that leadership is essential to the exercise of authority in government, and any discussion of governance would be incomplete without it.

This chapter presents a new conceptual model of public sector leadership, which we call "grounded" or "integrative" leadership. The model of leadership presented here draws upon and is illustrated by findings of the Government Performance Project (GPP). The study focused on capacity building within each of the management systems studied, but also on the ability to create integrating linkages across these systems, thus building capacity government-wide. We anticipated that two major systems—information technology and managing for results—would provide the most likely linking mechanisms. We found, in fact, that financial management systems and budgets frequently served the same function. We also found that there were distinct differences in the ability to create integrative capacity between the high performance governments in our study and those that did not do well (Gill and Meier 2001; Moynihan and Ingraham 2003). One of the most significant differences, we found, was the presence and quality of leadership (Ingraham 2001). Before we explain this model in further detail, the following section describes previous studies of leadership that have illuminated some of the leadership behaviors and styles that inform our approach.

Choices about Leadership Styles and Behaviors

There are almost as many models of leadership as studies on the subject. Scholars have explored the personal characteristics of leaders (a trait-based approach), the relationships between leaders and subordinates (leader-member exchange), the role of leadership in organizational change, and the differing effectiveness of various leadership styles in different settings and environments (Likert 1961; Stogdill 1974; Yukl 1998; Atwater et al. 1999; Ulrich, Zenger, and Smallwood 1999).

Very generally, however, conceptual models of leadership style and behavior can be summarized into four broad categories. The first category is the traditionally hierarchical, command-control model commonly associated with large bureaucratic entities, a model that emphasizes rules, regulations, structure, and stability. Leadership, per se, is related to the authoritative giving of orders and the expectation that those orders (or decisions) will be followed (or implemented). In Follett's (1997 [1926]) terms, the relationship between leader and subordinates is one of "power over," not "power with." Power or authority sharing diminishes the quality and the strength of this directive leadership; participation in the decision-making process is limited.

Another common model, transactional leadership, focuses on the leader/subordinate exchange in the interests of rewarding desirable behavior (in pursuit of leader or organizational goals) and punishing or engaging in corrective action to discourage behavior and activity not deemed productive (Bass 1985). In public organizational terms, behavior and characteristics of transactional leaders are closely related to adherence to procedures and commitment to process; internal organizational relationships reflect essentially standardized patterns. Although the leader-member relationship under transactional leadership is clearly not participative or shared leadership, the needs or actions of the subordinates are recognized as influencing the actions of the leader in this model.

Transformational leadership (Bass 1985) moves beyond the hierarchical and transactional leadership models, focusing more proactively on linking leadership or leader behavior to positive change. In transformational leadership the personal characteristics of the leader (including charisma), individualized consideration of follower needs, the ability to view problems or objectives from multiple perspectives, and the ability to communicate a vision or a path/purpose to change are significant factors, inspiring followers to work harder and enact change in their daily operations. Although transactional and transformational behavior are not completely separable patterns—effective leadership behavior and style often must be contingent on context—studies of transformational leadership have produced some empirical evidence that suggests that transformational behavior can be linked to higher organizational commitment, productivity, and performance in ways that transactional behavior cannot (Hater and Bass 1988; Yammarino and Bass 1990; Howell and Avolio 1993; Bycio, Hackett, and Allen 1995; Sosik, Avolio, and Kahai 1997, Waldman et al. 2001).

Because transformational leadership places an emphasis on change and innovation, it can be argued that this model of leadership coincides with the values inherent in models of administrative and organizational change underpinning many public sector reform efforts (Halligan 2004; Osborne and Gaebler 1992; Pollitt and Bouckaert 2000). Numerous scholars have produced evidence of increased innovation or entrepreneurial leadership on the part of managers and employees in all levels of public organizations, with some evidence of increased public sector effectiveness and efficiency (Sanders 1998; Thompson 1998; Borins 2000).

However popular, transformational leadership theories and behaviors are currently being challenged by new models of organizational structure emphasizing nearly constant change, changed patterns of communication, shared horizontal authority and responsibility, and the challenge presented to leadership within organizations whose boundaries are open to complex and often unpredictable pressures and demands (Milward and Provan 2000). Still other perspectives focus specifically on leadership in such settings and argue that effective leadership is not a free-floating phenomenon or based on transitory charisma, but must be more specifically linked to organizational performance (Ulrich, Zenger, and Smallwood 1999). Therefore, integrative leadership perspectives argue that leadership is a function of both leader attributes and the results that leaders (or leadership teams) can create by altering organizational conditions and capacities. Ulrich, Zenger, and Smallwood (1999) define successful leaders as those that pursue a framework that includes setting direction clearly, demonstrating personal character, mobilizing individual commitment, and creating what they call "organizational capability."

Many of the concepts included in this leadership model ring particularly true for public leaders, who are often faced with managing change created and directed externally. Public leaders depend upon a systemic organizational base for which they have only partial authority. In most public organizations, political (elected or appointed) leaders with short tenures must work with career civil servant leaders, with much longer tenure and, frequently, a different sense of the rules of the game (Ingraham, Thompson, and Eisenberg 1995). All public leaders must, however, utilize and build upon these conditions if critical organizational capacities are to be created and higher levels of performance achieved. Critical systemic capacities to be utilized in this regard include the organization's human capital, its internal management capabilities, information and knowledge management skills, and the ability of the organization and its members to evaluate and learn from previous efforts and experience. A key role of the leader is to integrate all of these into broader organizational strength and potential, while recognizing that leadership authority with regard to management change will to some degree be constrained. Building for future capacity as well as present performance is a continuing challenge, but the ability to do so is a core characteristic of a public sector integrative leadership model.

Forging the Links to Performance in the Public Service: The Changing Face of Leadership

A discussion of leadership in the public sector must address the rethinking of the definition of effectiveness or success. Demands for better accountability and improved performance have resulted in administrative reforms that strongly emphasize leadership and leadership development in many governments around the world (Pollitt and Bouckaert 2000). A primary target of such efforts—often lumped together as "new public management" reforms—is the narrow traditional model of leadership found in many national bureaucracies. In this pattern, sometimes referred to as "growing your own" leaders, leadership capacity occurs or develops in tandem with ever-increasing skills and expertise in program, policy, or administrative functions. Long-term service to the organization results in promotion up through narrow "stovepipes" of expertise or experience and culminates over time in promotion to management, upper-management, and finally senior leadership positions. Leadership development and training opportunities occur at specific promotion points. The strong points of this pattern include long-term development of public service values and creation of an intense institutional knowledge and memory base about specific programs, policies, and administrative practices. But there are two main drawbacks to this model. The first is that downsizing of the public sector or the relative attractiveness of private organizations for job candidates creates risks for the "grow-your-own" approach. A combination of both these factors has led to a well-documented crisis of human capital in the federal government and a growing concern about where the next generation of public leaders will come from (U.S. Office of Management and Budget 2001; U.S. General Accounting Office 2003). The second drawback of the model is its reliance on the stove-piped structures that fostered its growth and the constraints they place on managers. Integrating across boxes, structures, or systems is simply not a consideration (Ingraham and Donahue 2000).

Some early reforms, such as the creation of senior executive services in many countries, were intended to combat the narrow organizational and performance perspectives of the "grow-your-own" model. Better management skills, greater ability to bridge organizational boundaries and to communicate more effectively with elected officials and other public leaders, and an improved capacity for creative leadership skills were perceived to be necessary for more effective leadership in the public service. In addition, because members of the senior executive services were more directly accountable to political officials—and therefore also to external measures of performance—important early connections between leadership and performance were established (Ingraham 2001).

In effect, the reforms and their proponents argued that neither hierarchical nor transactional models of leadership behavior and performance reflected the real needs of modern public service and governance. In some way, a move toward more transformational, performance-based leaders and leadership development was necessary. Much of the rationale for the reforms directed at the higher service was based on the assumption that there was some tension between public service based values and commitment—valued and strengthened in the "grow-your-own" models—and the new demands for performance.

Many national governments initially addressed this tension not only by hiring in, but also by explicitly adopting private sector contract models for an executive cadre of the public service. New discretionary authority and flexibilities were created to facilitate performance-based behavior and to more accurately reflect conditions found in private sector organizations. Recruiting into executive positions from outside the public sector was not just one part of, but critical to, the creation of more effective leaders and higher levels of performance, institutionalizing the idea that competition and performance mattered more than continuity and traditional public sector values. Reforms in Canada, New Zealand, the United Kingdom, and the Netherlands are examples. Just as the "grow-your-own" approach has limited ability to produce the broad strategic perspective now deemed significant, however, the practice of hiring in or buying leadership talent produces limited capabilities in terms of core public service values. Further, the blending of internal and external talents and perspectives in a leadership cadre, while theoretically energizing and refreshing, has proved to be somewhat difficult in practice (Halligan 2004).

Although such performance reforms have not been abandoned, more recent developments place leadership in a more complex and more specifically public context. New perspectives on both performance and on the role of leaders in achieving high performance results emphasize the *preconditions* for performance and the extent to which leaders and managers have the necessary tools, skills, and organizational capability to attain performance objectives. Improved performance, in other words, relies upon not just leadership, but also a combination of factors. The integration of these factors and the synergy among them contribute to an improved performance dynamic and to positive performance potential. In this perspective, capacity assumes substantial significance as an interim objective that effective leaders can work to develop, but also as an effective launch pad for improved performance in the longer term. This conceptualization of leadership encompasses what we are referring to as the "public sector integrative leadership model."

Public Sector Integrative Leadership

The conceptual model presented in the following section is derived both from the work of scholars focused on the linkages between leadership and results and the work of public management scholars focused on the construction of management capacity in public organizations in the United States (Ulrich, Zenger, and Smallwood 1999; Ingraham and Donahue 2000; Ingraham, Joyce, and Donahue 2003). In developing a model of public management capacity, Ingraham and Donahue (2000) specifically adopt an integrated perspective concerning management capacity, arguing that a core component of capacity is created by the management systems found in most governments: human resource management, financial management, infrastructure management, and information technology. Results-based management is identified as fundamental to the ability to create improved performance and integrate these management systems around a common set of goals. How leadership develops, drives, and fosters this results-based management is at the core of our model of public sector leadership, with the focus on how leaders promote and create improved organizational capacity and performance potential.

This model of leadership is based upon the assumption that leaders in the public sector necessarily operate in some ways that are different from their private sector counterparts. In the private sector, leaders frequently have the flexibility and authority to create organizations that reflect their vision. In the public sector, these conditions must be created and the ability to do so is often constrained. Further, leaders in public organizations must work to ensure that the systems put in place or the capacity created can survive the movement of political tides.

Data and Methodology

In developing a public sector integrative model of leadership, we utilized data collected on managing for results and performance management systems in state governments. Information and conclusions about leadership were drawn from questions relating to sources and/or incentives for change, framing visions for creating capacity and improving performance, understanding of overall organizational goals and objectives, and managing for results.

Both public managers and scholars are more interested in learning from those who perform well more than from those who perform poorly (Gill and Meier 2001). Accordingly, we began our analysis by contrasting states that received a B+ or higher grade in the GPP assessment of managing for results practices in 2000 with those that received the lowest grades. Table 7.1 presents the distribution of both the managing for results and overall grades given to the high-performing states.

Table 7.1
Cases Selected, Managing for Results Grades, and Overall Capacity Grades

Case	Managing for Results Grade	Overall Grade
Michigan	B+	A–
Washington	A–	A–
Missouri	A–	B+
Utah	B+	A–
Virginia	A–	B+

The data used in this chapter—from structured open-ended survey questions, semistructured interviews, and extensive document review—were analyzed through both inductive and deductive coding (Strauss and Corbin 1990; Miles and Huberman 1994). The data were reviewed and the general categories comprising the stages of the conceptual model were developed. These categories comprised the initial coding scheme for analysis using the computer software program QSR NUDIST (Gahan and Hannibal 1998). The QSR NUDIST software allows for systematic coding of qualitative data and continuing modification of the coding structure as new information and understandings are developed from the data. Therefore, although the stages of the conceptual model were in place when we conducted the analysis, we allowed the data to surface the exploratory findings that will be presented in the next section.

The Team-Based Character of Integrative Leadership

A basic assumption that underpins our model is that leadership interacts with management systems as an ongoing process. There is no clear beginning or end, although it may be possible to identify points of intervention. This point is apparent in the conceptual model of public sector integrative leadership illustrated in figure 7.1.

A second assumption illustrated in figure 7.1 is that leadership is not exclusive to any particular part of the organizational hierarchy. Although studies of leadership have emphasized the leader at the top of the organization as crucial to the development of a long-term vision, leadership can also come from other levels of the organization. Essentially, leadership has the potential to be exercised anywhere authority exists. The separation of political powers, combined with hierarchical organizational structure, therefore creates multiple opportunities for leadership in the U.S. setting. For multiple actors to exert effective leadership requires a team-based approach, emphasizing different abilities to respond to external demands, different kinds of expertise, and different capacities and timetables for change. The leadership teams that

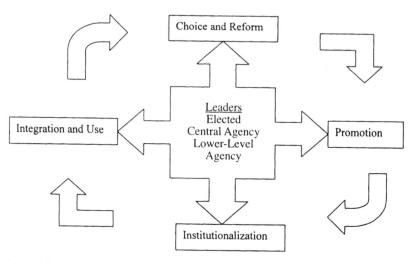

Figure 7.1
Integrative Model of Leadership

emerge may be political, bureaucratic, or a mix of individuals from both political and bureaucratic positions.

Evidence from the GPP supported this team-based approach. No single
leader can move a mountain. Instead, leadership needs to be at several levels
of the organization to create capacity and to achieve results. Although this
finding does not suggest that top-level leadership is unimportant, in our cases,
a mixture of political and bureaucratic leaders tended to work together, such
as governors or high-profile legislators and managers at different levels of the
government. An insight of the implementation literature was replayed in the
GPP findings: although political leaders seek to build systems designed to enable managers to be more flexible and effective, they can do so only with the
participation and assistance of managers and operating staff. Managers will
assume some leadership responsibilities in being more proactive, more accountable, and more directly connected to organizational performance. They
can be effective only if leaders are willing to share authority and responsibility. Jointness of managing and leading is one contributor to improved organizational capacity for change and performance, but assumes unusual skills
for both leaders and managers.

Apart from agency employees, senior leaders in the executive branch also
sought other reliable supporting actors, including central agency staff and external reform committees. Central agencies played a key role in this regard. A
designated central agency can reaffirm and lead the movement for better performance; it can communicate the vision and major goals of the government's
plan to achieve good government. The Commonwealth of Virginia, which has

term limits for its governor, has created strong administrative leadership in both financial management and planning to link gubernatorial visions with institutional strengths of state agencies and to link both to results-based management. Each of the other four high-performing states examined in this chapter have a similar state agency that coordinates the performance improvement efforts of these governments.[1]

Our analysis demonstrated that there are stages, or steps, in the systematic building of capacity that recurred across the high-capacity governments. They include system choice and reform; promotion of the vision and system; institutionalization and integration and use.

Step 1: System Choice and Reform

All governments have existing management systems in place, and the first choice that leaders will make is whether and how to adjust those systems. System choice is the decision to create a new management system or reform an existing one. Even the most effective system requires oversight. Not adjusting management systems, whether out of indifference or satisfaction, is essentially a leadership choice that existing systems are adequate. In recent years, however, leaders have tended toward deciding to change existing systems. Sometimes these changes are prompted by vague election promises to combat the shortcomings of bureaucracy. In seeking to fine-tune ideas about just what needs to be changed, leaders will frequently look to central agency staff or others for specific ideas about how to reform government. Such ideas will always exist, but it usually takes the willingness of a policy entrepreneur to choose to take on reform as an issue and to spend political capital on it before major change occurs (Kingdon 1984). Of course, it is also possible for agency level leaders to seek to adjust management systems within their agencies, but the constraints of state financial and personnel controls mean the impact may be limited.

Two types of decisions are made during this stage. One involves defining the governance problems that require a new or reformed system; the other involves defining the management solution. The GPP and others have found that the in the last decade the major governance problem for state governments was defined in terms of poor performance of bureaucracy. Most prominent among the perceived solutions was performance information systems that supported the creation of strategic goals and performance measures (Brudney, Hebert, and Wright 1999; Moynihan and Ingraham 2003).

In the high-performing governments, we found that executive branch elected officials were leaders in choosing, promoting, and driving the establishment of managing for results systems. In Washington, Governor Gary Locke entered office in 1997 with both a clear management agenda and a policy agenda. He consistently emphasized the importance of results in the governance process and promoted numerous results-based reforms, including legislation on performance-based budgeting. The top-level leadership can shore up support for results-based management and can be the driving force to create the means to monitor or direct this management, such as the establishment by the late Governor Mel Carnahan of a commission on management and productivity to oversee the movement to improve government efficiency in Missouri.

As noted above, however, teamwork is crucial. Top-level leadership may be necessary in making definitive choices to reform, but it does not ensure that results-based management will fully take hold in a government or that progress toward improved performance will be achieved. Political leadership, due to electoral tides or legislative requirement, can be transitory and cannot be assumed to be a constant support. Therefore, among the high performers, there is demonstrated action to involve departments and employees in the process of setting priorities and developing the performance measures that they will use to drive their actions. It is clear that, although political leaders may set the stage and agency level leaders may inspire their employees to create innovations directed toward the achievement of better performance, true results-based management and the creation of capacity to achieve results occur when there is cooperation and shared authority between both political and bureaucratic leaders.

Step 2: Promotion of the Vision and Systems

The next step in our model of public sector integrative leadership is promotion of a clear message. In changing organizations, that message is often one of changed expectations and new objectives. The promotion generally involves three substeps: (1) message creation, (2) message translation, and (3) message transmission. Message creation is similar to the drafting of a vision or mission or the setting of direction as articulated by advocates of strategic management. In the case of the current performance movement within the public sector, we argue message creation has generally proclaimed the commitment of the leader or leadership team to higher performing, more effective government. Leaders will communicate the choice of a performance framework and the particular strategic goals it seeks to achieve. More broadly, leaders will create or reinforce organizational values and norms associated with the idea of effectiveness. The nature of these values and the form that they take for each organization may be somewhat individualized; however, overall the espoused values underpinning many current public sector reforms are similar: performance, results, value-for-money, customer service, responsiveness, and efficiency.

Message translation involves taking actions to make this vision of better government a more concrete reality, setting priorities for the achievement of better results or performance, and developing reforms and strategies that will implement the message. Finally, message transmission involves publicizing the message, making it available to those who will be involved in the implementation of the vision of good government. The actions involved in message transmission generally include making it clear that management is a priority. Capacity does not evolve overnight and, as many studies of administrative reform have demonstrated, does not often succeed through fiat. Those who are to be enlisted in the implementation of the message and the creation of this new capacity directed toward the achievement of results must be persuaded as to the efficacy of this message or vision. Therefore, the message must be transmitted to all of those individuals in the organizations whose cooperation is essential for success (Denhardt and Denhardt 1999). One leader interviewed during the GPP analysis summed it up by saying, "Communicate, communicate, communicate. And when you think you can't bear to hear yourself say it one more time, say it one more time."

In addition, for public organizations, the message also must be transmitted externally. Getting the message to the citizenry to convince them of the importance of the movement toward achieving higher performance and to enlist their support and even assistance in the development of priorities for good government is another important aspect of the promotion role of the leader or leadership team. Enlisting the support of the citizenry will allow for another line of defense to assist in the next stage of the model, institutionalization of the systems or capacity for high performance.

Another lesson from the high-performing states is that leaders' promotion of high-capacity internal systems must be sustained. The fundamental message here was "build while changing." In the high-performing states, there are numerous examples of the promotion of the effort to achieve better results in government operations, while reinforcing what works well. The first step in each of these high-performing states is the need to get the message out to the citizens. In each of these cases, the elected leaders (usually governors) generally began to create momentum for managing for results by emphasizing the need for consistently high performance in high-profile speeches and public meetings, using such forums as the State Address, their inaugural addresses, and the publication of the annual executive budget. In addition, this message was then reiterated through numerous documents produced by these governments, including budgets, strategic plans, and performance reports. These reports were disseminated through many different venues, including the media, government publications, and the Internet. These dissemination efforts generally focused both within the government and to outside parties, with such examples as the monthly newsletter, *Capitol Connections*, which is distributed to all Utah managers and employees and describes the vision of the state and highlights excellent performance, Missouri's "Show Me Results" website, which outlines the vision for results in Missouri, and the use of websites and public mailing in Virginia, Michigan, and Washington.[2]

In addition, in each of these high-performing states, leadership has taken steps to ensure that the citizenry is both the recipient of these promotional activities and is involved in the creation of them. The emerging concerns with the link between performance and governance—rather than the more simple definition of performance as productivity—have placed the citizen and citizen satisfaction with public performance very squarely into the effective leadership equation. For leaders of public organizations, this broad external—sometimes instantaneous via the Web—evaluation of organizational performance is a new dimension. In this setting, organizational boundaries and constraints alone do not define parameters for performance; citizen expectations also contribute. The need for effective communication, listening, and learning is exponentially increased. The ability of leaders to acquire, process, disseminate, and use good information effectively, while always significant, becomes even more critical. Each of these high-performing states has annual citizen surveys in order to understand how their citizens feel about the progress of the governments toward improved results. In addition, each of these states operate multiple citizen advisory boards connected to many of their departments to provide forums for citizens to become involved in government and to get their views and concerns addressed.

Step 3: Institutionalization

Once the leader or the leadership team has created the message that high performance is a priority for the public organizations and has established the plans and priorities that underlie the capacity they wish to build, the next step in the leadership process is to take action that will lead to the institutionalization of the message. Because the term has taken on many meanings, it is worth clarifying what we mean by "institutionalization." In the context of management systems, institutionalization means the implementation of appropriate rules and procedures as a matter of routine.

This institutionalization may take many forms, but the inherent characteristic underlying any action promoting institutionalization must be that the action conveys that building these systems is a priority and that the systems should be embraced by all involved in the operation of the organizations. Moynihan and Ingraham (2004) find that the level of the governor's involvement in strategic planning process led executive branch officials to take performance information more seriously and use it in their decision-making processes. Some forms of institutionalization may include such actions as formal codification of management systems, process or reporting requirements through legislation, administrative regulations or executive orders, formalized training processes to assist employees in embracing and utilizing these systems, and agency-level reinvention laboratories that allow front-line employees to experiment with different ways to achieve the overall vision.

The variety among state governments implementing managing for results, and even the high-performers, suggests that, although there is not necessarily one best system or one best way to create capacity, a key factor lies in how the leadership institutionalizes the process. Among all of the cases, there are a variety of approaches to results-based government. Some states focus on using the executive budget or the budget process as a strategic method of ensuring that performance is a clear focus for agencies. Others have separate strategic planning systems for managing for results, including both government-wide and agency-level plans. The most important choices undertaken by these high-performing states do not lay in the system that they choose, but in how they put that system into operation and how they institutionalize the system in the agencies of government to create constant change and innovation in the effort to achieve improved performance. One key aspect of institutionalization is the formalization of the systems through legislation or other methods of formal recognition. Virtually all states now have formal legislative or administrative requirements for managing for results on the books; high-performers have implemented them, and the leaders have taken responsibility for effective implementation (Moynihan and Ingraham 2003).

Finally, a key aspect of institutionalization is to create systematic ways to observe and improve system capacity. All of the high-performers produce annual performance reports to track the progress of agencies and departments toward results. In addition, performance audits are in place not only to verify data but also to advise agencies on the performance framework system and ways to improve outcomes. Other leaders have instituted practices to ensure that constant learning occurs to improve performance. Leaders in the high-performing states have demonstrated that it is not sufficient to simply create a system and assume that performance will improve; creating management capacity requires care and monitoring by the leadership to ensure that progress will be made toward improved performance.

Step 4: Integration and Use

The fourth step of the public sector integrative leadership model involves putting the systems or the created capacity to use. If leaders promote and institutionalize a new system but then do not use it or pay attention to it, the previous efforts lose credibility in the view of managers. The leader or leadership team can use the management systems or management capacity to make decisions designed to achieve better government action. In the case of managing for results systems, this implies using performance information to make corrective changes to programs or to enact programs where there is an identified deficiency. But leaders also need to regularly assess system capacity and integration. Leaders need to be willing to ask, "How well are our systems working? Can they be improved? Can we better coordinate these systems?" Again, the insights and information that arise from central agency staff and agency managers are crucial. Leaders who are willing to undertake such inquiries recognize the ongoing nature of integrative leadership and will, sooner or later, return to the first stage of our model: making decisions about whether and how to adjust a management system.

Integration is the most difficult step of the leadership process because it requires a level of continued dedication and attention to management matters rare even among the best-intentioned reformers. It also calls on leaders to think about management not in terms of single, stove-piped systems that work in isolation, but in terms of interconnected systems that require coordination (Poocharoen and Ingraham, forthcoming). It needs, therefore, to reward coordination and teamwork.

The strongest evidence of integration comes from efforts to align managing for results with human resources and financial management systems. Efforts to integrate performance management with financial management systems seek to inform resource allocation decisions. This is the concept underlying the Government Performance and Results Act in the federal government (U.S. Office of Management and Budget 2001). Among the state high-performers, all have sought similar integration of the financial management and budget systems to drive performance. Virginia is clear about their choice of budget as primary driver, noting in the GPP survey, "You create one excellent system and others will follow." In Virginia, Washington, and Michigan, the budget process, strategic planning, and performance reporting are part of the same system. Most states seek to make some sort of link between performance information and the budget process, but even the high-performers were frank in admitting that building links between performance information and budget decisions was a challenge.

There are also efforts to integrate human resource management systems with managing for results, with the goal of motivating and rewarding employee performance that aligns with the goals and priorities established by the leader or the leadership team. In each of these high-performers, there is evidence that leaders have promoted the integration of their performance measurement and management systems with their human resource management systems in order to improve performance. Although creating strategic planning and performance management systems is a necessary step toward tracking the performance of government agencies, the leaders in these high-performers realize that they must take these systems a step further in order to promote their use and to achieve results. Integration of the performance management system with their human resource system was demonstrated by use of performance information in employee evaluations and pay-for-performance plans. In the state of Washington, the governor created annual performance agreements between himself and his cabinet to focus their attention on key strategic goals and cascade those goals down to the agency level.

Another potential tool to enable integration across systems is the use of information and the enhanced ability of governments to store and disseminate up-to-date information (especially performance information) through information technology. Integration implies that information technology systems reflect a cross-system perspective, providing decision makers with a broad range of performance and other types of information in as timely a manner as is feasible (Moynihan and Ingraham, 2004). Each of the high-performers identified the important role that information technology systems can play in supporting and energizing the integration of management systems.

Conclusion

In this chapter, we have argued that it is necessary to rethink public sector leadership and that the attention of public management scholars should be focused on understanding how leadership interacts with capacity to achieve higher performance in government. Leadership represents a crucial piece of the puzzle in exploring government performance and therefore is integral to exploring the governance framework presented by Lynn, Heinrich, and Hill (2000). In seeking to contribute to this empirical study of governance, by focusing on leadership in action, we have presented a new conceptual model focused on leadership interaction with administrative systems rather than personality traits, a model that seeks to show how leaders can undertake certain steps to put in place lasting management infrastructures to promote better results into the future. The simple fact that leadership is frequently referenced as crucial to performance lends credence to our argument that a better understanding of leadership is the next step in developing a more complete and nuanced understanding of management and performance in public organizations.

Evidence about public sector leadership action, drawn from a comparison of states with strong management systems to those with low capacity, informs this model. Clearly, more research is needed, with one of the next steps being to develop an understanding of the attributes of the leadership teams, how they form, and how they work and stay together. In addition, it is important to note that the stages in this model may not always work in a linear progression, but will overlap or occur simultaneously.

Constant promotion and institutionalization appear to be crucial in distinguishing the high performers from the low. The standout lesson in this regard is that building commitment to priority actions, and communicating constantly about their significance, is a constant characteristic of systems with strong systems and leaders. In a public setting, as the conceptual model presented here makes clear, the need for a team approach with the ability to span electoral cycles and membership changes is also central.

The empirical study of governance pursued by many public management scholars today has illuminated many new paths and avenues for developing a better understanding of the way in which public authority is exercised and the way in which institutions and actions shape government performance and accountability (Heinrich and Lynn 2000; Lynn, Heinrich, and Hill 2001; Hill and Lynn 2004). With this chapter, we have sought to add leadership to the many facets of governance that should be modeled and measured to better develop our scholarly understandings of governance and better improve government operation.

Notes

1. The agencies are, respectively, the Washington Office of Financial Management, the Michigan State Government Affairs Office and the State Budget Office, the Missouri Center for Performance and Innovation, and the Utah Office of Planning and Budget.

2. A particularly creative way to get the governor's strategic vision for performance out to the citizenry was developed by Missouri, who includes a description of the "Show Me Results" vision in an annual tax booklet mailed to all citizens at tax time by the Department of Revenue.

References

Atwater, Leanne E., Shelley D. Dionne, Bruce Avolio, John F. Camobreco, and Alan W. Lau. 1999. "A Longitudinal Study of the Leadership Development Process: Individual Differences Predicting Leader Effectiveness." *Human Relations* 52:1543–62.

Bass, Bernard M. 1985. *Leadership and Performance beyond Expectations.* New York: Free Press.

Behn, Robert D. 1998. "What Right Do Public Managers Have to Lead?" Symposium: Leadership, Democracy, and the New Public Management. *Public Administration Review* 58:209–25.

Borins, Sanford. 2000. "Loose Cannons and Rule Breakers, or Enterprising Leaders? Some Evidence about Innovative Public Managers." *Public Administration Review* 60:498–509.

Boyne, George. 2003. "Sources of Public Improvement: A Critical Review and Research Agenda." *Journal of Public Administration Research and Theory* 13:367–94.

Bycio, Peter, Rick D. Hackett, and Joyce S. Allen. 1995. "Further Assessments of Bass's (1985) Conceptualization of Transactional and Transformational Leadership." *Journal of Applied Psychology* 80:468–78.

Brudney, Jeffrey L., F. Ted Hebert, and Deil S. Wright. 1999. "Reinventing Government in the American States: Measuring and Explaining Administrative Reform." *Public Administration Review* 59:19–30.

Denhardt, Robert B., and Janet Vinzant Denhardt. 1999. *Leadership for Change: Case Studies in American Local Government.* Arlington, Va.: PriceWaterhouseCooper.

Doig, Jameson W., and Edwin C. Hargrove, eds. 1990. *Leadership and Innovation: Entrepreneurs in Government.* Baltimore: Johns Hopkins University Press.

Follett, Mary P. 1997 [1926]. "The Giving of Orders." In Jay M. Shafritz and Albert C. Hyde, eds., *Classics of Public Administration,* 4th ed. Fort Worth, Tex.: Harcourt Brace College, 53–61.

Gahan, Celia, and Mike Hannibal. 1998. *Doing Qualitative Research Using QSR Nudist.* London: Sage.

Gill, Jeff, and Kenneth J. Meier. 2001. "Ralph's Pretty-Good Grocery versus Ralph's Super Market: Separating Excellent Agencies from the Good Ones." *Public Administration Review* 61:9–17.

Halligan, John, ed. 2004. *Civil Service Systems in Anglo-American Countries*. London: Edward Elgar.

Hater, John J., and Bernard M. Bass. 1988. "Superiors' Evaluations and Subordinates' Perceptions of Transformational and Transactional Leadership." *Journal of Applied Psychology* 73:695–702.

Hill, Carolyn J., and Laurence E. Lynn, Jr. 2004. "Governance and Public Management: An Introduction." *Journal of Policy Analysis and Management* 23:3–11.

Heinrich, Carolyn J., and Laurence E. Lynn, Jr., eds. 2000. *Governance and Performance: New Perspectives*. Washington, D.C.: Georgetown University Press.

Howell, Jane M., and Bruce J. Avolio. 1993. "Transformational Leadership, Transactional Leadership, Locus of Control, and Support for Innovation: Key Predictors of Consolidated-Business Unit Performance." *Journal of Applied Psychology* 78:891–902.

Ingraham, Patricia W. 2001. "Linking Leadership to Performance in Public Organizations." Paper presented at the Human Resources Management Conference of the Organization for Economic Cooperation and Development, Paris, June 27–29.

Ingraham, Patricia W., Phillip G. Joyce, and Amy Kneedler Donahue. 2003. *Government Performance: Why Management Matters*. Baltimore: Johns Hopkins University Press.

Ingraham, Patricia W., and Amy Kneedler Donahue. 2000. "Dissecting the Black Box Revisited: Characterizing Government Management Capacity." In Carolyn J. Heinrich and Laurence E. Lynn, Jr., eds., *Governance and Performance: New Perspectives*. Washington, D.C.: Georgetown University Press, 292–318.

Ingraham, Patricia W., James R. Thompson, and E. F. Eisenberg. 1995. "Political Management Strategies and Political/Career Relationships: Where Are We Now in the Federal Government?" *Public Administration Review* 55:263–72.

Kaufman, Herbert. 1981. *The Administrative Behavior of Federal Bureau Chiefs*. Washington, D.C.: Brookings Institution.

Kingdon, John. 1984. *Agenda, Alternatives, and Public Policies*. Boston: Little, Brown.

Lambright, W. Henry. 1995. *Powering Apollo: James E. Webb of NASA*. Baltimore: John Hopkins University Press.

Likert, Rensis. 1961. *New Patterns of Management*. New York: McGraw Hill.

Lynn, Laurence E., Jr. 1981. *Managing the Public's Business: The Job of the Government Executive*. New York: Basic Books.

Lynn, Laurence E., Jr., Carolyn J. Heinrich, and Carolyn J. Hill. 2001. *Improving Governance: A New Logic for Empirical Research*. Washington, D.C.: Georgetown University Press.

———. 2000. "Studying Governance and Public Management: Why? How?" In Carolyn J. Heinrich and Laurence E. Lynn, Jr., eds., *Governance and Performance: New Perspectives*. Washington, D.C.: Georgetown University Press, 1–33.

Miles, Matthew B., and A. Michael Huberman. 1994. *Qualitative Data Analysis*, 2d ed. Thousand Oaks, Calif.: Sage.

Milward, H. Brinton, and Keith G. Provan. 2000. "Governing the Hollow State." *Journal of Public Administration Research and Theory* 10:359–80.

Moynihan, Donald P. and Patricia W. Ingraham. 2004. "Integrative Leadership in the Public Sector: A Model of Performance Information Use." *Administration & Society* 38:4 (September):427–53.

———. 2003. "Look for the Silver Lining: When Performance Based Accountability Systems Work." *Journal of Public Administration Research and Theory* 13:469–90.

Osborne, David, and Ted Gaebler. 1992. *Reinventing Government: How the Entrepreneurial Spirit Is Transforming the Public Sector*. Reading, Mass.: Addison Wesley Longman.

Pollitt, Christopher, and Geert Bouckaert. 2000. *Public Management Reform: A Comparative Analysis*. New York: Oxford University Press.

Poocharoen, Ora-Orn, and Patricia W. Ingraham. Forthcoming. "When Does Integration Happen?" In Patricia W. Ingraham, ed., *In Pursuit of Performance: Management Systems in State and Local Government*. Baltimore: Johns Hopkins University Press.

Riccucci, Norma. 1995. *Unsung Heroes: Federal Execucrats Making a Difference*. Washington, D.C.: Georgetown University Press.

Sanders, Ronald P. 1998. "Heroes of the Revolution: Characteristics and Strategies of Reinvention Leaders." In Patricia W. Ingraham, James R. Thompson, and Ronald P. Sanders, eds., *Transforming Government: Lessons from the Reinvention Laboratories*. San Francisco: Jossey-Bass, 29–57.

Sosik, John J., Bruce J. Avolio, and Surinder S. Kahai. 1997. "Effects of Leadership Style and Anonymity on Group Potency and Effectiveness in a Group Decision Support System Environment." *Journal of Applied Psychology* 82:89–103.

Stivers, Camilla. 1997. "Leadership: Myth and Vision." *International Journal of Public Administration* 20:881–86.

Stogdill, Ralph M. 1974. *Handbook of Leadership: A Survey of the Literature*. New York: Free Press.

Strauss, Anselm L., and Juliet M. Corbin. 1990. *Basics of Qualitative Research: Grounded Theory Procedures and Techniques*. Newbury Park, Calif.: Sage.

Thompson, James R. 1998. "Ferment on the Front Lines: Devising New Modes of Organizing." In Patricia W. Ingraham, James R. Thompson, and Ronald P. Sanders, eds., *Transforming Government: Lessons from the Reinvention Laboratories*. San Francisco: Jossey-Bass, 5–28.

Ulrich, Dave, Jack Zenger, and Norman Smallwood. 1999. *Results-Based Leadership*. Boston: Harvard Business School Press.

U.S. General Accounting Office. 2003. *High Risk Series: Strategic Human Capital Management*. GAO-03-120. Washington, D.C.: U.S. General Accounting Office.

U.S. Office of Management and Budget. 2001. *The President's Management Agenda*. Washington, D.C.: U.S. Office of Management and Budget.

Waldman, David A., Gabriel G. Ramirez, Robert J. House, and Phanish Puranam. 2001. "Does Leadership Matter? CEO Leadership under Conditions of Perceived Environmental Uncertainty." *Academy of Management Journal* 44:134–60.

Yammarino, Francis J., and Bernard M. Bass. 1990. "Transformational Leadership and Multiple Levels of Analysis." *Human Relations* 43:975–95.

Yukl, Gary. 1998. *Leadership in Organizations*, 4th ed. Upper Saddle River, N.J.: Prentice Hall.

Part IV

The Map for Future Analysis

Eight

Putting Performance Measurement in Context

Edward T. Jennings, Jr. • Meg Patrick Haist

Performance measurement is perhaps the most significant administrative re-form of the new public management because it provides a means to judge the success of programs and to hold both public managers and contracting ser-vice providers accountable for the outcomes of their activities. The emphasis on outcomes rather than inputs shifts attention from resource commitments and processes to the consequences of those commitments and activities. The focus is on results rather than on processes and outputs. Thus, the movement to foster attention to performance has come to be called "results-oriented gov-ernment." The Government Performance and Results Act is often touted as a symbol of the reinvention of the national government. Reformers everywhere believe that it and similar initiatives at the state and local levels herald a new era of accomplishment and accountability that will ensure the wise use of pub-lic funds and help restore citizen confidence in government.

Analysts and practitioners alike have pointed to many potential uses of per-formance information in public policy and administration. Joyce and Tomp-kins (2002) suggest many ways that performance data can be used in the bud-get process. Gormley and Weimer, in *Organizational Report Cards* (1999), suggest that performance measures provide information for those who need it to enhance policy control and accountability both from the top-down and from the bottom-up. Hatry (1999) offers ten possible uses, including ac-countability, budgeting, operational decisions, building public trust and oth-ers. More recently, Behn (2003) has argued that performance information has eight basic purposes: to evaluate, control, budget, motivate, promote, cele-brate, learn, and improve. The driving purpose, as he sees it, is to improve performance. The other purposes are simply means to that end.

An extensive literature informs managers about principles of performance measurement (Broom and McGuire 1995; Newcomer 1997; Hatry 1999). Much of that literature explores the difficulties involved in developing mea-sures that are valid, reliable, comprehensive, and useful. There is considerable emphasis on best practices. A variety of books and articles attempt to portray factors that affect the use of performance measurement (Poister and Streib 1999; Julnes and Holzer 2001; Newcomer et al. 2002). Case studies are full of insights into performance measurement processes (Governmental Ac-

173

counting Standards Board; Hatry et al. 2003). A variety of studies and books have reported on features of effective measurement and technical difficulties of developing valid and reliable measures.

In the context of this explosion of performance measurement, there has been surprisingly little effort to develop a theory of performance management. By that, we mean a theory that would help predict the ways in which performance measures will be used and the consequences of that use. Gormley and Weimer (1999) make the most extensive effort of this nature, drawing heavily on concepts of accountability, incentives, and competition to structure their argument. Dixit (2002) also offers an extensive discussion of the role of incentives in performance measurement. We draw on their work, but also move beyond it to examine the effect of political context, agency type, organizational characteristics, and leadership on performance.

Thus, we seek to examine the theoretical underpinnings of performance measurement, the assumptions that provide the basis for expectations about impact. Why do we expect measurement to make a difference? What assumptions about accountability and the behavior of administrators and service providers drive our expectations about performance measurement? When do we expect it to make a difference? In other words, what factors are likely to affect the impact of performance measurement? When might we expect performance measurement to have negative consequences for performance?

In the pages that follow, we briefly set performance measurement in the context of a theory of governance and develop a theoretical grounding for expectations about the consequences of measurement. Along the way, we suggest a variety of hypotheses about the conditions under which performance measurement makes a difference and the factors that affect the nature of its impacts. This should lead us toward systematic empirical studies to test relevant hypotheses.

Measurement in the Governance Process

As described earlier in this volume and in a series of papers and manuscripts, Lynn, Heinrich, and Hill (1999, 2000a, 2000b) have integrated a vast array of studies of governance into the framework of a model that specifies the types of factors that affect policy outcomes. It is a model of governance in which the path to performance (P) is mediated by structure (S), treatments (T), environment (E), client characteristics (C), and management (M): $P = S + T + E + C + M$.

Public policy creates a set of incentives and services that constitute the treatment. That treatment is provided through a structure of organizational arrangements that distributes authority and other resources. The impact of the program depends on the socioeconomic, cultural, technological, and physical environment in which it is implemented. Client characteristics mediate the effects of the treatment. The management of the program is critical in the delivery of services and application of incentives. Performance management is the use of management tools and policy instruments to enhance organizational or policy accomplishments. As such, it is part of the M in the Lynn, Heinrich, and Hill formulation.

The broad features of the governance model suggest that performance measurement or management is only one of many factors that shape the impacts of a policy. As such, the effects are likely to be at the margin. It may indeed be the case that performance management will often be challenged to overcome barriers raised by administrative structures, the available treatments, environmental features, and client characteristics.

Theoretical Expectations: Incentives and Accountability

Performance measures are, in many senses, one more tool in the vast array of approaches that have been developed over the years to ensure the accountability of public servants. They are comparable to the external mechanisms of control that were one side of the classic Friedrich-Finer debate over how best to ensure that public administrators are faithful to public ends and the public good. On the one hand, Finer (1941) argued that the only effective way to ensure faithful adherence to public purposes was to impose formal mechanisms of external control. On the other hand, Friedrich (1940) suggested that effective pursuit of public purposes could be achieved only if public administrators internalized a set of values consistent with those purposes.

The types of incentives and sanctions that might be advocated by adherents of Finer's approach to accountability would include formal, externally imposed controls outlined in statutes or regulations. To the extent that it is externally imposed, the new mechanism of performance measurement is similar to traditional mechanisms of this kind. Such mechanisms depend on sanctions and incentives for their effectiveness. For those whose persuasion is similar to Friedrich's, however, the effectiveness of performance measures will depend on the values and orientations of administrators and street-level operators. It is that internal light, rather than the imposition of sanctions or the offer of rewards, that will motivate movement toward high performance, as we discuss later in this chapter.

Gormley and Weimer (1999) provide a particularly helpful perspective for discussing theoretical expectations about the consequences of performance measurement. They suggest that organizational report cards, performance measures, are accountability mechanisms for dealing with information asymmetry. Performance measures provide information that consumers (public officials, service recipients, citizens) can use to make judgments about the effectiveness of an organization or program. They can be used to enhance both top-down and bottom-up accountability. The information enables more effective oversight by citizens, elected officials, and organizational leaders. That oversight should lead to enhanced performance.

If it is oversight that leads to enhanced performance, service recipients, citizens, and officials have to (1) receive performance information (which will be affected by how widely it is distributed) and (2) use the information. Or, at least, service providers and administrators have to believe interested groups and individuals will use it. In addition, those using the data for accountability purposes have to be able to shape the behavior of administrators and service providers. In other words, they need mechanisms of control, the capacity to replace, reward, or punish service providers. The service providers or administrators have to be susceptible to the rewards and punishments. This leads to the following hypotheses:

H1: The more widespread the sharing of performance information, the greater the likelihood of positive effects on performance.

H2 : The greater the belief of service providers and administrators that officials or citizens care about and will use performance information, the greater the likelihood of positive effects on performance.

H3: The more extensive the mechanisms of control available to principals, the more likely it is that agents will react positively to performance measurement.

Incentives, which can include inducements and sanctions, are central to the theoretical expectations of performance measurement (Dixit 2002). Incentives can be of various types: monetary rewards for administrators or service personnel, more funding to support additional activities, greater control over the ways money is to be spent, resources to enhance agency facilities, organizational growth, and enhanced prestige. Sanctions might include increased oversight or program takeover by the supervising agency, transfers or replacement of personnel, or loss of resources to other organizations. Poor performance can affect the prestige of an organization and its members.

The savvy manager or agency executive will estimate the likelihood of being rewarded for exceeding performance standards or penalized for failure to meet specific standards and, if the likelihood is low, may be unwilling to move agency resources toward the attainment of targeted measures, especially if the manager faces unpleasant tradeoffs in attempting to move the organization toward the new goal.

Anecdotal reports have suggested that fear of sanctions may be a greater motivating mechanism than desire for rewards. Cornett and Gaines (1997) report that legislators in Kentucky believe the threat of school closings and job loss are more motivating than what may amount to small bonuses for teachers under the Kentucky Education Reform Act (KERA). One critic claims that few states have been able to develop reward systems that can compete with the publication of test scores in motivating teacher behavior (Cohen 1996).

As Gormley and Weimer argue, organizational report cards have the potential to affect organizations and their leaders because they can affect the flow of resources to the organization and its reputation. Reputation can influence financial resources and authority. Because organizations require finances and authority to achieve their goals and meet the needs of their members, dependence of resources on performance should impact the effect of performance measurement. Because of their implications for resources, Gormley and Weimer (1999) and Dixit (2002) are particularly sensitive to the effect of markets on the impact of performance measures. The more the organization faces a competitive market, the more likely it is that performance measures will influence behavior. The need to attract customers is an important influence on behavior. When organizations have a monopoly position, information about performance will have much less impact. Thus, for example, performance information about the accomplishments of schools should have more impact in metropolitan areas rich in school choices than in smaller communities with few public or private options. This leads to hypotheses about resource dependency and competition:

H4 : The more an organization's resources are dependent on measured performance, the greater the impact of performance measurement.

H5 : The greater the competition faced by the organization, the greater the impact of performance measurement.

Of course, incentives and rewards can have undesirable consequences. Abt, Capron, and Rivlin (1976) suggest that careless application of rewards and sanctions can backfire when, for example, putting more money in better-managed social programs places participants in poorly managed programs at a double disadvantage, as they become subject to both inferior management and funding. Heinrich (1999) has demonstrated that performance measures can produce activities that are not consistent with broad, long-term objectives of policy. Others have pointed out that performance measurement can lead to gaming behavior that distorts policy and leads to a false image of accomplishment (Courty and Marschke 2004; Figlio and Winicki 2002). It can also lead to outright cheating, as shows up from time to time in educational settings.

This leads to design issues. It seems self-evident that the selection of an appropriate set of measures will be critical to successful performance management. Hatry (1999) and others who write manuals on how to conduct performance measurement devote considerable attention to the qualities of an effective management system. Critical issues in design include (1) selecting indicators appropriate to vision, goals, and objectives (Abt, Capron, and Rivlin 1976; Hatry 1999); (2) selecting benchmarks or standards by which to assess performance (Carter, Klein and Day 1995; Hatry 1999; Morley, Bryand, and Hatry 2001); (3) deciding whether and how to adjust measures to take into account factors beyond the agency's control that affect outcomes (Clotfelter and Ladd 1996; Steifel, Rubenstein, and Schwartz 1999); and (4) avoiding gaming, goal displacement, and other distorting effects (Barnow 1992; Gormley and Weimer 1999; Courty and Marschke 1996, 2004; Dixit 2002; Heinrich 2002).

H6: Incomplete systems of performance measures are likely to distort agency behavior and reduce attainment of policy goals.

The impact of performance measures should turn critically on the relationships of principals and agents to the measures: the attention that principals give the measures, the resources they have available to shape the behavior of agents, and the skill with which they use those resources. Viewed in terms of the behavior of the agents, the impact of performance measures should depend on: the validity and importance the agents attach to the measures, their susceptibility to the resources or blandishments and incentives of principals, and the costs and benefits they attach to the attainment of high performance as measured by the chosen indicators.

Rewards are widely considered to be a critical component of performance measurement systems. The Job Training Partnership Act (JTPA) was predicated in part on the assumption that the availability of rewards would enhance performance. Education reformers, like those who shaped the KERA of 1991 and the U.S. No Child Left Behind Act of 2002, assume that financial rewards will stimulate teachers and administrators to improve educational outcomes. The question is why administrators and service providers should care about the rewards. In many cases, the rewards cannot be used to reward individuals. If that is so, to have an impact, administrators and service providers must care because they want the resources to improve their programs. Alternatively, they may care about the professional prestige and enhanced mobility that come with managing an organization that wins awards.

Unless the potential exists for significant resource impacts, or for highly disruptive outside interference with the functioning of the organization, externally imposed sanctions may prove ineffective as incentives for compliance with the use of performance measures. Friedrich's (1940) emphasis on the importance of professional legitimacy and reputation may play a key role in motivating organization leaders. This is reinforced by Mosher's (1968) assessment of the role of professions in the public service. Research has suggested that members of professions are particularly sensitive to performance measures that may impact their reputation among peers. Gormley and Weimer discuss the theme of reputation at length. Good performance positively affects a leader's prestige and career mobility. In addition, positive reports enhance the prestige of his or her organization, which in turn affects his or her ability to recruit and retain talent, which has managerial benefits. Significantly, with enhanced prestige may come greater discretion over the use of resources. Particularly important for public agencies, greater prestige may bring a reduction in the costs of the organization's governance relations, presumably as enhanced trust and confidence free bureaucrats from legislative or executive oversight.

This line of thought leads to the following hypotheses:

H7: Performance measures have greater impact when principals give them more attention, have more resources to shape agent behavior, and use the resources to pursue performance goals.

H8: Performance measures have greater impact when service providers and managers believe they are accurate reflections of performance.

H9: Performance measures have greater impact on outcomes when managers believe that the organization's performance on the measures affects their own economic well-being, career opportunities, power, or professional prestige and the organization's access to resources of authority and finance.

The Political Context of Performance Measurement

Nowhere do managers and their organizations exist in a vacuum. Especially in the public sector, where executive action or legislation is responsible for the genesis, maintenance, and monitoring of programs, managers may expect frequent external interference in the form of new legislation, restructuring, and the institution of a variety of accountability mechanisms, including performance indicators. This principal role for the external political environment, however, presents the potential for diverse responses to performance measures.

In discussing the origin of educational reforms, Lourie (1976) writes that decisions about the need to change the system are seldom the result of research findings. Instead, extrinsic factors such as policymakers' sense of timing, or nationally directed policies, drive reforms. In recent decades, the courts, media, and public advocacy organizations have all acted to pressure a wide variety of public agencies to become more accountable, most recently through the development of program performance measures. Naturally, this external pressure will have implications for acceptance by the organization, especially when attention to new indicators may require a major organizational upheaval.

Because governance turns critically on politically defined goals, the first challenge of performance measurement is to find a mutually agreed upon definition of good performance. This question, while partly technical in nature, is mostly a political issue. Agencies that have multiple or competing goals, or agencies that face diverse interests, may see actors vying for a specific focus in performance management that will best serve their agendas. Carter, Klein, and Day (1995) note that the primary concerns of the most powerful interest will determine the development of the performance indicators to be implemented. Thus, the dominant advocacy coalition is critical in defining both the goals to be pursued and the indicators of success. Disputes can take place over either goals or indicators.

This means that the performance orientation is subject to changes in political direction, because the priorities of a new administration or legislative committee may differ from those of the previous controlling body. In other words, for some policy areas, the political and ideological context may fluctuate; as control shifts, attention to performance indicators may suffer. Rewards may not be provided for good results and sanctions may not be imposed for poor results. Alternatively, performance indicators may become the

Goals

Validity	Agree	Disagree
Agree	Positive impact	Uncertain impact
Disagree	Uncertain impact	No impact

Figure 8.1
Effect of Political Agreement with Respect to Policy Goals and Measurement Validity on Performance Measurement Impact

subject of enhanced political scrutiny, with positive or negative consequences diligently brought to bear. As Perrow states, "Power effects the definition of effectiveness." Beyond shifts in political control and variations in the power of actors, there is the simple fact that much of American public policy operates in a context of dispersed power and authority (Bryson and Crosby 1992), a setting in which no one is in charge. With multiple political principals, diverse venues of appeal, and public disagreement over many issues, performance measurement is not likely to be simple or noncontroversial.

Thus, we expect that the impact of performance measures will be shaped by the political context in which they are created and operate. The impact of performance measures will vary depending on the degree of political agreement over the goals of the policy and the validity of the measures of goal attainment. It is helpful to consider the simple case of a four-cell table and several sets of relationships.

This is very similar to the framework that Waterman and Meier (1998) provide for thinking about the relationship between principals and agents. They note that typical treatments of agency theory assume some degree of conflict between principals and agents. Information asymmetry, moral hazard, and the like are supposed to lead agents to less than fully pursue the intent of principals (see Dixit 2002). They point out, however, that principals and agents may share goals, rather than being in conflict over them. In addition, principals may have more information than agents.

When there is general agreement in the political order about the means and ends of policy, it should be easier to design performance measures and use them to guide performance. Disagreement in the political order should render the use of performance measurement much more problematic. Radin (2000) argues that disagreement of this type is a significant impediment to successful implementation of the Government Performance and Results Act. Dixit

(2002) treats this as a problem of multiple stakeholders and points out how the presence of multiple stakeholders shapes efforts to judge performance.

Consider broad political alignments. How does disagreement about the general goals of policy among the general public, attentive publics, and political activists affect performance management? And, with respect to the validity of indicators, what difference does it make if left and right, Republican and Democrat, libertarian and communitarian disagree? What happens to the impact of performance measures if there is agreement?

Transferring this to the principals in typical governance settings, what are the implications of agreement and disagreement? If the governor and legislature agree, for example, on the goals of education reform, they will be in a more powerful position to sanction low performance and reward high performance. When principals agree on appropriate indicators of performance, they are better placed to send a unified signal about performance expectations and outcomes to agents. Thus, agreement should lead to greater impact. Disagreement, however, over goals or measurement makes it difficult for the principals to guide the performance of agencies (see, e.g., Wooley 1993). This may have been the case with welfare policy throughout the 1980s and early 1990s, as Congress, the president, governors, and state legislatures struggled with each other over the goals of reform. As they came together in agreement that self-sufficiency and reductions in the welfare rolls were the central goals to be pursued, they sent a clear signal to managers. Concerted action followed (Nathan and Gais 1999). When there is disagreement, the effect of measurement may well be muted and will depend upon which principal is able to exercise greater control over the agency.

H10: The greater the agreement among principals with respect to goals and measures, the greater the effect of measurement.

Even when principals are in agreement, success will depend upon the degree to which agents agree with principals. Once again, when there is agreement between or among principals and agents, we would expect positive impact. When there is disagreement, we would expect less impact.

If the agents are in agreement with the principals on goals, they are more likely to respond to messages from the principals. The likelihood will increase even further if they are in agreement on the indicators of performance. When agents disagree with principals, however, they have a diverse array of possibilities for subverting attention to the performance measures. In these cases, the effect of measurement depends critically on the attention principals give the measures and the resources they bring to bear to move agents in desired directions.

H11: The greater the agreement between principals and agents with respect to goals and measures, the greater the impact of performance measurement.

Once the information obtained from the performance measures is in the hands of political interests, the data might not necessarily be utilized in a socially desirable manner. Gormley and Weimer note that audiences pay varying degrees of attention to performance measures, with some indicators being more salient to certain interests. This is good when audiences with informed preferences move the organization in the appropriate direction; however, as Abt, Capron, and Rivlin (1976) warn, policymakers have constraints (in particular, they suffer from cognitive dissonance) on their perceptions. The implication is that depending on what information is provided by performance measures, such indicators may have either no impact, or even socially undesirable impacts, if interests perceive the reported results as contrary to their ideological position, or as harmful to some other agenda, goal, or belief of the interest. Interest mobilization in response to measurement will shape the impact of performance measurement.

H12: Significant mobilization of interests adverse to the measures will reduce the impact of performance measurement.

What Kind of Work? Agency Type and the Role of Performance Indicators

Reformers' focus on output and outcome indicators, as opposed to attention paid to input or process measures, requires the assumption that outputs and outcomes may be easily observed and that they can be attributed to the organization. James Q. Wilson's development of four agency types provides a starting point in developing expectations for positive versus negative responses and, on a higher level, for substantive versus symbolic impact on the direction of the agency (Wilson 1989; Dixit 2002). Wilson develops his typology along two dimensions—whether outputs (the direct activities of the agency, such as number of claims processed) and/or outcomes (the results of the policy, such as self-sufficiency for welfare clients) are directly observable to managers (and, in the case of outcomes, directly attributable to the program treatment). In production agencies (the Internal Revenue Service, the U.S. Postal Service), both outputs and outcomes are clearly observable, according to Wilson. In craft agencies (the Army Corp of Engineers, the Antitrust Division of the Justice Department) outcomes are observable, but outputs are difficult to observe and, therefore, to control. The military during wartime is an excellent example; it is usually clear whether a battle has been won, but accounting for the actions of each soldier toward that goal is impossible. Procedural agencies (Occupational Safety and Health Administration, the Army in peacetime), have observable outputs, but outcomes are difficult to attribute to the program. Finally, coping agencies (schools, most of the work done by police departments) have relatively unobservable outputs and outcomes (due in part to input into the process from external sources, such as a student's home environment). For these agencies, formal measures may be only loosely related to the real work being done.

Wilson addresses agency type from the perspective of a single program and goal. As Dixit (2002) and others point out, however, programs can have multiple goals; this complicates in a variety of ways the assessment of the observability of outputs and outcomes.

One difficulty with Wilson's formulation is that he shifts back and forth between agency and worker. This creates an interesting dilemma, well illustrated by the U.S. Army Corps of Engineers. Wilson discusses it as an agency where the outputs are unobservable but the outcomes can be observed. This is true at the individual level, where the outputs of engineers, for instance, cannot be observed readily, but the final product (for example, a dam) can. On the other hand, at the agency level, both output and outcome are observable. One of the outputs of the corps is a dam. Outcomes of this might be flood control and recreation, each of which is observable. Another difficulty is that Wilson talks about observable outcomes in two different ways. For example, he says that schools have both unobservable outputs and unobservable outcomes. The outcomes are unobservable, he says, because, even though we can test students for their knowledge, the test scores do not differentiate between what the teacher taught and what the student learned otherwise (Wilson 1989). On the other hand, he cites Coleman's findings that private and parochial schools do a better job than public schools as evidence that they perform better, presumably accepting test scores at the school level as valid measures of outcomes. Here he seems to want it both ways—outcomes cannot be attributed to the schools, and outcomes can be attributed to the schools. Certainly, most observers would agree that educational outcomes are not solely a product of schools or teachers. They are co-produced by teachers, students, and parents. They are influenced by social context.

Untreated in Wilson's discussion is the difficulty introduced when agencies or programs have multiple goals, as is typically the case for public programs. This means, as Dixit (2002) points out, that it can be more than difficult to decide which outcomes to observe. Different stakeholders will emphasize different dimensions and dimensions will vary in their observability.

Although they do not categorize agencies into groups in their discussion, Downs and Larkey (1986) nicely illustrate in a similar manner best and worst-case scenarios involving the use of performance measures. They compare garbage collection (a production agency under Wilson's typology) and policing activity (a coping agency) with regard to the difficulties inherent in using performance data to determine agency effectiveness. To begin, the technology of waste removal is relatively straightforward and easily understood and, therefore, is accessible to city councils making decisions based on performance measures. Outputs are directly observable, and outcomes may be directly attributed to the agency. Policing is on the opposite extreme, first because, to quote Downs and Larkey, "the absence of a refined technology of law enforcement usually means that interpretation and appropriate adjustment are not possible. It is like trying to learn how to play the game of baseball solely by studying box scores" (Downs and Larkey 1986, 89). In addition, there exists a high probability that changes in outcomes of interest are not entirely due to policing behavior, making performance measures less useful for decision making. Changes in burglary rates, for example, cannot solely be attributed to alterations in patrolling or crime-prevention programs, but are subject to the impact of other factors, including the weather or economic conditions (Downs and Larkey 1986, 89). This is similar to the point that Wilson was actually making about education: it is not that we cannot measure outcomes; the difficulty is that there are other things contributing to the outcomes besides what goes on in the school (and there is considerable disagreement about which outcomes to measure).

Downs and Larkey point out that where there are at least several valuable or high-quality innovations in performance measurement available to policymakers or managers, there is a greater likelihood that utilization of productivity measures will make a significant contribution to the program. The production versus coping agency example is compounded here, because the greater complexity and less-understood technology in policing, or education, means such programs come up against the truth that the quality of ideas to improve performance is a function of how well the system is understood. Although not employing Wilson's terminology, Downs and Larkey are in effect stating that, because production agency activity is better understood, innovations in performance measurement have the greatest effect for these programs, making the payoff for performance measurement in sanitation greater than for police departments.

This adds a third dimension to Wilson's concern with the degree to which outputs and outcomes can be observed. The degree to which outcomes can be attributed to the program or agency should affect the degree to which performance measures are used and the effects they have. If Downs and Larkey are right about police and garbage, we should find that performance measures are likely to be applied to garbage collection and disposal and less likely to be applied to police activity. We are a bit skeptical about this, because we know that many law enforcement agencies track a variety of activities and outputs (arrest rates, clearance rates, response time), and outcomes (crime rates) and use this information to guide strategy and action.

Understanding that variation in other factors affecting the adoption or implementation of performance measures may alter the ultimate effect of performance measurement systems, our expectations for the impact of performance measures using the Wilson typology are represented by figure 8.2.

The degree to which outputs and outcomes can be attributed to the agency will affect the degree to which performance measures are used and the impact that they have. They should be less likely to be used and have less impact in settings where agency control over outcomes is weak.

	Outputs Observed	Outputs Unobserved
Outcomes Observed	Production Agency: Substantive impact is clear; measures likely to be used and to have impact.	Craft Agency: Because outputs are difficult to observe (and therefore to control), expectation is for symbolic impact or the adoption of outcome-focused performance incentive systems as a means of improving agency effectiveness.
Outcomes Unobserved	Procedural Agency: Substantive impact on procedures or outputs, but may be difficult to assess whether *outcomes* are impacted by performance measurement-driven changes in outputs being measured. Attention will focus on efficiency, the relationship of inputs to outputs.	Coping Agency: Because neither outputs nor outcomes can be observed, indirect measures may be used, but impacts will be unclear; or measures will be at the activity level.

Figure 8.2
Expected Impact of Performance Measures by Type of Agency

H13: The extent to which performance measures are used and the types of measures used will depend on the degree to which outputs and outcomes can be observed.

H14: Measurement will be more common and will have greater impact when agencies have greater control over outcomes.

We note here that politics and public interest can be critical. The importance attributed to a function can override the degree of controllability. Performance measurement has become widespread in education despite the fact that (1) teachers and schools only partially control outcomes, (2) there is disagreement over which dimensions of performance to measure, and (3) there is disagreement over the validity of performance measures. This is because of the societal and political importance of education. Leaders under these conditions insist on performance accountability. Of course, increased use of performance measures may also be a function of misguided beliefs about the extent to which outcomes are controllable by the schools.

Agency type leads to a consideration of the types of measures that are appropriate to the organization or program. Measures can focus on process, activity, output, or outcome. The relevance of each type of measure and issues related to its use depend on the nature of the program or the nature of the organization's work. The current wave of reform in performance measurement systems is to focus on outcomes as a means of accountability. For some programs, output, process, or even input measures may remain the best indicator of whether the mission of the organization is being fulfilled, despite the recent emphasis on outcomes. Carter, Klein, and Day (1995) suggest that, if service delivery is the most important feature of an organization's work, process indicators may supersede outcome indicators in importance. In such instances, the appropriate measure might indicate the level of competence in routine activities. This would also be the case with Wilson's procedural agencies.

Nevertheless, Grizzle (1982) contends that outcomes are the most likely dimension to be left out of performance measurement systems because they are difficult to measure, costly to collect, are often contaminated by factors outside the program's control, and frequently involve time lags. She warns, however, that the adverse consequences of excluding outcome measures where relevant may include the misuse of information or the distortion of agency activity and resources (1982). Hatry (1980, 314) agrees, stating dryly that "partial control is the usual situation in government." Where measures may not be controllable in the short run, he suggests, government may still have enough influence to affect the outcome, and the measure may serve as an accountability mechanism. What researchers appear to have discovered is that performance measures (and especially extremely targeted kinds of measures) must not become so important as to eclipse any overall evaluation of a program and its attempt to achieve both statutory and de facto program objectives.

The simple fact of the matter is that the effectiveness of performance management will depend on the adoption of measures appropriate to the tasks and goals of the agency.

H15: The impact of performance measurement depends on the design of a set of measures appropriate to agency task and goals.

Organizational Compatibility

In addition to the broad types of organization discussed above, general features of an organization's structure and its interaction with the implementation of performance indicators will impact successful implementation of performance measures and accompanying goals. There is a vast literature on the adoption of innovations by organizations, but for our purposes three aspects of organizational structure are important to the impact of performance indicators. First, especially for hierarchical organizations, the closeness of the measure to the level of service delivery is critical. The higher up in the hierarchy a performance indicator is implemented, the more difficult it becomes to assign responsibility for the outcome. In part, this is due to the increasing difficulty in monitoring the behavior responsible for specific outputs. Gormley and Weimer (1999) suggest that, in general, the closer to the operatives the performance measure is targeted, the greater impact it will have. This supposition is in line with related findings by service delivery–level researchers such as Lipsky (1980).

H16: The closer to the level of service delivery a performance measure is implemented, the greater the impact on output or outcomes.

Second, a performance measure's compatibility with existing organizational capability is essential to its incorporation. Indicators that require the use of underdeveloped skills, or skills not in practice, may be attended to only selectively. Similarly, measurement systems that require significant reorganization of tasks among individuals or between organizations may suffer in implementation. This need to adapt the capacities of the organization may be a significant contributor to what Carter, Klein, and Day (1995) term the "innovations cycle." During an innovation cycle, there may initially be only perfunctory compliance with the development of performance indicators, followed by resistance to their use, subsequent refinement of measures, and, finally, acceptance.

H17: Performance measures that are compatible with the existing use and distribution of skills, tasks, and resources will result in greater and more immediate impact. Conversely, performance measures that require significant disruption of skill utilization or task organization may experience delayed or dysfunctional response in adoption.

Finally, the aims of a performance measure may conflict with the execution of formal program objectives, particularly in organizations characterized by significant heterogeneity of products or services, forcing managers to make tradeoffs between attentiveness to existing goals and new indicators of success.

H18: Performance measures will have greater impact in more homogeneous organizational settings.

Organizational Assent: Culture

We noted early in this chapter Friedrich's (1940) argument that the effective, accountable pursuit of public purposes depends on the degree to which administrators have internalized a set of norms consistent with the public purposes. Gormley and Weimer explain that the impact of report cards depends on the ability of leaders to change the behavior of organizations. This, in turn, is likely to depend on the ease with which behavior in the organization can be targeted. The ability of leaders to do this is likely to be a function of the compatibility of the measures with the organization's internal culture. Has agency staff internalized a set of norms that supports pursuit of the goals reflected in the measures?

Agency cultures are composed of norms, beliefs, and routine patterns of action that guide the behavior of organization members. When there is a strongly shared culture, there will be consistent normative orientations and beliefs. Kaufman's (1960) classic study, *The Forest Ranger,* illustrates the importance of organizational efforts to socialize staff in a shared set of norms, beliefs, and behaviors. Not all agencies, of course, enjoy the same degree of internal harmony. In agencies faced with multiple or competing objectives, diverse professional perspectives, or weak socialization, members may have opposing ideas about the importance of various outputs or outcomes, leading some to be less attentive than others to certain performance measures.

We may think of internal harmony as revolving around internalization of mission. As Wilson (1989) puts it, the great advantage of mission internalization is that it permits the agency head to be more certain members will act in specific instances in ways that he would have behaved had he been in their place. Because all members share common understandings, the transmission of information is more accurate. In their study of mission statements, Weiss and Piderit (1999) describe these statements as engaging employees' commitment, encouraging them to "identify with the organization, even making performance at work a significant component of self concept." In their discussion of effective government agencies, Rainey and Steinbauer (1999, 17) write that "a strong organizational culture will be related positively to agency effectiveness when the culture is *effectively linked* to mission accomplishment" (emphasis added). The effectiveness of this link may be strengthened by the adoption of performance measures that manifest or help make specific the mission of the organization.

H19: The more consistent performance measures are with an agency's culture, the greater the likelihood of a positive impact.

H20: Performance measures that enhance the mission of the organization will have a positive effect on outcomes.

H21: Agencies with low agreement among members regarding the organization's mission (agencies experiencing low policy consensus) are more likely to experience dysfunctional responses to performance measurement.

Gormley and Weimer (1999), in discussing the contribution of professional subcultures to the implementation of performance indicators, suggest that functional responses are possible when professionals whose norms are consistent with the desired direction of behavior are empowered by the performance measures, perhaps helping to prevent dysfunctional responses such as goal displacement or deceit. Alternatively, Carter, Klein, and Day (1995) note that, the greater the autonomy of actors in the agency (which often occurs in cases involving professionals), the greater may be the resistance to performance indicators.

H22: Agencies staffed by professionals whose norms are aligned with the goals of performance measures are more likely to experience positive response in adoption of performance indicators.

H23: Agencies staffed by professions with strong norms of autonomy are more likely to experience delayed or negative response to adoption of performance measures.

Focusing and Mobilizing Support: Agency Leadership

In chapter 7 of this volume, Ingraham, Sowa, and Moynihan offer an analysis of the role of leadership in performance management. They suggest that integrative leadership links leadership to performance in public organizations. Their model focuses on the role of top level and agency level leadership in promoting, institutionalizing, integrating, and using results-based management. We try here to supplement their insights by offering some theorizing about the impact of leaders and leadership on the impact of performance measurement. We do this with caution, recognizing that leadership may be subsumed by other factors of the governance model or that it is specific activities, rather than an overarching set of characteristics or orientations that we call leadership, that are important; however, such astute observers of public management as Lynn (1987) have suggested that leadership is critical to performance.

The statutory and personal powers of the manager(s) or executive may act as mediating or transforming forces through his or her interaction with both the internal and external environment. Although Weiss and Piderit (1999) were unable to measure the role of leadership in articulating and mobilizing support for the aims of school mission statements, they note this as a recurring theme in their study. We have already suggested the importance of a leader's ability to foresee the potential impact of performance measures on her organization, a point also mentioned by Gormley and Weimer (1999) in their treatment of organizational report cards. A leader whose personal ideology or attitudes are aligned against the aims of a performance measurement system has great opportunity to hinder its effective use. In contrast, the executive who supports the use of performance indicators can, as Gormley and Weimer describe it, use the measures as a focal point to create a desired cultural transformation within the agency. Carter, Klein, and Day (1995) place great emphasis on the acceptability of performance indicators to organization members and, in instances where acceptability entails the internalization of a completely new way of thinking, no individual has greater power to articulate and formulate that new mission for the organization than the executive.

In the public sector, the leader's critical role in the functional adoption of performance measures is a product of his or her position as the agency's champion. She or he is the mediator and buffer between the external environment and the agency, including its multiple levels of responsibility and coordination. Political pressure from outside the agency and the accompanying minimization of discretion place what Sharkansky calls a premium on the manager's capacity to "identify opportunities and pursue effective strategies" (1982, 119). Rainey and

Steinbauer's (1999) thesis on effective government organizations implies that the impact of performance measurement will be positive if management is free to direct the implementation of such measures, but this necessitates a leader who possesses the requisite skills and commitment to accomplish the task.

Although the literature is replete with lists of leadership qualities central to agency success (Barnard 1938; Wilson 1989), three of those mentioned by Rainey and Steinbauer seem important to the successful utilization of performance measures. They include commitment to mission, effective goal setting, and effective administrative and political coping (1999, 18). First, leadership must be able to articulate for and focus the agency's members on the central policy mission guiding the day-to-day tasks of the agency. Leadership's failure to align mission with the adoption of program measures can lead to the potential for dysfunctional response, including goal displacement and other forms of misdirection. Maintaining the centrality of mission, on the other hand, may lead to what Gormley and Weimer call "mission enhancement," bringing about marked change in organizational performance. Second, a leader who is an effective goal setter can use performance measures to direct improvement of processes or to reallocate organizational activity or resources, or, importantly, to perform what Gormley and Weimer call managerial focusing, enabling more effective coordination among units or more efficient use of resources. Finally, as our discussion of political context makes evident, the executive's ability to navigate and mediate the effects of the political environment, and to deal with subsequent administrative challenges, is the agency's most important resource in remaining true to its mission and avoiding catastrophic forms of goal displacement.

H24: Leadership that demonstrates high commitment to mission, effective goal setting ability, and ability to cope with (external) political and (internal) administrative challenges specific to performance measures will result in positive impact of performance measures.

One additional leadership characteristic may be important within certain types of agencies, particularly those staffed and supervised by individuals of the same profession or agencies relying on large numbers of specialists. That characteristic we call professional competence, which indicates that demonstrated expertise by leadership is necessary to afford the exercise of influence. In their thorough study of school leadership and performance, Friedkin and Slater (1994) show that expert status of principals is critical in school settings because of professional norms of autonomy, privacy, and equality. Although his or her hierarchical designation is necessary to the principal's leadership role, it is not sufficient, but is conditional on the teacher's knowledge of his or her expertise. We would expect recognition of professional competence to be important in procedural and some coping agencies, where professionals look to experts for guidance in implementing new standards within complex and often uncertain policy arenas.

H25: For organizations staffed largely by professionals, recognition of professional competence of the leader is critical to the impact of performance measures.

Conclusion

In the context of governance, the attainment of policy objectives will be shaped by a variety of important considerations. With all of the attention that public officials have given a new public management that incorporates significant components of performance measurement, it is critical to consider the factors that affect the implementation and impact of performance measurement systems. In this chapter, we have highlighted significant features of the governance system that are likely to mediate the impact.

Incentives are surely an important component of performance management. Without incentives of one type or another, managers and service providers would have little reason to respond to performance measurement. As we point out in our discussion, the important questions about incentives are what kind, what effect, and under what conditions? As we and others have suggested, a perspective grounded in incentives suggests that the impact of performance measures will depend on how widely the information is shared, the degree to which service providers and administrators believe that officials and citizens care about and will use the performance information, and the degree to which principals have effective mechanisms of control. The degree to which resources are dependent on measured performance should affect the impact of performance measurement, as should the degree of competition faced by the organization. Because public servants respond to incentives, the design of measurement systems is critical. Incomplete measurement systems can affect performance adversely by distorting behavior. Finally, attention, resources, and confidence in the measures will increase their impact. Perhaps most importantly, the impact will be greatest when managers believe the performance of the organization affects their own economic well-being, career opportunities, power, or professional prestige.

In governance, politics rules. For us that means the impact of measures depends on the degree to which political interests agree on the goals of policy and the validity of measures selected to chart progress toward the attainment of goals. Agreement among principals and between agents and principals will also increase the likelihood of a favorable impact.

Organizations provide the vehicles for the pursuit of public purposes. The types of agencies assigned responsibility for a policy and the nature of their work have a lot to do with the possibilities for measurement. As we point out, Wilson's distinction among production, craft, procedural, and coping agencies provides important insight. The degree to which outputs and outcomes can be observed (measured) affects the potential for performance measurement. Also important is the degree to which outcomes can be attributed to the efforts of the agency.

General features of an organization's structure and operations will also affect performance measurement. This depends, in part, on the design of the performance measurement system. The closer to the actual delivery of services that measures are implemented, the greater the likelihood for impacts. In addition, the effect of performance measures depends on their compatibility with the skills, tasks, and resources of the organization.

As we argue, incentives are important, but their impact will be shaped by the culture of the organization. The more consistent the measures are with the dominant norms, beliefs, and orientations in the agency, the greater we can expect their impact to be. When there is agreement on mission and the measures support the mission, there is likely to be greater positive impact. And, professional norms in the agency will affect impact.

Finally, we turn to the role of leadership. We suggest in our discussion of leadership that its impact is potentially great when leaders demonstrate high commitment to mission, demonstrate effective goal-setting ability, and the ability to cope with external and internal political and administrative challenges. As suggested by Ingraham, Sowa, and Moynihan, leadership that promotes, institutionalizes, integrates, and uses results-based management will go far to ensure positive impacts of performance measurement systems.

References

Abt, Clark C., William Capron, and Alice Rivlin. 1976. "Discussion: Payoffs of Evaluation Research." In Clark C. Abt., ed., *Evaluation of Social Programs*. Beverly Hills, Calif.: Sage, 242–46.

Barnard, Chester. 1938. *Functions of the Executive*. Cambridge, Mass.: Harvard University Press.

Barnow, Burt S. 1992. "The Effects of Performance Standards in State and Local Programs." In C. Manski and I. Garfinkel, eds., *Evaluating Welfare and Training Programs*. Cambridge, Mass.: Harvard University Press, 227–309.

Behn, Robert. 2003. "Why Measure Performance? Different Purposes Require Different Measures." *Public Administration Review* 63:586–606.

Broom, C. A., and L. McGuire. 1995. "Performance-Based Government Models: Building a Track Record." *Public Budgeting and Finance* 15:3–17.

Bryson, John M., and Barbara C. Crosby. 1992. *Leadership for the Common Good: Tackling Public Problems in a Shared-Power World*. San Francisco: Jossey-Bass.

Carter, Neil, Rudolf Klein, and Patricia Day. 1995. *How Organisations Measure Success: The Use of Performance Indicators in Government*. London: Routledge.

Clotfelter, Charles T., and Helen F. Ladd. 1996. "Recognizing and Rewarding Success in Public Schools." In Helen F. Ladd, ed., *Holding Schools Accountable: Performance-Based Reform in Education*. Washington, D.C.: Brookings Institution, 23–63.

Cohen, David K. 1996. "Standards-Based School Reform: Policy, Process, and Performance." In Helen F. Ladd., ed., *Holding Schools Accountable: Performance-Based Reform in Education*. Washington, D.C.: Brookings Institutions Press, 99–127.

Cornett, Lynn M., and Gail Gaines. 1997. *Accountability in the 1990s: Holding Schools Responsible for Student Achievement.* Atlanta: Southern Regional Education Board.

Courty, Pascal, and Gerald Marschke. 2004. Gaming and Performance Incentives. *Journal of Labor Economics* 22:23–56.

———. 1996. "Moral Hazard under Incentive Systems: The Case of a Federal Bureaucracy." In Gary Libecap, ed., *Advances in the Study of Entrepreneurship, Innovation, and Economic Growth,* vol. 7. St. Louis: JAI Press, 157–90.

Dixit, Avinash. 2002. "Incentives and Organizations in the Public Sector: An Interpretative Review." *Journal of Human Resources* 37:697–727.

Downs, George W., and Patrick D. Larkey. 1986. *The Search for Government Efficiency: From Hubris to Helplessness.* New York: Random House.

Figlio, David N., and Joshua Winicki. 2002. "Food for Thought: The Effects of School Accountability Plans on School Nutrition." Working Paper 9319. Cambridge, Mass.: National Bureau for Economic Research.

Finer, Herman. 1941. "Administrative Responsibility in Democratic Government." *Public Administration Review* 1:335–50.

Friedkin, Noah, and Michael R. Slater. 1994. "School Leadership and Performance: A Social Network Approach." *Sociology of Education* 67:139–57.

Friedrich, Carl. 1940. "Public Policy and the Nature of Administrative Responsibility." In Carl Friedrich and E. S. Mason, eds., *Public Policy.* Cambridge, Mass.: Harvard University Press, 3–24.

Governmental Accounting Standards Board. http://accounting.rutgers.edu/raw/gasb. (Accessed February 2002.)

Gormley, William T., Jr., and David L. Weimer. 1999. *Organizational Report Cards.* Cambridge, Mass.: Harvard University Press.

Grizzle, Gloria A. 1982. "Measuring State and Local Government Performance: Issues to Resolve before Implementing a Performance Measurement System." *State and Local Government Review* 14 (September):132–36.

Hatry, Harry P. 1999. *Performance Measurement: Getting Results.* Washington, D.C.: Urban Institute Press.

———. 1980. "Performance Measurement Principles and Techniques: An Overview for Local Government." *Public Productivity Review* 4 (December):312–39.

Hatry, Harry P., Elaine Morley, Shelli B. Rossman, and Joseph S. Wholey. 2003. *How Federal Programs Use Outcome Information: Opportunities for Federal Managers.* Washington, D.C.: IBM Endowment for the Business of Government.

Heinrich, Carolyn J. 2002. Outcomes-Based Performance Management in the Public Sector: Implications for Government Accountability and Effectiveness. *Public Administration Review* 62 (November–December):712–25.

———. 1999. "Do Government Bureaucrats Make Effective Use of Performance Management Information?" *Journal of Public Administration Research and Theory* 9:363–94.

Joyce, Phillip, and Susan Sieg Tompkins. 2002. "Using Performance Information for Budgeting: Clarifying Terms and Investigating Recent Experience." In Kathryn Newcomer, Edward T. Jennings, Jr., Cheryle Broom, and Allen Lomax, eds., *Meeting the Challenges of Performance-Oriented Government.* Washington, D.C.: American Society for Public Administration, 61–98.

Julnes, Patria de Lancer, and Marc Holzer. 2001. "Promoting the Utilization of Performance Measures in Public Organizations: An Empirical Study of Factors Affecting Adoption and Implementation." *Public Administration Review* 61:693–708.

Kaufman, Herbert. 1960. *The Forest Ranger.* Baltimore: Johns Hopkins University Press.

Lipsky, Michael. 1980. *Street Level Bureaucracy: Dilemmas of the Individual in Public Services.* New York: Basic Books.

Lourie, Sylvain. 1976. "Policy Research and Decision Making in Education." In Clark C. Abt, ed., *Evaluation of Social Programs.* Beverly Hills, Calif.: Sage, 83–90.

Lynn, Laurence E. 1987. *Managing Public Policy.* Boston: Little, Brown.

Lynn, Laurence E., Carolyn J. Heinrich, and Carolyn J. Hill. 2000a. "Studying Governance and Public Management: Why? How?" In Carolyn J. Heinrich and Laurence E. Lynn, Jr., eds., *Governance and Performance.* Washington, D.C.: Georgetown University Press, 1–33.

———. 2000b. "Studying Public Management: Challenges and Prospects." *Journal of Public Administration Research and Theory* 10 (April):233–62.

———. 1999. "The Empirical Study of Governance: Theories, Models and Methods." Paper prepared for Workshop on Models and Methods for the Empirical Study of Governance. Tucson, Arizona, April 29–May 1.

Morley, Elaine, Scott Bryand, and Harry P. Hatry. 2001. *Comparative Performance Measurement.* Washington, D.C.: Urban Institute.

Mosher, Frederick C. 1968. *Democracy and the Public Service.* New York: Oxford University Press.

Nathan, Richard P., and Thomas L. Gais. 1999. *Implementing the Personal Responsibility Act of 1996: A First Look.* Albany, N.Y.: Nelson A. Rockefeller Institute of Government, State University of New York [www.rockinst.org/publications/welfare_and_jobs.html]. (Accessed May 13, 2004.)

Newcomer, Kathryn. 1997. *Using Performance Measurement to Improve Public and Nonprofit Programs.* San Francisco: Jossey-Bass.

Newcomer, Kathryn, Edward T. Jennings, Jr., Cheryle Broom, and Allen Lomax, eds. 2002. *Meeting the Challenges of Performance-Oriented Government.* Washington, D.C.: American Society for Public Administration.

Poister, Theodore, and Gregory Streib. 1999. "Performance Measurement in Municipal Government: Assessing the State of the Practice." *Public Administration Review* 59:325–35.

Radin, Beryl. 2000. "The Government Performance and Results Act and the Tradition of Federal Management Reform: Square Pegs in Round Holes?" *Journal of Public Administration Research and Theory* 10 (January):111–36.

Rainey, Hal G., and Paula Steinbauer. 1999. "Galloping Elephants: Developing Elements of a Theory of Effective Government Organizations." *Journal of Public Administration Research and Theory* 9:1–32.

Sharkansky, Ira. 1982. *Public Administration: Agencies, Policies and Politics.* San Francisco: W. H. Freeman.

Stiefel, Leana, Ross Rubenstein, and Amy Ellen Schwartz. 1999. "Using Adjusted Performance Measures to Evaluate Resource Use." *Public Budgeting and Finance* 19 (fall):67–87.

Waterman, Richard W., and Kenneth J. Meier. 1998. "Principal-Agent Models: An Expansion?" *Journal of Public Administration Research and Theory* 8:173–203.

Wooley, John. 1993. "Conflict among Regulators and the Hypothesis of Congressional Dominance." *Journal of Politics* 55 (February):92–114.

Weiss, Janet A., and Sandy Kristin Piderit. 1999. "The Value of Mission Statements in Public Agencies." *Journal of Public Administration Research and Theory* 9:193–223.

Wilson, James Q. 1989. *Bureaucracy.* New York: Basic Books.

Nine

Conceptual Issues in Modeling and Measuring Management and Its Impacts on Performance

Kenneth J. Meier • Laurence J. O'Toole, Jr.

Organization and management influence the effectiveness of public programs. Of this assertion there is little doubt, in light of the accumulation of evidence in recent years—as presented in this volume and others (see, for instance, Hill and Lynn 2000; Hill and Lynn 2004; and Lynn, Heinrich, and Hill 2001). Validating this proposition in general terms, nonetheless, is only the beginning of the story. The larger challenge is to dig more deeply: to explore some of the detailed questions about how to conceive of structural arrangements, public management, and political and other environmental influences on program performance; address the specification challenges implied in any serious empirical study of governance; and consider some of the knotty measurement issues at the heart of the task.

Any thoroughgoing effort to grapple with the concept of management and its impact on performance in public programs needs to consider an array of conceptual, theoretical, and measurement matters. This chapter examines several such issues that have arisen or lie implicit in the burgeoning research literature. To limit the analysis to reasonable bounds and render the coverage as specific as possible, we use our own research agenda as grounding, but all public management and governance research faces the same issues. Our work has sprung from an effort to model and test for the effects of public management, the institutional arrangements in which managers operate, and the broader setting of public programs—all on program performance. The modeling work has been developed in earlier studies (O'Toole and Meier 1999, 2000, 2004b) and is being tested in several others (Meier and O'Toole 2001, 2002, 2003, 2004; Meier, O'Toole, and Nicholson-Crotty 2002, 2004; Nicholson-Crotty and O'Toole 2004; O'Toole and Meier 2003b, 2004a, 2004b; O'Toole, Meier, and Nicholson-Crotty 2003). We do not review that work or its myriad findings in any systematic form here. Rather, we use the research effort as a basis for explicating an array of issues that need to be considered in *any* mature development of the study of how organization and management affect public program performance.

Accordingly, although the discussion and the examples follow, and are framed in terms of, our own research agenda, the challenges are not unique to this particular set of studies or our way of approaching research. The questions explored here, in fact, are issues that must be addressed, no matter what theoretical approach may be adopted by governance researchers. Qualitative and small-n empirical investigations crafted to aid in theory development and reasoned guidance for practice are not immune to these matters. The challenges are more explicit and direct, however, for those interested in engaging in the effort to move the study of public management to systematic, scientific large-n designs.

The coverage is structured here in four parts. Three are directly linked to the major concepts in the model we have been developing (management, stability, and the environment) and the fourth is related to more general issues—the purpose of empirical theory, the complexities of the network level of program implementation, the use of organizations as the unit of analysis, and the question of nonlinear relationships. We do not include a discussion of performance measurement, because it has already been the focus of considerable attention by many researchers for some time (see, e.g., Heinrich 2002). We largely ignore this topic in favor of other, less well-developed issues. The other chapters in this volume, then, offer some specifics from various program settings, delivery mechanisms, and performance metrics.

A Base Model

Because this discussion draws heavily on and is framed in terms of our theoretical and empirical work, a brief exposition of our base model is in order. In seeking to understand the relationship between public management, as well as the associated institutional arrangements, and public program performance, we begin with the following:

$$O_t = \beta_1 (S + M_1) O_{t-1} + \beta_2 (X_t/S)(M_3/M_4) + \varepsilon_t, \qquad [1]$$

where O is some measure of outcome; S is a measure of stability; M denotes management, which can be divided into three parts—M_1 (management's contribution to organizational stability through additions to hierarchy/structure as well as regular operations), M_3 (management's efforts to exploit the environment of the organization), and M_4 (management's effort to buffer the unit from environmental shocks; X is a vector of environmental forces; ε is an error term, the other subscripts denote time periods, and β_1 and β_2 are estimable parameters.

The model is autoregressive, nonlinear, and contingent. The autoregressive component is captured by the lagged dependent variable, thus requiring time-series data for estimation purposes. The nonlinear elements are represented by various interaction effects, some designated as reciprocal functions. The model is contingent simply because the stability term can be considered one end of a continuum, with fluid arrays on the opposite pole. As the stability variable moves toward zero, the model estimates how management affects programs in settings marked by great and unpredictable changes over time.[1]

In the model, S can be considered a composite of the various kinds of stability in an organizational setting. Stability means constancy in the design, functioning, and direction of an administrative system over time. At least five types were identified in an earlier study: structural stability, mission stability, production or technology stability, procedural stability, and personnel stability (O'Toole and Meier 2003b). In that analysis, we investigated the impact of personnel stability on the performance of administrative systems and developed empirical evidence of its positive contribution.

The model contains three different functions of management. They are efforts to manage the internal operations of the organization (M_1), efforts to exploit opportunities in the environment (M_3), and efforts to limit the negative impact of environmental changes (M_4). The latter two functions in the second, environmental portion of the model are often combined as M_2—defined as the ratio of M_3 to M_4.

The objective in presenting the original formal model, and the impetus behind this research agenda, is the idea that it is crucial to be precise about one's ideas regarding exactly how management might relate to performance and how it might interact with other factors to affect performance.[2] We have stated from the outset of this work that we care less about being right in the final analysis than about being precise in what is being said (O'Toole and Meier 1999). An unfalsifiable theory is of little use in a scientific effort to understand phenomena, including such a complex and important phenomenon as public management. Indeed, this model has been modified in certain respects as evidence has been documented regarding the various specified relationships.

Although this model incorporates some rather specific and potentially controversial elements—for instance, the several kinds of nonlinearities evident in [1]—it is also purposely constructed upon some widely recognized features of governance systems. As such, exploring conceptual and measurement issues through this perspective should shed light on challenges to be faced by other researchers approaching similar agendas from other directions. For example, the model builds on the widely noted tendency of managerial systems to operate in inertial fashions; it incorporates multiple managerial functions (via the Ms), thus reflecting some of the rich arguments about causality found in the public management research tradition; and it treats structural features (through the S term) as offering stabilizing influences on program performance—in both the first and second terms of the model. Whether such stability is a good or worrisome thing depends, of course, on one's perspective and the current performance of a system. In short, this model represents a precise and somewhat reductionist specification that nevertheless incorporates widely recognized tendencies of public programs and their operations.

What issues are conjured by this representation that should be of general interest to those desirous of systematic scientific work on public management and performance? We turn now to these, organized in terms of portions of this model as well as more general themes.

M & M: Issues of Management

The perspective of this volume is that both organizational/structural features and managerial moves or efforts can shape program outcomes. Indeed, as the model suggests, we think that structure and management interact over time (O'Toole and Meier 1999). In particular, this model indicates that management matters in the implementation of programs, but this core notion does not rely on some simplistic image of managerial invincibility. Rather, the impact of management is expected to be multiple and contingent, but also subject to estimation. Demonstration of this relationship must be found through systematic and replicable studies. What issues must be faced in undertaking this sort of work? Many could be sketched, starting from exceedingly broad questions such as, What is management? How should it be conceptualized? For present purposes, we assume basic agreement on a general notion of management encompassing both externally and internally oriented efforts to coordinate people and resources to achieve public purposes. From such a perspective, and using the model presented above, fourteen conceptual issues can be explored.

Conceptual Issue 1: How to Conceive of "Managing Outward"

Our theory includes as one component what Moore (1995) has called "managing outward": managerial effort and talent directed toward the external—that is, outside the organizational—world.[3] The theory holds that efforts to manage the environment (M_2) are of two kinds: attempts to buffer the producing organization against the ill effects of environmental changes (M_4) and efforts to exploit opportunities that the environment offers (M_3). Both exploitation and buffering may include elements of "political" action by managers—building support or reducing opposition—and also efforts to encourage enhanced production—eliciting the contributions of others, for instance, or minimizing negative externalities from the actions of other organizations on the production of the home unit. This ratio of exploitation to buffering, we suggest, can be termed the risk orientation of the public manager. These concepts of external management would appear to be quite important in understanding managerial influences on performance. To date, however, our research agenda has not offered a measure of either M_3 or M_4. Rather, we have relied thus far on a measure of M_2 for external management on the basis of how frequently the manager interacts with various key actors in the environment.[4] This pattern of interactions is akin to setting up a behavioral network to facilitate organizational performance.

We are confident that our measure of M_2 taps a crucial aspect of managers' efforts to deal with their environments. The measure is related to organizational performance on a wide range of outputs under dramatically varying model specifications (Meier and O'Toole 2001, 2003). The measure interacts with organizational resources and constraints, personal traits of the manager, the stability of the organization, and even the basic autoregressive nature of the system (O'Toole and Meier 2003b). Additional unpublished research demonstrates that this measure of external management is an individual rather than an organizational characteristic (Meier and O'Toole 2004). The correlation between environmental management for the same managers over a period of two years is strong and positive; the correlation of this measure for different managers in the same position in the same organization is virtually zero. Unpublished data also demonstrate that the number of nodes included in the data gathering (five in the original measure versus eight in a second survey) matters little (Meier and O'Toole 2004). Although some nodes can have unique and different influences on organizational performance, any measure that combines interactions with two or more nodes produces similar empirical results.

These findings derive from one set of empirical cases in one policy field. Still, they carry implications for how to conceive of and measure managers' efforts in complicatedly networked settings. Researchers on networks and network management often indicate that the only way one can tap networks and networking is via laborious field research that involves validation of every interaction at both ends of each dyad (Provan and Milward 1995; Milward and Provan 2000). This requirement, however, is very expensive to fulfill, even in small-n studies, and is simply not feasible for large-n investigations. If a reasonable approximation to managerial networking behavior can be attained via survey work with key managers themselves, however, opportunities for multivariate analyses across large numbers of cases are substantially increased. This issue is definitely worth further investigation, since it may be crucial to the prospects for advancing systematic research on this topic.[5]

Despite the encouraging performance of the M_2 measure, three caveats need to be entered here. First, the M_2 measure taps managerial effort only, not managerial talent or skill. The theory implies that external management requires both effort and ability to contribute to program performance. The studies conducted thus far include only the former in the measure. Some progress regarding managerial quality, however, can also be noted. The issue is addressed more fully under the next two conceptual issues treated in this chapter: M_2's discriminant validity, and how contingencies might influence the impact of M_2.

Second, the measure taps a behavioral dimension of networks, not a structural dimension (see O'Toole and Meier 2004b). It also measures only network nodes rather than network processes. The use of this stripped-down measure of network management permits one to capture the general outlines, but not the nuances.

Third, the failure to distinguish empirically between M_3 and M_4 is troublesome simply because that distinction is an essential element in managerial strategy (O'Toole and Meier 1999; see also Boyne and Walker 2002). More refined empirical work, for instance via further survey research, might produce discrete measures of these two components. Nevertheless, at the basic theoretical level, one might even be skeptical that $M_2 = M_3/M_4$, simply because this ratio makes no allowances for the level of effort. If the manager increases efforts to exploit the environment by a factor of ten and increases efforts to buffer the environment by a factor of ten, for example, the net impact on the network management measure is nil.[6] This logic suggests that while the research agenda may have tapped a valid measure of M_2, the decomposition of external management into exploitation and buffering efforts remains problematic.

One possible avenue of empirical research might be that the ratio is in itself contingent on the level of effort. Managers might first decide to allocate their efforts to internal (M_1) and external (M_2) management; only after the decision to allocate x percent of time to environmental management does the strategic question of exploitation versus buffering come to be decided. Alternatively, most of a manager's initial effort in the environment will be monitoring and buffering; only as the amount of effort increases above a certain level will efforts to exploit opportunities become realistic. The current specification in this circumstance would be adequate because increases in M_2 would essentially be exploitation or M_3 actions. A further possibility is that this ratio is continually changing and is contingent on the nature of the composition of the environment (X) or the extent of stability in the organization $(S;$ see O'Toole and Meier 2003b).

The first possibility can be framed formally. Consider the X vector at any time t to be composed of a set of discrete external forces, resource-providing or -constraining. For each element i in the set, the impact of any particular exploitive or buffering-oriented managerial effort directed at X_i at time t depends on what kind of impact the X_i can be expected to have on the system. Exploitation and buffering efforts, that is, are likely to be chosen on the basis of a manager's expectation of the sign (and magnitude) of various X_i's at t. Thus, the model can be framed as

$$O_t = \beta_1(S + M_1)O_{t-1} + \Sigma\beta_i(X_{it}/S)(M_{3i}/M_{4i}) + \varepsilon_t , \qquad [2]$$

where the summative (Σ) term indicates that exploitation and/or buffering by managers is/are directed at each discrete component of X, and the M_3 and M_4

values, as well as their ratio of course, are contingent on managers' assessment of the value and direction of each X_i. Here, of course, the measurement and estimation challenges are compounded. Skillful managers who interpret their external environment correctly can boost performance by the properly diagnosed application of M_3 or M_4 effort to the appropriate external forces. Inept diagnosis, however, should lead to suboptimal impacts of the same overall levels of managerial effort toward the environment.

This situation—Ms contingent on X—will be discussed more in "Conceptual Issue 3," shortly. In this instance, as well as the possibility that Ms are contingent on organizational stability or that exploiting greatly exceeds buffering, however, we think the questions are as much empirical as theoretical. We simply need to know more about how managers react to changes in an organization's environment.

Conceptual Issue 2: M_2's Discriminant Validity

As noted above, a strong case can be made that managing the environment is a critical part of what public managers contribute to assist performance. Our measure of managing outward, or what one might call managing the network, meets many of the criteria for a good empirical concept. It is reliable; the same managers get generally the same result when responding to the survey two years apart. It is robust to the number of nodes asked; deleting one or more interactions has little effect on the overall measure. Most importantly, it has a great deal of empirical import; it performs as predicted in our theory of public management in the face of numerous controls and with a wide variety of organizational outputs.

One question that remains is the discriminant validity of the measure: whether it contains aspects of variables other than managing the network. Why might we suspect that discriminant validity is an issue? The network management measure only taps the extent to which managers interact with important actors in their environment.[7] It does not reveal the content of the interactions and, perhaps more importantly, does not indicate the quality of the interactions. A manager who interacts with external actors and does so poorly could adversely affect the performance of the organization rather than help it. Our measure consistently produces positive relationships with performance even in poorly performing organizations, which suggests that the measure might contain factors other than merely the frequency of interaction.

One possibility is that managers recognize their own limitations and, therefore, interact with the environment less when they perceive they do a poor job of it. Such a strategy would induce a bias toward more effective interactions. At the same time, expecting managers to be more astute about the strategy of network interactions than they are about the quality of interactions when they do so is asking a lot. Another possibility is that the time period in question for our empirical investigations thus far, 1995–1999, was a very favorable one for these organizations; budgets were growing, and schools were improving on most indicators of performance. In such a situation the relative effort to exploit the environment could exceed efforts to buffer so that the M_2 measure might actually be largely a measure of M_3. The explanation, however, is contradicted by unpublished results for 2000–2002, which are also consistently positive.

The discriminant validity question with regard to the external management measure suggests that a priority should be placed on unpacking the measure into its buffering and exploiting components. Doing so would transform this discussion into a series of empirical questions. The central question, then, becomes how to measure M_3 and M_4 as distinct from simply the frequency and number of managerial interactions.

Conceptual Issue 3: Contingencies and External Management

The public manager's decision about how much to buffer versus exploit the environment can be expected to be contingent on both the composition of environment (X) and the degree of stability (S) in the public-program system (see O'Toole and Meier 2004b). One managerial skill is the ability to decipher the environment or the signals emanating from it and then decide whether any aspects should be ignored, buffered to protect the core organization, or exploited to the organization's benefit. The correct reading of such signals and the appropriate matching of strategy to the situation is, from this perspective, a fundamental management skill.

As noted earlier, our M_2 measure used thus far contains no skill component. We have developed a broad measure of managerial quality, however, that has been validated in the setting of public education, where top managers' salaries are set in a context approximating a neoclassical labor market (for details and justification, see Meier and O'Toole 2002). This quality measure was not developed with specific reference to external management but presumably includes both internal and external aspects.

We do not explore further here the thorny question of what quality public management is or the complications associated with trying to measure it in all settings (but see Meier and O'Toole 2002). Rather, the quality measure can be mentioned here in connection with the contingencies of external management, because the discussion of managerial skill at environmental surveillance must be qualified in response to one of our key empirical findings. In a sample of more than 500 public school systems, our salary-based measure of management quality is uncorrelated with the measure of the extensiveness and frequency of network management, the M_2 measure (Meier and O'Toole 2002).[8] The skill of environmental management, therefore, must be something different from the current quality measure and, as a result, something that is not recognized by school board members with increases in salary. The distinct nature of the quality measure from what would comprise a hypothetical quality-of-external-management measure is underscored by the lack of a consistent positive interaction between the quality measure and M_2 (as they relate to organizational performance). That is, if management quality were to tap the skill of the manager in dealing with the environment, then one would expect managers scoring highly on both to have more impact on organizational performance than the sum of their quality and network contributions taken separately.

Introducing a measure of manager's skill to the M_2 relationship has two implications. First, the ratio of exploitation to buffering is likely to vary over time rather than remain constant. Although such ratios might be relatively stable for organizations that emphasize a consistent approach to a placid environment, even the most consistent organizations vary some over time. Second, that variation should be contingent on the nature of the environment, whether it is supportive or threatening or some combination of the two. From a modeling perspective, this means that not only does M_2 interact with the environment to influence organizational performance but that M_2 itself (or, rather, the M_3/M_4 ratio) changes as perceptions of the environment change. Correct specification of public management externally, as a result, is likely to include a two-step process whereby changes in the environment influence the M_3/M_4 ratio and that ratio (or the separable components) then affects performance in the next period. The complications of a dynamic M_3/M_4 ratio are considerable if we cannot develop nonsurvey measures of the ratio simply because no public agency is likely to allow researchers real-time access to the organization. The alternative is to assume that the M_3/M_4 ratio is relatively stable in the short run; this limits the complexities to just matching the environment to the M_3/M_4 ratio, a task that is not simple in itself and will require substantial analysis of the organization's environment (see "The X Files: Issues with the External Environment," below).

Conceptual Issue 4: Measuring Internal Management (M_1)

Internal management of the organization plays a vital role in the field of public management and in any explanation of how management might affect program performance. It also features prominently in our theoretical work. Internal management functions include establishing organizational structures and routines, creating appropriate incentives to attract and retain staff, motivating them, setting and refining the organization's goals and priorities, monitoring individual and group performance, crafting and updating financial and information systems that facilitate efficient and effective production, and countless other tasks. To date, we have not offered a measure of internal management.[9] Our measure of managerial quality, of course, is likely to reflect in part skills at managing the internal workings of the organization (see Meier and O'Toole 2002). Separating the quality measure into internal and external components, however, is not possible with the data collected thus far, because we cannot obtain two separate judgments of managerial quality from salary data. Only direct surveys of those evaluating the manager could obtain such assessments.

Measurements of M_1 could have numerous elements. Questions related to establishing or shaping norms, procedures, or even organizational culture are possible (Khademian 2002), although in each case the researcher would need detailed information about the organization to write appropriate questions. The anything-but-parsimonious research literature on leadership offers innumerable possibilities, including many varieties of people-centered and production-focused styles and behaviors (for details, see Rainey 2003; Brewer and Selden 2000; Rainey and Steinbauer 1999). Even in the best of circumstances, however, internal management encompasses such an enormous set of potentially significant tasks that the best feasible measures will surely be quite incomplete. Systematic work on merely the venerable elements of POSDCORB-ian management, for instance, would require a substantial effort, not to mention what would be needed to extend beyond this rather staid range. Note that the gargantuan data-gathering task of the Government Performance Project, involving hundreds of pages of survey instruments and many other forms of documentation for even a single case at a single point in time, necessarily omitted numerous aspects of standard internal management (see Ingraham, Joyce, and Donahue 2003). The task, furthermore, of relating what was gathered in that effort about management capacity to actual performance is yet to be accomplished. It is clear that the task of defining and measuring internal management, let alone testing for links to performance, is unlikely to be accomplished easily, completely, and in the short run.

One central question in measuring M_1 is how management might contribute to stability or structure (O'Toole and Meier 1999).[10] We have begun an exploration of this key question through some of our empirical work in public school systems. One of our surveys includes questions about the degree of discretion given by top managers to subordinates, the desire for consistent processes in the organization, the degree to which the manager sees the role as one of a change agent, the managerially perceived separation of policy from administration, and other items. Unfortunately, these questions rarely produced consistent answers; as an example, superintendents both desired every school to do things the same way and also desired that principals exercise more discretion. An implication may be that tapping actual orientations toward internal management, not to mention behavioral aspects, may require data gathering beyond occasional forays into samples of managerial respondents with the typical approaches.

In measuring M_1, therefore, how much can one can rely on the responses by managers without having corroborating information from knowledgeable subordinates? Managers are clearly aware of the most recent trends in management, either in general or for the specific types of organizations they run; as a result, they are likely to give socially or managerially desirable responses—answers that show they are up on the latest kernels of managerial conventional wisdom. The difference between what the manager claims to do as a manager and what happens in actual practice could be substantial. Getting corroborating data from subordinates would require much larger (and more expensive) surveys. The willingness of a manager to respond to a survey could also decline if attempts were initiated to tap subordinates' perspectives also; alternatively, limiting such investigations to organizations where top management agreed to permit the administration of the survey might well induce selection bias into the results.

The measurement issues related to M_1 are substantial. No solution other than trial and error is immediately obvious. A first step might be to collect numerous existing management questionnaires and peruse them for questions that tap aspects of what we have termed M_1.[11]

S: Issues Involving Stability

Stability, one of three central concepts in the model, contributes to the autoregressive nature of the system in the internal part of the model and affects the organization's ability to buffer the external portion of the model. Stability can be a manifestation of structure, standard operating procedures, organizational norms, or other factors. In empirical work, two aspects of personnel stability were measured and shown to be related to organizational performance—street-level personnel stability and managerial stability (O'Toole and Meier 2003b).[12] We have not investigated or even measured structural stability, mission stability, production/technology stability, or procedural stability. It is worth noting, nonetheless, that we regard stability as a too-often-denigrated aspect of the performance challenge. Although a great deal of contemporary and popular management thought emphasizes innovation and castigates bureaucratic forms and functions (for instance Barzelay 1992; Altshuler and Behn 1997), the theory and empirical results indicate that stability can contribute to results. Accordingly, selected stability-related issues can be identified.

Conceptual Issue 5: Are Both Stability Measures the Same?

Our general model of management includes stability in both its first, internal term (here denoted as S_j) and in its second, environmental term (denoted as S_x).[13] The former regularizes operations that contribute to production, whereas the latter supports ongoing processes and approaches in the face of potential perturbations from the external world. Logic suggests that the two forms of stability are overlapping but distinct, given the different functions that each is hypothesized to perform. In the environmental term, stability performs a buffering function, absorbing uncertainty from the environment and triggering responses to negative impacts.[14] That function differs from the internal uses of stability that regularize the work patterns, relationships, and expectations for individuals in the organization. Production stability especially, and also procedural stability, are likely to be a large part of the first term S_i and a relatively small part of the S_x term. Structural stability, mission stability, and personnel stability might play a large role in both S_i and S_x. Whatever the mix in the two terms, the overall composition of the two stability terms is unlikely to be identical simply because in large organizations those structures and processes that are devoted to production are generally not the same ones that are used to monitor and respond to the environment (see O'Toole and Meier 2003a). Two conceptual issues that, if resolved, would seem to promise significant empirical gains with regard to stability, therefore, are specifying the relative composition of each in terms of the five (or possibly more) types of stability and creating measures that tap each of these types separately. Certain stabilizing forces are likely to be more important than others in shaping performance over the long run.[15] Only systematic analyses of discrete contributions can provide confirming or rebutting evidence.

Conceptual Issue 6: The Reciprocal Relationship

The reciprocal relationship for structure in the second, or environmental, term suggests that as stability in a program system increases, external influences have less effect. This logic was developed in terms of how organizations deal with environmental perturbations (O'Toole and Meier 1999, 2000). A stable organization can take a much larger jolt from the environment and continue its operations, perhaps because organizational leadership can let the internal processes run themselves, whereas managers tend to environmental shocks or perhaps because structure itself absorbs environmental forces and dissipates them (O'Toole and Meier 2003a). The reciprocal relationship specified, with the S in the denominator of the second term reducing the impact of X forces from the environment, is isomorphic with this theoretical relationship. At the same time, it is not the only functional form for a buffering relationship. A summative relationship with the environment as shown in equation [3] would work equally well. If one interprets shocks as having a negative value, an additive relationship for stability would serve as the equivalent of a levee, keeping shocks below a certain level out of the organization.[16]

$$O_t = \beta_1(S_i + M_1)O_{t-1} + \beta_2(X_t + S_x)(M_3/M_4) + \varepsilon_t .$$ [3]

An implication of a summative relationship is that the same structure that buffers environmental shocks also facilitates positive environmental factors. This pattern might be interpreted as generating the capacity to permit resources to be used. A third modeling possibility is that stability interacts with the M_3/M_4 ratio in a manner similar to a switch. The ratio takes on a negative value when facing a constraint or a negative shock and a positive value when facing resources (with the manager making decisions to interpret whether the inputs are constraints or resources). Structure in this situation might fit into a pure multiplicative role (equation [4]).

$$O_t = \beta_1(S_i + M_1)O_{t-1} + \beta_2(X_t)(S_x)(M_3/M_4) + \varepsilon_t \ . \qquad [4]$$

Needless to say, the empirical work conducted thus far has not gotten into these issues and, therefore, offers no guidance regarding which specification is most likely.

The *X* Files: Issues with the External Environment

In work to date, we have paid little attention to explicating the environment of the core production organization except for a recent empirical study that includes a treatment of how intergovernmental structures affect organizational management and performance (O'Toole and Meier 2004b). That study examines the source, and diversity of sources, of funds for an agency's programs. In so doing it distinguishes between a structural network in and with the intergovernmental environment (the diversity of and dependence on other levels of government) and the behavioral networking activities of the manager (that is, M_2).

Thus far, we have ignored additional nuances in the organization's environment to press the research agenda forward on the themes of management and stability. Any comprehensive study of public management and performance, however, needs to take seriously the composition, organization, and valence of the "environment" and its forces with which core units may be interdependent.[17] This section considers how scholars might go about differentiating and examining the external environment in a way that could reveal a great deal about how organizations are managed and what difference it makes.

Conceptual Issue 7: The Structure of the Environment

Our consideration of the environment focuses on four concepts—resources, constraints, shocks, and networks. An important consideration about the first three is how they are aggregated in the environment; the fourth notion has to do with the collective structure of the set of environmental actors in conjunction with the core organization and thus also brings up issues of aggregation. Are the resources (or constraints) at the disposal (or in the way) of the agency merely a sum of all available resources, or are some of them contingent on the presence of others? This question about resources can be generalized and is thus connected in turn to the patterns of interdependence between the core unit and other organizational actors that may be relevant to performance. Attending to such patterns is one way of unpacking important parts of the X term.

Thompson (1967) sketched a simple typology of such patterns for organizations, and his notions can be applied across units as well. Whether agency environments are pooled, sequential, or reciprocal carries significant implications for how one models management. Pooled environments, where multiple external organizational actors contribute to impacts on the targets of public policy, but do not deal directly with each other during their own efforts, are by definition less interdependent than other patterns; thus resources (or constraints) from them can likely be summed. Maintaining a supply of a particularly strategic resource from one part of a pooled environment does not require managing relations with the remainder of the actors; similarly, controlling the impact of constraints imposed from a particular direction does not necessarily entail orchestrating coalitions of actors across multiple units. Sequentially structured environments—arrays in which an output of one unit serves as an input for the next, and so on—suggest certain other critical management issues: eliminating any blockages in the flows of production between units in the environment, and taking advantage of how resources may be aggregated. Sequential environments should be aggregated in a multiplicative manner; a probability of failure (or success) in one relationship affects the probability of failure (or success) of all subsequent units in the sequential chain. Reciprocal environments, where outputs of some units serve as inputs for others, which in turn provide critical inputs for the first set, cannot be modeled in such simple ways. These require mathematical techniques that permit both positive and negative feedback in a pattern where the resources are not wholly exogenous to the organization.

The implications of these various archetypes of environments for management (separate from their implications for modeling) should be obvious. In a pooled environment, the manager merely has to be concerned with factors that directly affect the organization. Unless other organizations are linked into its environment, the actions that they take are of little concern to the organization except as competitors. In a sequential environment, the manager has to be concerned with the operations of all other organizations in the sequence and must either convince an errant organization to change or adapt his or her own organization to the change in inputs. In reciprocal environments, organizational management becomes similar to network management with a web of relationships and concerns that must be incorporated into any decisions.

Of course, any organization's environment can contain resource (or constraint) linkages that fit all three types of interdependence. Aggregation questions become even more important when one moves from the organizational level to the network level (see conceptual issue 14, below) because the question of aggregation and its form applies not only to the environment of the core organization of interest but to the network itself (for instance, regarding how the management function is aggregated across units).

Among other properties, the structure of an organization's environment also includes its degrees of density, diversity, and stability.[18] Some agencies operate in heavily populated—dense—environments where numerous other organizations compete for the same resources or seek to affect the same clientele, possibly in partially divergent ways (Downs 1967); the welfare-to-work and the family-planning arenas are two examples. Other organizations operate virtually as monopolies with few competitors or colleagues; examples here include some bureaus of the Department of State (although of course other departments and the national security adviser do compete with the State Department on certain functions) and the meat inspection activities of the Food Safety and Inspection Service of the U.S. Department of Agriculture. As an organization's environmental density increases (with rivals, coproducers, or other interested parties of all sorts), one would hypothesize that the importance of the M_2 function should increase.

The diversity of an environment considers the relative heterogeneity of the actors; the environment of an urban public school system, for example, contains a wide range of interests and institutions, each concerned with how the schools perform; in contrast a suburban school district usually has a more homogeneous environment. In both cases the environment makes demands on the organization, but in the latter case the demands are likely to be more consistent and thus easier to accommodate (see Chubb and Moe 1990). Environmental diversity as an aspect of the X term, therefore, is likely to increase the importance of both management and resources.

The stability of the environment affects the agency by determining whether the organization can routinize its environmental interactions. To the degree that environments are stable, resources and constraints are likely to be stable, and structures plus procedures can be established to deal with both. As the turbulence of the environment increases, organizational structures, procedural regularity, and stability in general become less important (or at least less functional for performance); management is likely to become more important. Rather than making a few decisions and then following established procedures, in a changing environment managers need to adapt as the environment shifts.

Conceptual Issue 8: Environmental Shocks

Managing environmental shocks is an integral part of public management. How an organization responds to shocks from its environment indicates a great deal about the resilience of the unit, and possibly of the program it runs. The basic tenet is that managerial choices matter for how well the organization performs and thus whether the organization survives and flourishes.

The first conceptual issue regarding shocks is what the idea itself means. Shocks are changes in either the organization or its environment that have the potential to disrupt the day-to-day workings of the unit. One operational definition of an *environmental* shock might be a change in organizational inputs larger than a given size. This general definition, covering both positive and negative events, could be applied to a wide range of phenomena from budgets, to clientele composition, to missions, to a collapse of outputs.[19] The general nature of the measure, however, does not solve the issue of what magnitude of change should be considered a shock. A budget change of 5 percent is clearly within the realm of normal, and one of 50 percent is clearly a shock. The exact cut point, however, is ambiguous and undoubtedly contextual.[20] One promising theoretical approach might be the work of Jones (2001) on punctuated equilibria. Although Jones does not define a precise level of change in his theory, he does provide a set of probability distributions that could be used to tell how unusual an event might be.

Related to the size issue in defining environmental shocks is the question of symmetry. "Stability" in organizations usually means modest growth over a period of time. Negative events, as a result, are likely to be more unusual, and thus more readily interpretable as "shocking," than positive ones. An unanticipated increase in resources, as an illustration, merely requires the organization to respond by increasing its effort as quickly as bureaucratic procedures permit (that is, hiring restrictions, the availability of trained personnel, and so forth). Negative changes in revenues are more pressing; they require the use of slack resources or, absent slack, an actual reduction in organizational size. Thus, for instance, economic and governmental organizations in Taiwan were shaken during 2002 by the shock of negative growth, albeit at a modest level of approximately 5 percent, after many years of uninterrupted increases—most of which were larger in increments than 5 percent annual growth.

How to model shocks of a nonquantitative nature also poses an issue. The terrorist attack on the Pentagon counts as a shock to the U.S. Department of Defense from its environment, but any attempt at quantification in defining such an event is likely to face difficulties. The role of the Arthur Andersen accounting scandal in the performance of the Securities and Exchange Commission is a similar example. Sometimes these shocks are generated by choices made at other governance levels; local law-enforcement units' receipt of directives from Washington during 2002 to interview and keep tabs on Arab immigrants within their jurisdictions would count as a controversial instance of such a pattern.

Although shocks have been treated thus far as emanating from the environment, they can also be generated internally—from within the organization. A change in leadership might constitute a shock, a likely situation in a nonprofit agency when the founder of the organization decides to retire. An internal scandal that results in massive personnel changes constitutes another example. Some shocks can be consciously self-induced (after all, the entire field of organizational development seeks to create planned change in an organization). The decision by the Young Women's Christian Association (YWCA) to change its mission from recreation to social services is a case in point.

Conceptual Issue 9: Governance Levels as an Aspect of the Environment

Management and the core agency are often not the only set of actors seeking to shape public program performance. Even in the simplest circumstances, all such organizations are embedded in a "governance system" that includes several levels of authority—voters, elected officials, agency heads, midlevel management, and street-level operatives—even in what are essentially unitary, hierarchical organizations (see Lynn, Heinrich, and Hill 2001). Programs may also be ensconced in a network of multiple organizations; one of these may have lead authority, or the responsibilities of leadership may be shared among several organizational actors. Even if a single unit is formally charged with the obligation of delivering performance, technical requisites or political realities may mean that numerous organizations in various sectors coproduce outcomes or collaborate in some significant program-relevant activities. Such patterns are common in the United States (Hall and O'Toole 2000; Agranoff and McGuire 2003) and other countries (Kickert, Klijn, and Koppenjan 1997; Bogason and Toonen 1998). In a program designed to be implemented in a network-like structure, the number of governance levels proliferates further. Indeed, in complex networks the notion of "level" itself, implying a hierarchy within the governance setting, oversimplifies. The consideration of governance, in both empirical and normative senses, is considerably complicated in network contexts (O'Toole 1997).

Sorting out the concepts and measures here and clarifying appropriate modeling approaches has only just begun (see the brief coverage of this subject later in the chapter). The importance of the topic, however, can be seen by recognizing that many uses of the third sector in the management and delivery of social policy involve such intricately patterned arrays. Contracting for goods and especially services, a growing governmental phenomenon, impels attention to more complex governance forms. Increasing use of subcontracts and multiple extragovernmental parties in putatively public tasks requires modeling attention (Light 1999). Collaborative public-private partnerships of all sorts call for systematic attention, and in Europe the "social partners" of government have become increasingly involved in the management and delivery of key public programs as well (Nicolaidis and Howse 2001).

Still, even where one can treat governance systems as sufficiently ordered as to be hierarchical, so that lower levels of governance cluster within the bounds of upper strata, governance levels are more complex than indicated thus far. Such levels can be considered as chains of principal-agent relationships, and such links are by definition reciprocal. The policy-implementation literature clearly demonstrates that lower levels of governance shape program performance in ways different from that intended by higher levels (O'Toole

2000; Hill and Hupe 2002)—and that this reality can sometimes actually improve program performance (Stoker 1991). Lower levels also frame the choices available to upper levels and control a large amount of the information that superordinates receive (Downs 1967), so much so that some argue that authority comes from below rather than being asserted from above (Barnard 1938; Simon 1996a).

Governance levels also contain an overall feedback system whereby the results of programs contribute to shaping citizen preferences that then influence political choices (Lynn, Heinrich, and Hill 2001). One should not forget in this process that public-organizational employees might be agents of political actors, but that they are also voters and thus principals in the political process. These reciprocal relationships among the levels of governance mean that a precise separation of the influence of management from the influence of political principals may not always be possible. In light of the web of interrelationships, preferences across the levels are likely to be somewhat similar, thus inducing collinearity in any attempts to sort out the relative degrees of influence precisely (see Meier, O'Toole, and Nicholson-Crotty 2004). It also means that studies that fail to include all levels of governance incur a substantial risk of spurious results (Meier, O'Toole, and Nicholson-Crotty 2002). This complication is likely to get more rather than less important. The emergence of new multilevel governance arrangements like the European Union adds levels that have become more influential over time. Even in the United States, the development of international agreements has meant that in literally thousands of cases, formal ties and direction for national and subnational action extend beyond the nation-state and its boundaries (O'Toole and Hanf 2002). Systematic empirical work in many policy fields needs to take these developments into account.

Conceptual Issue 10: The Reactivity of the Environment

Organizations are open systems, units influenced by their environment as well as acting on that external world. A portion of the setting, however, consists of strategic actors who seek to manipulate the organization and its actions for their own benefit or, at minimum, for purposes other than enhanced program performance. Interest groups lobby legislatures to change framing statutes; other agencies seek to cultivate and perhaps to capture the organization's clientele; still additional actors may desire to work with the core unit on some tasks of joint salience, but typically support a somewhat different schedule of values and operate from a somewhat different world view than the agency in question. In a networked system of program implementation, the reactivity of the network increases even more because the organization lacks the capacity to coerce these other actors. Decision making in an environment that contains strategic actors becomes vastly more complex than decision making in a passive or merely reactive environment.

In such settings, "management" designates a more indirect and facilitative set of actions than has typically been implied in the field of public management (see Agranoff and McGuire 2003). What constitutes the most appropriate strategies, and under what conditions, is a prime topic for theory building and research (for an agenda here, see McGuire 2002). Even leaving aside the major behavioral management tasks of such settings, the cognitive challenges facing managers in complicatedly networked settings are daunting. When program demands require that managers sort out, in effect, the causal paths important for diagnosing wicked problems and their likely solutions, and when these paths include contingencies grounded in the strategic choices made by other actors over whom the managers have no direct control, the complications escalate rapidly. Do transaction costs heavily shape managerial choices in such contexts? Do opportunity costs dominate the strategic calculus of such decision makers? Is reality shaped by some of both? These and many more issues await systematic investigation.

General Conceptual Issues in the Empirical Study of Management

Along with the conceptual issues raised with regard to the first three basic variables in our theory of public management, plus the complication of networked program arrays, a set of more general issues can be identified that clearly transcend any particular model and research agenda. A few of these deserve brief attention in this chapter. What is the purpose of theory in empirical research on management and performance? What is the appropriate unit of analysis for the study of public management? What advantages does a nonlinear logic offer over strictly linear models? And how does one move theories from the level of the organization upward—to deal with the multiactor networks that characterize a great deal of policy implementation?

Conceptual Issue 11: The Purpose of Theory

Empirical research agendas can have varying views of the most appropriate purpose of theory. Some, such as those entailed by the advocacy coalition approach (Sabatier and Jenkins-Smith 1993) or institutional rational choice theory (Ostrom 1990), seek a comprehensive explanation of all social-scientific, policy-relevant phenomena. In contrast, we value parsimony, an explanation that covers a large portion of the relationships of concern using relatively few variables. Our theoretical model, as a result, has only four variables, with the remaining factors that affect organizational performance absorbed in the general environment or in the error term. To the charge that we have omitted parts of the complete explanation, we plead premeditated guilt. We do so, however, knowing the tradeoff between comprehensiveness and parsimony; most theories in this field have emphasized the former over the latter—with some costs. It is appropriate, we believe, to see what progress can be made by placing weight on the latter.

Theory, in our view, differs from a more general logic of governance (see Lynn, Heinrich, and Hill 2001) in that it makes relatively precise predictions about variables and their relationships. A "logic" of governance is not a theory of governance. The former integrates existing research and provides a checklist for future work to consider (Lynn, Heinrich, and Hill 2001). Other than clarifying a listing of relevant variables that should be considered in theory building, it does not generate specific research hypotheses and is largely agnostic in choosing between theoretical perspectives—as, for instance, between socialized-choice and rational-choice theories of governance. Governance work, broadly speaking, as well as our own theory-building and -testing research effort are both inductively driven. Both generate their basic notions by generalizing from existing research. Multiple theories could fit within, say, the Lynn, Heinrich, and Hill logic of governance; our version is only one of them.

What advantages attend an approach such as the one we have adopted, if one is interested in explaining program performance? First, as should be obvious, a logic of governance is useful but insufficient; theory building is necessary. Our theoretical perspective explicitly incorporates management into the process, provides precise predictions about how the variables relate to each other, allows and specifies that many relationships could be nonlinear, frames a set of research questions so that conceptual and measurement issues can be identified and addressed (as in this chapter), and mimics in the abstract how organizations operate in practice (contingent decision making that takes place in an autoregressive system open to environmental influences). These advantages, we would argue, are not inconsiderable; but the ultimate test is empirical.

Conceptual Issue 12: The Unit of Analysis

Our initial theoretical work took the program as the unit of analysis (see O'Toole and Meier 1999); more recent empirical work clearly treats the organization as the unit of analysis while at the same time considering the multiple programs that can operate within an organization. In part, this shift from programs as a unit of analysis was dictated by the availability of data for empirical settings in which programs have been implemented primarily by organizations rather than multiactor networks. Whether the focus is on programs or organizations, the units of analysis of primary interest are decidedly not individuals. The theory, as a result, does not fit easily within the rubric of either rational choice theory or psychologically based theories. Those approaches seek to explain individual behavior and in the process reduce actions and activities to the individual level. We are explicitly interested in the behavior and actions of collectivities, be they organizations or networks for policy implementation, albeit sometimes in response to efforts of individual managers. Management, by definition, is a process for motivating collective action; the impact of management, therefore, is properly evaluated by its influence on that collective action, that is, on the outputs of the organization(s) rather than the outputs of individuals.

This theoretical orientation guides the empirical strategy adopted in our work. Organizations or similar collectivities, not individuals, are the units of analysis. Relationships need to operate at the organizational level to be relevant to the phenomena under investigation. Such relationships might have origins, indeed are likely to have origins, in individual behavior, but the perspective we have adopted is that to understand organizations, or clusters of them, one must study organizations rather than individuals.

Conceptual Issue 13: Taking Nonlinearity Seriously

Much of social science implicitly or explicitly assumes or tests for linear relationships, despite the fact that many qualitative depictions of the world in which public programs operate suggest the likelihood of a more complex reality. The theory we have developed specifies a set of nonlinear relationships linking management, stability, and the environment to past performance. Any nonlinear theory will confront difficulties during empirical research simply because testing for nonlinear relationships puts a great deal of stress on a data set. In particular many specifications of nonlinear relationships generate high levels of collinearity, which renders regression estimates unreliable. One solution is generating better quality data. In the short run, one can address this problem via another route: relying on sample splitting and the flexibility of techniques like substantively weighted least squares (SWAT; for a complete explanation with multiple illustrations, see Meier and Gill 2000), which provides a systematic method of overweighting parts of a sample to see how relationships might change. One of the clear benefits of large-n research is sufficient instances, so the set of cases can be segmented by various key characteristics to check for alterations in the patterns of relationships.

To illustrate, we have demonstrated a wide variety of interactions between the various terms in our model. Our measure of network management (M_2) interacts with the resources and constraints of the environment in what seem to be strategic ways (Meier and O'Toole 2001, 2003). In these studies management appears to be one way to free the organization from the constraints of past performance. The network-management variable also interacts with the structure of the environment, in particular the distribution and diversity of funding arrays created by the intergovernmental relations setting (O'Toole and Meier 2004b). In empirical analysis, four managerially relevant terms—

managerial networking, managerial quality, top-managerial constancy, and front-line personnel stability—each interact with each other to generate nonlinear relationships with performance (O'Toole and Meier 2003b). These patterns by no means exhaust the possibilities. Alternative specifications of different nonlinear relationships are possible (O'Toole and Meier 2000), and some of our theoretical concepts have yet to be operationalized.

Conceptual Issue 14: Moving On Up: The Network Level

Moving public management theory to the network level involves increasing its complexity by an order of magnitude. Although the core concepts and the basic ideas remain the same, the number of possible relationships and the demands that these place on data and models increase significantly. This section merely indicates the direction that such modeling and estimation may need to take; a full elaboration would require at minimum a second chapter. Again we rely on our model, which seeks large-n validations of the insights of small-n research.

The basic model can first be reintroduced, but with the subscript h to indicate that the concepts are measured for a formal hierarchy (that is, at the organizational level). This modification in symbolization but not conceptualization yields equation [5]:

$$O_{th} = \beta_{1h}(S_h + M_{1h})O_{(t-1)h} + \beta_{2h}(X_{th}/S_h)(M_{3h}/M_{4h}) + \varepsilon_{th} . \qquad [5]$$

For the sake of simplicity, one can define the internal (that is, first-term) nonoutput portion as Y and the external (environmental) term as Z, yielding the following simple equation for a hierarchy:

$$O_{th} = \beta_{1h}(Y_h)O_{(t-1)h} + \beta_{2h}(Z_h) + \varepsilon_{th} , \qquad [6]$$

where $Y_h = S_h + M_{1h}$, and $Z_h = (X_{th}/S_h)(M_{3h}/M_{4h})$.

A network established or used to implement a program would also have similar internal and external terms. We theorize in terms of the same kind of functional form, now subscripted with an n to reference the network level:

$$O_{tn} = \beta_{1n}(Y_n)O_{(t-1)n} + \beta_{2n}(Z_n) + \varepsilon_{tn} . \qquad [7]$$

Even networks should be expected to be somewhat inertial, although less so than individual formal organizations. The internal term of the model, however, becomes much more complex because it must now include both the internal management terms for the network ($S_n + M_{1n}$), and also the same terms for the hierarchies that compose the network:

$$Y_n = [(S_n + M_{1n}) \oplus \Phi (S_h + M_{1h})] , \qquad [8]$$

with two new symbols introduced, as explained shortly. Similarly, the environmental term must now include both the environmental factors for the network $(X_{tn}/S_n)(M_{3n}/M_{4n})$ and the environmental factors for the hierarchies that comprise the network:

$$Z_n = [(X_{tn}/S_n)(M_{3n}/M_{4n})] \oplus \Phi \, [(X_{th}/S_h)(M_{3h}/M_{4h})] \, . \tag{9}$$

When combined, the overall formal presentation of network work management becomes:

$$O_t = \beta_{1n}[(S_n + M_{1n}) \oplus \Phi \, (S_h + M_{1h})]O_{(t-1)n}$$

$$+ \, \beta_{2n}[(X_{tn}/S_n)(M_{3n}/M_{4n})] \oplus \Phi \, [(X_{th}/S_h)(M_{3h}/M_{4h})] + \varepsilon_t \, . \tag{10}$$

The two new symbols require explanation. The Φ term is used to indicate that the internal management terms of the individual organizations comprising a network are aggregated in some manner, as yet undefined; the external management terms of these units are also aggregated in some manner. The form of aggregation, we theorize, depends on the type of interdependence among the units comprising the network (see the coverage under "Conceptual Issue 7," above). In a simple pooled relationship, this aggregate operator is likely a simple vector summation (Σ);[21] in a pure sequential relationship, the aggregation parameter is likely a multiplicative one (Π). Mixed relationships are likely to have some combination of these aggregation operators or others. The Φ aggregation parameter also appears in the environmental term of the model and indicates that the environments of the hierarchies must also be aggregated. A second term $(\oplus)$ is included to show that the internal network management needs to be related to the aggregated internal management of the hierarchies, and that the environment of the network needs to be related to the aggregated environments of the hierarchies. Exactly how these elements are combined (addition, multiplication, and so forth) remains to be discovered.

The network-level model outlined sketchily here suggests why deciphering management in and of networks is more complex and demanding than management of simple hierarchies. In a two-node network, the demands might not be insurmountable; but as the number of nodes increases, the ability of either analysts or managers to consider all factors simultaneously soon exceeds the bounds of rational capacity. Managers, we think, use a variety of coping techniques to allow them to manage the network. Possibilities include satisficing, rational shielding from nodes, ignoring some of the interdependencies, decoupling or "negative coordination" (Scharpf 1993) from nodes, adding structure to the network environment, and so forth. The exact strategies can only be determined via empirical analysis of how managers operate in these networked situations.

Conclusion

This chapter indicates that many of the interesting conceptual and measurement challenges linked to understanding, theorizing, and testing for the influence of public management on performance have yet to be directly addressed, yet alone resolved. Treatment of the performance theme in much of the research literature sometimes inadvertently implies that the core intellectual challenge surrounds developing adequate measures of performance. Important as such measures are, however, we argue that a wide array of other issues should be moved to center stage for systematic attention by researchers.

Our theoretical approach and the associated developing empirical investigations provide one concrete perspective to unpack these issues. As this chapter indicates, doing so highlights some core questions about how scholars and practitioners should think about the basic functions of public management, how these are most appropriately measured, and what affects how much managerial efforts and ability are likely to make a difference in results. Forces encouraging system stability, an often-neglected theme in recent research and injunctions for practice, are also relevant to the core question at stake. How to theorize about the Janus-faced impacts of stability is a matter well worth systematic attention. The "environment" of public programs and public agencies typically consists of multiple levels and often multiple strategic actors. The importance of such political and economic forces has been a standard emphasis in the field, but just how to conceptualize the impact of the environment, particularly as it delivers perturbations to administrative systems, poses intriguing modeling and measurement puzzles. Beyond all these matters lie several fundamental questions regarding how to theorize about management and performance, what kinds of relationships to treat seriously, and what to do—theoretically speaking—about the networked nature of so many program settings.

This chapter delivers more a sketch of the terrain than a detailed map revealing solutions, although we have not been shy about indicating some of the points on the compass. As should be obvious, underlying most of the issues identified here are several more matters in contention or at least in play. Still, it is helpful to remember that this work does not constitute the tiny initial steps in a long inquiry. Sufficient work has been done thus far to demonstrate clearly that management does indeed have practical impacts, that managerial efforts on operations as well as on and in the environment can pay dividends in performance, that nonlinear patterns can be detected and analyzed with profit, and that the multiple levels and actors in the environment of public agencies must themselves be considered potentially crucial shapers of results. The huge set of questions yet to be addressed cannot all be answered quickly or perhaps even clearly. Many of the chapters in this volume offer detailed empirical treatments of some of the issues under contest. Much further work will be required, nonetheless, before one can draw to a close this research agenda.

Notes

This chapter is part of an ongoing research agenda on the role of public management in complex policy settings. We have benefited from the helpful comments of George Boyne, Stuart Bretschneider, Amy Kneedler Donahue, H. George Frederickson, Carolyn Heinrich, Patricia Ingraham, J. Edward Kellough, Laurence E. Lynn, Jr., H. Brinton Milward, Sean Nicholson-Crotty, David Peterson, Hal G. Rainey, and Bob Stein on various aspects of this research program. Responsibility for the ideas and interpretations here, of course, lies solely with the authors.

1. Modeling the performance of overall networks of organizations, including efforts to manage the network, is considerably more complex than modeling the performance of an organization operating within an interdependent setting. We are at work on aspects of the first-mentioned subject and note some preliminary efforts in the coverage of Conceptual Issue 14 below.

2. In our own work, we have used the formal presentation neither to irritate others who study public management, nor to mimic economic modelers—who too often rely on formal presentations that amount to elegant depiction of relationships that have no referents in the real world. Rather, our modeling effort has been inductively generated. The formal approach offers an important advantage: it forces theorists to be precise about what they say and, if validated, can be more relevant to how managers operate in public organizations. The issue is treated further under coverage of Conceptual Issue 11 later in the chapter. Our perspective fits with the notion of public management scholarship as a design science (Simon 1996b). Those who prefer an intuitive rather than precise characterization of relationships might seek solace with the "best practices" literature of public management (Osborne and Gaebler 1992); those who have little interest in improving practice can find fellow travelers among those advocating a disciplinary approach to scholarship.

3. Moore also notes another component of what might be deemed external management: "managing upward"—managerial influence directed toward superordinate levels within a larger hierarchy. This element is certainly real and combines, in effect, aspects of internal and external management. Managing upward is influence within a hierarchical array but exerted external to the formal jurisdiction of the manager. We ignore this issue here (but see O'Toole, Meier, and Nicholson-Crotty 2003). One reason is that in our empirical work thus far we have been examining the impact of top management in administrative units.

4. For our published empirical work on public education, this measure is a factor score of how frequently school superintendents interact with the Texas Education Agency, state legislators, local business leaders, other superintendents, and members of the school board. Application to other types of organizations simply requires a modification so that the actors fit those in the organization's environment. A related measure of the same concept, derived from survey responses from law-enforcement agencies, is developed in Nicholson-Crotty and O'Toole (2004). We expect that survey-based M_2 measures can be developed in most fields of policy.

5. It is also important to keep in mind what is *not* being asserted here. Surveying managers to determine their activity managing outward is not the same as measuring the structural interdependencies across two or more organizational units. As indicated later in this chapter, structural dimensions of networks are not the same as behavioral aspects.

6. We thank Zhirong Zhao for suggesting this issue.

7. We have recently gathered data on who initiates the interactions with network actors and can now distinguish between active and passive strategies of managerial interaction. We plan to report results from these data in future research.

8. The quality measure was constructed by regressing superintendent salary on those factors that should be related to salary such as the size of the district, the demands of the job, human capital, and personal characteristics. In this residual, we contend, is an implicit

judgment by a school board as to the quality of the superintendent's management. We have since replicated this measure with data from 2000 to 2002 and get similar results.

9. In related work Nicholson-Crotty and O'Toole (2004) have developed a measure of some aspects of M_1 for local law enforcement agencies that is positively related to performance.

10. Note that M_1 is treated in the model as a component of management that supports the autoregressive nature of administrative systems. Some aspects of internal management, even in well-running operations, however, are likely devoted to changing things rather than re-producing current operations over time. Internal management directed toward performance-improving innovations is omitted in the basic model but can be considered an additional issue worthy of exploration. See Nicholson-Crotty and O'Toole (2004).

11. Another partial approach is to rely on those limited aspects of internal management deemed so important by professional managers in the policy field that they take pains to gather it systematically themselves. This idea has been used to explore some aspects of law-enforcement management (Nicholson-Crotty and O'Toole 2004).

12. Street-level stability was measured as 100 minus the teacher turnover percentage; leadership stability was measured as the number of years the superintendent had been em-ployed by the organization in any capacity.

13. We use the term "stability" rather than "structure" because we are interested in the actual behavior exhibited rather than formal manifestations. That is, one can regularize processes in an organization by creating more highly structured relationships (a formal ap-proach), by instilling similar values and allowing individuals to exercise discretion (see Kauf-man 1960), and other means. Multiple paths lead to stability, the core notion included in the model.

14. Alternatively, and less helpfully, S_x may inhibit an organization's ability to take ad-vantage of opportunities in the environment to ratchet up performance. This theme has been prominent in the critiques of bureaucratic sluggishness and lack of entrepreneurial creativ-ity in recent years.

15. Interactions between or among different stabilizing forces are possible. The theory as sketched thus far has not explored or even speculated on the internal form of the stabil-ity term in either part of the model. Evidence for rather complex nonlinearities among sev-eral terms in the model is available, however, in O'Toole and Meier (2003b).

16. Again, X forces containing opportunities for *improving* performance are also pos-sible. We primarily emphasize in this portion of the coverage the situation when public pro-grams confront a set of environmental threats rather than fortuitous possibilities. The lat-ter are treated shortly.

17. As Rainey (2003) notes, attention to the environment as a salient concept for orga-nizational researchers was high several years ago but has been treated by some analysts re-cently as passé (for instance Aldrich 1999). It is not clear that this shift represents an im-provement, and we believe that the notion should remain an important focus for theory building and testing.

18. Analysts of social networks have proliferated an impressively large number of con-cepts to characterize patterns of interdependence across units: reciprocity, centrality, multi-plexity, and so on (see, for instance, van Waarden 1992). In our view, this conceptual pro-liferation has largely surpassed its empirical utility (note the coverage in Bressers, O'Toole, and Richardson 1994). Studies of networks frequently incorporate substantially more net-work concepts and dimensions than networks actually being analyzed, thus precluding val-idation of theoretical ideas.

19. Working primarily in the United States should not blind one to the notion that the entire output side of the organization could collapse. The hyperinflation characteristic of some Latin American countries, for examples, renders the outputs of many corresponding government agencies in those countries irrelevant. When organizations can no longer influ-ence the outcomes that they are designed to affect, the result should be a massive increase in negative feedback—in short, a shock to the system.

20. One aspect of contextuality is this: the size of a shock probably depends on what degree of change the agency is used to. In mathematical terms, this treatment of shock would allow one to link the notion to the second derivative of change in inputs with respect to time. Alternatively, one might consider as a "shock" a change in inputs larger than two (or more) standard deviations from the median change in a relatively long time series. An organization that regularly sees the size of its clientele increase or decrease by 20 percent per year would see a 25 percent change as within normal ranges whereas an organization with a clientele that varied on average by 1 or 2 percent would view this level of change as dramatic.

21. Different organizations may have managers pulling their units in quite different directions, so directionality should be included in such summations.

References

Agranoff, Robert, and Michael McGuire. 2003. *Collaborative Public Management: New Strategies for Local Governments.* Washington, D.C.: Georgetown University Press.

Aldrich, Howard E. 1999. *Organizations Evolving.* Thousand Oaks, Calif.: Sage.

Altshuler, Alan A., and Robert D. Behn, eds. 1997. *Innovation in American Government: Challenges, Opportunities, and Dilemmas.* Washington, D.C.: Brookings Institution.

Barnard, Chester. 1938. *The Functions of the Executive.* Cambridge, Mass.: Belknap Press of Harvard University Press.

Barzelay, Michael. 1992. *Breaking through Bureaucracy: A New Vision for Managing in Government.* Berkeley: University of California Press.

Bogason, Peter, and Theo A.J. Toonen, eds. 1998. "Comparing Networks." Symposium in *Public Administration* 76:205–407.

Boyne, George, and Richard Walker. 2004. "Strategy Content and Public Service Organizations." *Journal of Public Administration Research and Theory* 14 (April):231–56.

Bressers, Hans, Laurence J. O'Toole, Jr., and Jeremy Richardson. 1994. "Networks as Models of Analysis: Water Policy in Comparative Perspective." *Environmental Politics* 3 (winter):1–23.

Brewer, Gene A., and Sally Coleman Selden. 2000. "Why Elephants Gallop: Assessing and Predicting Organizational Performance in Federal Agencies." *Journal of Public Administration Research and Theory* 10 (October):685–711.

Chubb, John, and Terry M. Moe. 1990. *Politics, Markets, and America's Schools.* Washington, D.C.: Brookings Institution Press.

Downs, Anthony. 1967. *Inside Bureaucracy.* Boston: Little, Brown.

Hall, Thad E., and Laurence J. O'Toole, Jr. 2000. "Structures for Policy Implementation: An Analysis of National Legislation, 1965–1966 and 1993–1994." *Administration and Society* 31 (January):667–86.

Heinrich, Carolyn J. 2002. "Outcomes Based Performance Management in the Public Sector." *Public Administration Review* 62:712–25.

Hill, Carolyn J., and Laurence E. Lynn, Jr. 2004. "Governance and Public Management: An Introduction." *Journal of Policy Analysis and Management* 23 (winter):3–12.

———. 2000. *Government and Performance: New Perspectives.* Washington, D.C.: Georgetown University Press.

Hill, Michael, and Peter Hupe. 2002. *Implementing Public Policy.* London: Sage.

Ingraham, Patricia W., Philip G. Joyce, and Amy Kneedler Donahue. 2003. *Government Performance: Why Management Matters.* Baltimore: Johns Hopkins University Press.

Jones, Bryan D. 2001. *Politics and the Architecture of Choice: Bounded Rationality and Governance.* Chicago: University of Chicago Press.

Kaufman, Herbert. 1960. *The Forest Ranger.* Baltimore: Johns Hopkins University Press.

Khademian, Anne. 2002. *Working with Culture.* Washington, D.C.: CQ Press.

Kickert, Walter J. M., Erik-Hans Klijn, and Joop Koppenjan, eds. 1997. *Managing Complex Networks: Strategies for the Public Sector*. London: Sage.

Light, Paul C. 1999. *The True Size of Government*. Washington, D.C.: Brookings Institution Press.

Lynn, Laurence Edwin, Jr., Carolyn J. Heinrich, and Carolyn J. Hill. 2001. *Improving Governance: A New Logic for Empirical Research*. Washington, D.C.: Georgetown University Press.

McGuire, Michael. 2002. "Managing Networks: Propositions on What Managers Do and Why They Do It." *Public Administration Review* 62 (September–October):599–609.

Meier, Kenneth J., and Jeff Gill. 2000. *What Works: A New Approach to Program and Policy Analysis*. Boulder, Colo.: Westview Press.

Meier, Kenneth J., and Laurence J.O'Toole, Jr. 2004. "Managerial Networking: Issues of Measurement and Research Design." Unpublished manuscript, Department of Political Science, Texas A&M University.

———. 2003. "Public Management and Educational Performance: The Impact of Managerial Networking," *Public Administration Review* 63 (November/December):689–99.

———. 2002. "Public Management and Organizational Performance: The Impact of Managerial Quality" *Journal of Policy Analysis and Management* 21 (fall):629–43.

———. 2001. "Managerial Strategies and Behavior in Networks: A Model with Evidence from U.S. Public Education." *Journal of Public Administration Research and Theory* 11 (July):271–95.

Meier, Kenneth J., Laurence J. O'Toole, Jr., and Sean Nicholson-Crotty. 2004. "Multilevel Governance and Organizational Performance: Investigating the Political Bureaucratic Labyrinth." *Journal of Policy Analysis and Management* 23 (winter):31–48.

———. 2002. "Political Control versus Bureaucratic Values: Evidence from Latino Representation." Unpublished manuscript, Department of Political Science, Texas A&M University.

Milward, H. Brinton, and Keith G. Provan. 2000. "Governing the Hollow State." *Journal of Public Administration Research and Theory* 20 (October):359–79.

Moore, Mark H. 1995. *Creating Public Value: Strategic Management in Government*. Cambridge, Mass.: Harvard University Press.

Nicholson-Crotty, Sean, and Laurence J. O'Toole, Jr. 2004. "Testing a Model of Public Management and Organizational Performance: The Case of Law-Enforcement Agencies." *Journal of Public Administration Research and Theory* 14:1–19.

Nicolaidis, Kalypso, and Robert Howse, eds. 2001. *The Federal Vision: Legitimacy and Levels of Governance in the United States and the European Union*. Oxford: Oxford University Press.

O'Toole, Laurence J., Jr. 2000. "Research on Policy Implementation: Assessment and Prospects." *Journal of Public Administration Research and Theory* 10 (April):263–88.

———. 1997. "Treating Networks Seriously: Practical and Research-Based Agendas in Public Administration." *Public Administration Review* 57 (January–February):45–52.

O'Toole, Laurence J., Jr., and Kenneth I. Hanf. 2002. "American Public Administration and Impacts of International Governance." *Public Administration Review* 62 (September):158–69.

O'Toole, Laurence J., Jr., and Kenneth J. Meier. 2004a. "Parkinson's Law and the New Public Management? Contracting Determinants and Service Quality Consequences in Public Education." *Public Administration Review* 64:342–52.

———. 2004b. "Public Management in Intergovernmental Networks: Matching Structural and Behavioral Networks." *Journal of Public Administration Research and Theory* 14 (October).

———. 2003a. "Bureaucracy and Uncertainty." In Barry C. Burden, ed., *Everything but Death and Taxes: Uncertainty and the Study of American Politics*. New York: Cambridge University Press, 98–117.

———. 2003b. "*Plus ça Change*: Public Management, Personnel Stability, and Organizational Performance," *Journal of Public Administration Research and Theory* 13:43–64.

———. 2000. "Networks, Hierarchies, and Management: Modeling the Nonlinearities." In Carolyn Heinrich and Laurence Lynn, eds., *Governance and Performance: New Perspectives*. Washington, D.C.: Georgetown University Press, 263–91.

———. 1999. "Modeling the Impact of Public Management: The Implications of Structural Context," *Journal of Public Administration Research and Theory* 9 (October):505–26.

Osborne, David, and Ted Gaebler. 1992. *Reinventing Government*. Reading, Mass.: Addison-Wesley.

Ostrom, Elinor. 1990. *Governing the Commons: The Evolution of Institutions for Collective Action*. New York: Cambridge University Press.

O'Toole, Laurence J., Jr., Kenneth J. Meier, and Sean Nicholson-Crotty. 2003. "Managing Upward, Downward, and Outward: Networks, Hierarchical Relationships and Performance." Paper presented at the annual meeting of the American Political Science Association, Philadelphia, August 28–31.

Provan, Keith G., and H. Brinton Milward. 1995. "A Preliminary Theory of Network Effectiveness: A Comparative Study of Four Mental Health Systems." *Administrative Science Quarterly* 40:1–33.

Rainey, Hal G. 2003. *Understanding and Managing Public Organizations*, 3d ed. San Francisco: Jossey Bass.

Rainey, Hal G., and Paula Steinbauer. 1999. "Galloping Elephants: Developing Elements of a Theory of Effective Government Organizations." *Journal of Public Administration Research and Theory* 9 (January):1–32.

Sabatier, Paul A., and Hank Jenkins-Smith. 1993. *Policy Change and Learning: An Advocacy Coalition Approach*. Boulder, Colo.: Westview Press.

Scharpf, Fritz W., ed. 1993. *Games in Hierarchies and Networks*. Frankfurt am Main: Campus/Westview.

Simon, Herbert A. 1996a. *Administrative Behavior*, 4th ed. New York: Free Press.

———. 1996b. *Sciences of the Artificial*, 3d ed. Cambridge, Mass.: MIT Press.

Stoker, Robert P. 1991. *Reluctant Partners: Implementing Federal Policy*. Pittsburgh: University of Pittsburgh Press.

Thompson, James D. 1967. *Organizations in Action*. New York: McGraw-Hill.

van Waarden, Frans. 1992. "Dimensions and Types of Policy Networks." *European Journal of Political Research* 21 (February):29–52.

Ten

Analyzing Management Structures and Systems in a Governance Framework: What Have We Learned?

Patricia W. Ingraham

In the preface to this volume, we asked a series of questions related to the proposed framework for analysis, methodology, and potential theory building. We asked, Does a logic of governance, and the location of public management within such a logic, move us forward or distract us? Is research producing findings supporting the assumption that management matters; that is, that public management *should* be located within a framework for analysis? If so, how, when, and under which conditions can management choices make a difference? How do the ways in which government programs are organized and managed make a difference to governmental performance? We hoped—indeed, we argued elsewhere—that the logic of governance framework provided here would allow a parsimonious explanation of the multiple influences on performance (Lynn and Ingraham 2004). We argued further that the framework and the explanations it allowed—and excluded—could assist in a more nuanced understanding of the complex public policy processes and influences that add up to performance. The end objectives are straightforward: a better understanding of public policy and the influences that shape it, and an improved ability to offer useful information to key policymakers.

The complexity of these tasks is daunting. As both the authors in this book and others point out, already difficult to capture policy processes are made more opaque by multilevel service delivery arrangements, organizational networks, and lack of agreement about specific goals and priorities. In this setting, as Carolyn Heinrich warns, even evidential bases derived from rigorous empirical research do not necessarily lead to improved practice and performance. Nonetheless, the effort is worthwhile. The chapters in this book demonstrate not only that advances in understanding and methodology are likely, but also that linking disparate efforts with a common framework can enhance an incremental policy-learning process.

In fact, all of the empirical chapters in the book reinforce the relevance of the framing questions and logic. At the same time, they certainly discourage complacency about the undertaking. Chapter 1 takes us there immediately in warning that governments and governance are transforming; multiparty contracts and collaborations are increasingly the means for service delivery; and new performance expectations challenge traditional notions of hierarchy, authority, and accountability. This multilevel, multidimensional reality of contemporary governance, with its many decision-making structures and influences, poses a significant and continuing challenge for analysts (Peters and Pierre 1998; Kettl 2002). The several chapters in this book that address multi-level delivery arrangements and administrative structures bear testimony to analytical difficulty, but also demonstrate that levels can be picked apart, that elements of service delivery can be viewed with some degree of separation, and that lessons can be derived from the analyses.

So specifically what progress did we make here? We return to the most key questions we asked in the preface.

Does a logic of governance framework—and the location of management in such a framework—move us forward or distract us? Overall, the consistency with which major elements of the governance framework are found to be significant to program outcomes and other measures of intermediate or longer term performance suggests strong relevance to future governance and performance research. The policy analysis community has long been engaged in a cumulative endeavor, translating limited findings from limited observations into a broader understanding of complex policy processes and outcomes. Often, however, inclusion of measures of the activities of public management and administrative institutions and arrangements has been limited and blunt. Over a period of nearly ten years, authors involved with examination of the governance framework and with other efforts to link management to performance have utilized increasingly sophisticated analyses to fine-tune the linkages that define the ability to deliver on public policy promises (Kettl and Milward 1996; Brudney, O'Toole, and Rainey 2000; Heinrich and Lynn 2000; Ingraham, Joyce and Donahue 2003; Lynn and Ingraham 2004). The context of an explicit framework that delineates sets of influences and levels of interaction allows measure construction to be more sophisticated, more contextual, and more directly related to elements of policy that may be malleable. A more specific context permits greater clarity in the presentation of conceptual and theoretical linkages to be examined—and perhaps allows new linkages to be identified. As Meier and O'Toole argue in one of the concluding chapters here, the generation of more specific research questions is one of the fundamental needs of governance and performance research. The utility of common theoretical and empirical references in that regard cannot be overlooked. Research can be cumulative only if it is not completely scattershot.

Is research producing findings supporting the assertion that management matters? The chapters in this book support the conclusion that management matters in a variety of settings and in a variety of ways. Consider Ewalt's conclusions about welfare policy implementation in Kentucky in chapter 3: "This study shows that organizational structure and managerial arrangements clearly matter." Donahue and colleagues, reporting on two management functions within state governments and with data from all fifty states, build on earlier work by Meier, O'Toole, and Nicholson-Crotty (2004) and observe, "Most of our findings are clearly consistent with O'Toole and Meier's theory that managerial activities that contribute to functional stability and predictability improve . . . intermediate . . . outcomes" (chapter 6).

Heinrich's conclusions, dealing with different structural arrangements and different service delivery, demonstrate the complex paths through which managerial structures and arrangements can make a difference: "By linking program structure and management to treatment practice, this work further shows that the availability of medical services on site increases the length of treatment for patients, contributes to higher levels of counseling intensity, and increases their receipt of medical services, all of which increase the probability of abstinence and reduced drug use in the postprogram period" (chapter 4).

Ingraham, Sowa, and Moynihan examine leadership as a quality of management and find that it matters to creating *capacity* to perform, by creating internal organizational linkages and consistently reinforcing organizational priorities. They note, "While there is not necessarily one best system or one best way to create capacity, a key factor lies in how the leadership institutionalizes the process" (chapter 7). Suggesting the influence of lower levels of management as well, Donahue et al. note that their findings "suggest that administrative discretion increases attention to effectiveness and performance."

What do these findings say in summary? First, and significantly, that management appears to matter throughout the policy process. It is important in choices about policy design; in choice, arrangement, and operation of service delivery systems, in the location of authority and representation in decision systems; in the creation and development of integrated capacity within management themselves; and in the ability to measure quality and program performance. Second, the significance of the *structure* of management and administrative delivery and support systems emerges throughout the analyses. Even—or perhaps particularly—in the networks and horizontal linkages examined by the authors, the connections, or links, among hierarchical contexts and the more multidimensional network realities are significant. Work not reported here (Milward and Provan 2002) and earlier work by Heinrich (2000) hint that even in a strongly decentralized networked setting, the notion of center of authority or coordination emerges.

Third, influences of management and administration are different for different time points, different points of service, and different program outcomes. In earlier work, Meier, O'Toole, and Nicholson-Crotty pointed out that management influence appears to be present at multiple levels of governance. Its influence probably varies across those levels as well (2004). Donahue et al. and Ewalt examine two elements of this influence as proposed in still other work by Meier and O'Toole: the ability of management to stabilize or manage its own function (internal capacity); and the ability to manage externally, that is, into the broader environment, both hierarchically and horizontally (and probably in other directions as well!). These authors, and others in this volume, find substantial influence in each.

The influence on building internal capacity is not surprising; one would expect professionals to use their expertise wisely. An equally interesting conclusion is suggested by the idea that administrators and managers use their influence in the external environment in ways that enhance their capacity and systems even further. If, as Donahue and her colleagues hint—but do not conclude—one outcome of this multidimensional influence is a greater focus on effectiveness and performance, the implications for change and reform are substantial. Certainly, the idea that increased managerial discretion improves performance has underpinned new public management and reinventing government reforms across the world. In one sense, it is reassuring to have even preliminary confirmation of the positive relevance of this change. At the same time, it poses additional difficulties for analysis, since it is difficult to predict with any accuracy precisely where and when the impact of increased managerial discretion might be found in policy processes.

The findings presented in this volume also appear to confirm, at least in a preliminary way, that understanding contemporary governance means understanding alternative organizational forms for public policy delivery. The nature of the organizations that deliver government services and the effectiveness of governance are entwined. Management and administration have taken different organizational forms and characteristics in this set of research, but their compatibility with—indeed, their centrality to—many other qualities and components of governance is consistently clear. To the extent that governance must include influences on the overall effectiveness of public policies, therefore, the role that management, administration, and their various organizational forms play must also be acknowledged.

What is, or should be, the role of explanatory theory in governance and public management research? The logic of governance that frames the book, the many streams of research reported in the book, and the research forums that preceded this book are based on the conviction that better explanation of the policy process and of performance can provide important insight into the design, management, and evaluation of government programs and governance. Theoretical underpinning and understanding is crucial to this enterprise. A strong argument for a single encompassing framework is that it gathers relevant research and knowledge into one giant sifter and allows key information and findings to remain after "chaff" is eliminated.

Three chapters in the book—Rainey and Ryu, Jennings and Haist, and Meier and O'Toole—very specifically engage this debate. Challenging the "take my word for it" syndrome, Rainey and Ryu argue, "If we demand high levels of scientific rigor, large representative samples, clear conceptualization of concepts and variables and their hypothesized relations, very explicit empirical measures and analyses—we will be crying in the wilderness for a long time. Such conditions will remain difficult and expensive to attain for many reasons, such as the difficulty in establishing clear, widely accepted, and measurable performance indicators for many government organizations. At the same time, we need to consider the challenges in designing and carrying out research that clearly resolves such questions'" (chapter 2).

Similarly, Jennings and Haist cast a critical eye toward performance measurement per se and note "there has been surprisingly little effort to develop a theory of performance management" (chapter 8). They propose a framework for examining *measurement* that closely parallels and supplements the broader logic of governance. Again, this is a research agenda that mirrors Rainey and Ryu's challenge. Meier and O'Toole are the most forceful in their argument: "A "logic" of governance is not a theory of governance. The former integrates existing research and provides a checklist for future work to consider (Lynn, Heinrich, and Hill 2001). Other than clarifying a listing of relevant variables that should be considered in theory building, it does not generate specific research hypotheses and is largely agnostic in choosing between theoretical perspectives—as, for instance, between socialized-choice and rational-choice theories of governance" (chapter 9).

Thus, the broad recognition of the new need for theory building and for the discovery of elements of the theory that are at once robust and parsimonious leads to a reframing of the challenge for analysts of governance and performance, rather than to a conclusive theoretical solution. Nonetheless, the clarity of the maps leading to important elements of a theory is improved. Again, Meier and O'Toole argue that mapping particularly troublesome challenges does not solve the problem. They make their case more convincing by listing several very large challenges—the quality of internal and external management; the stability of the organization, the structure of the environment, for example. And, yes, it is true that the analyses included here are more tantalizing than conclusive in their findings. The findings are important for their coherence and cumulative contribution and for their ability to pinpoint specific challenges for potential theory. Again, a common framework and the iterative nature of the learning make a positive contribution to the longer-term theory building enterprise.

In chapter 1, for example, we presented a set of alternative frameworks for analyzing governance influences and contributions to effective government. Salamon's new governance framework, systems frameworks, and social choice frameworks all suggest different paths to explanation and theory. We have isolated elements from each of these, combined them in new ways, and started the examination of the interaction of both elements and larger models.

We also emphasized that elements of both traditional systems of hierarchical authority and more recently understood systems of network management would be necessary to a fully specified governance framework and to identifying components of a theory of public performance and governance. We have confirmed the significance of analyzing both horizontal and vertical structures and methods of organization. If the research is to contribute to policy decision making, however, as well as to broader theoretical explanations, more work is necessary.

Equally vexing for theory building is the difficulty in specifying the point at which management or administrative influences might be most important. It is useful to know that there is a consistent influence at several points in policy design and delivery processes. It is more difficult to understand lags between building internal capacity and stability and longer-term effect on performance or quality. Even more complex is the difficulty in understanding what internal capacity might be or how it looks in a more networked and open setting. All of these issues must be explored in more depth if the "black boxes" of government, governance, and performance are to be fully understood.

The Continuing Dilemma of the Black Boxes

Both public management and policy analysis strive to inform and shape the policy process. They often take different paths to do so—effective management of public organizations for example, versus rigorous empirical analysis of policy choice is one common way of summarizing the differences. As both endeavors have grown and advanced, however, it has become increasingly clear that their intersections are more significant than their differences. Effective management in a dismal policy environment is an exercise in frustration. The most elegant analysis in a desk drawer—or worse, the circular file— is of little use. In the final analysis, what matters for government is the ability to use knowledge and resources effectively to solve public problems.

For governance and performance, creating effective solutions draws on particularly elusive components: politics, effective leadership, relatively stable resources, to name a few. It also draws on the ability to adequately understand what happens inside an organization and what happens when that organization interacts with its environment. In this setting, it is easy to understand the attractiveness of the old black box theories: rigid boundaries closed off external influence, decision making was neutral and not intended to shape policy, individual motivations and incentives were not dysfunctional to the organization, and leadership unquestionably had the skills and ability to lead. Sheer beauty for an analyst more concerned with politics or the environment!

The organizations and the settings described in the research in this book are far messier. The research describes open organizations interacting fully with their environment, having—intentionally or not—an influence on policy at multiple points. Perhaps what they do not describe fully is the reality of these networked organizations coexisting with the traditional hierarchies that are larger government funding sources or decision makers. That remains a challenge for future work.

That there are remaining challenges, however, does not suggest failure. The findings of the chapters in this book have implications for policy design, administrative and managerial arrangements, service delivery, contemporary reforms such as contracting out, leadership development strategies, the design of management systems, efforts to assess the effectiveness of public programs, and continued efforts to build theories that link the institutional arrangements of government with performance. The book does not provide what Rainey (2003) terms "snappy aphorisms." That was not the intention. The combined contributions of the authors here are much more important than that and will have longer term impact on effective governance. Together, the chapters of this book are a powerful demonstration of the value of common theoretical and empirical reference. They demonstrate that the path ahead may be bumpy, but they also provide important guidance in finding our way.

References

Brudney, Jeffrey L., Laurence J. O'Toole, and Hal G. Rainey, eds. 2000. *Advancing Public Management: New Developments in Theory, Methods, and Research.* Washington, D.C.: Georgetown University Press.

Heinrich, Carolyn J. 2000. "Organizational Form and Performance: An Empirical Investigation of Nonprofit and For-Profit Job Training Service Providers." *Journal of Policy Analysis and Management* 19:233–61.

Heinrich, Carolyn J., and Laurence E. Lynn, Jr. 2000. *Governance and Performance: New Perspectives.* Washington, D.C.: Georgetown University Press.

Ingraham, Patricia W., Philip G. Joyce, and Amy K. Donahue. 2003. *Government Performance: Why Management Matters.* Baltimore: Johns Hopkins University Press.

Kettl, Donald F. 2002. *The Transformation of Governance: Public Administration for the Twenty-First Century.* Baltimore: Johns Hopkins University Press.

Kettl, Donald F., and H. Brinton Milward, eds. 1996. *The State of Public Management.* Baltimore: Johns Hopkins University Press.

Lynn, Laurence E., and Patricia W. Ingraham, eds. 2004. "The Influence of Management in Governance: A Symposium." *Journal of Policy Analysis and Management* 23 (winter): 13–97.

Meier, Kenneth J., Laurence O'Toole, Jr., and Sean Nicholson-Crotty. 2004. Multilevel Governance and Organizational Performance: Investigating the Political Bureaucratic Labyrinth." *Journal of Policy Analysis and Management* 23 (winter):31–48.

Milward, H. Brinton, and Keith Provan. 2002. "Private Principals, Nonprofit Agents." Paper presented at the 98th Annual Meeting of the American Political Science Association, Boston, August 29–31.

Peters, B. Guy, and Jon Pierre. 1998. "Governance without Government? Rethinking Public Administration." *Journal of Public Administration Research and Theory* 8:233–44.

Rainey, Hal G. 2003. *Understanding and Managing Public Organizations*, 3d ed. San Francisco: Jossey Bass.

Index

Printed in the United States
62516LVS00003B/109

9 781589 010345